Presented to

_____

By

_____

On the Occasion of

_____

Date

_____

Daily
Wisdom

FOR

Working
Women

MICHELLE MEDLOCK ADAMS
GENA MASELLI

BARBOUR
PUBLISHING

ISBN 1-59310-369-7

Published by Barbour Publishing, Inc., P.O. Box 719, Uhrichsville, Ohio 44683, www.barbourbooks.com

Our mission is to publish and distribute inspirational products offering exceptional value and biblical encouragement to the masses.

Member of the
Evangelical Christian
Publishers Association

Printed in China.
5 4 3 2 1

DEDICATION

For my best friend, Raegan Holiday Quan,
and my sister-in-law Barb Medlock—
wonderful elementary teachers
and a credit to today's working women.
I love you both!
Michelle (A.K.A. Missy)

To Patricia Irene Heinen and Alice Williams Pfeifer,
the most inspiring and hardest working women
I've ever known.
Gena

NEW YEAR'S RUSH

Sing to him a new song;
play skillfully, and shout for joy.

PSALM 33:3

Isn't the New Year a great time to reevaluate your life? You can think about the past year and remember what you liked or disliked, what you accomplished, and the things you'd like to change. It's a fresh start, a new song.

Each year, I contemplate these things. While reflecting on the past year, whether it's been a year full of joy or one that had its share of challenges, I still see God's hand on it. I know He was with me all the way. Though I don't necessarily make New Year's resolutions, I do set goals for the upcoming year. I think about where I want to be at the end of the year and what I want to accomplish. Often, these goals happen, but if they don't, well, I'll have another year to work on them.

This year as you reflect on the previous year or on the one yet to come, take time to joyfully thank God for His blessings and His direction. Seeing His provision in the past will help you meet the future with confidence, knowing that He is with you every day.

–GM

POWER PRAYER
Heavenly Father, thank You for Your provision and blessings this past year. I dedicate this next year to You and commit to following Your ways each day.

BIG CHANGES

*"Be strong and courageous. . .
for the LORD your God goes with you;
he will never leave you nor forsake you."*

DEUTERONOMY 31:6

As I watched the moving truck pull away, a pang of fear shot through my body. This pang was followed by waves of questions: Are we doing the right thing? How will we survive in a big city? Is this fair to our children? Will I even like my new job?

I had married my high school sweetheart. After graduating from college, we had settled into nice, comfy jobs in our hometown. My parents even lived next door to us. It was the perfect setup. We were sure we'd live and die in Bedford, Indiana. So when I was offered a tremendous magazine writing job in Fort Worth, Texas, we were unsure of what to do. After much prayer, we felt God calling us west.

Talk about a big change! Even though I knew we were in the center of God's will, I worried. But God was with us every step of the way, reassuring us of our decision. There are days that I still get homesick, but I'm never alone. If you're facing some major changes today—cross-country moves or job transfers—you won't have to go it alone, either. God will go with you.

–MMA

POWER PRAYER
*Lord, I am afraid of change. Help me to face these changes
with joy and strength. I love You. Amen.*

NEW KIDS ON THE BLOCK

*The end of a matter is better than its beginning,
and patience is better than pride.*

ECCLESIASTES 7:8

God bless new bosses and coworkers. They're in a tough place. They've just walked into new positions, not knowing the office history or procedures. They come with their own experiences and expertise. Many times, they've been hired to bring about change, improving productivity or sales.

For those who work with them, it can be challenging. You've done your job to the best of your ability, within the boundaries of the current organization, possibly carving out your own niche, only to have a newcomer decide to change everything. Your instincts tell you to resist the person and her ideas, because everything's been working just fine until now, right?

Remember that not all changes are bad. When Jesus came into your life, He made *big* changes. He completely changed the way you thought about your life. The ideas in His Word may have seemed foreign, but they worked—even better than you could have imagined.

So when that newcomer comes into your office, be patient. You never know. . .her ideas may improve things, too.

–GM

POWER PRAYER

Heavenly Father, please give me patience and insight to work with the new people who come into my office. Help me to listen to and discuss their ideas clearly and sensibly.

FOR EVERYTHING
THERE IS A SEASON

There is a time for everything,
and a season for every activity under heaven.

ECCLESIASTES 3:1

I wish I could say that I lived for change, that I was one of those remarkable people who thrive on learning new procedures and think a fun Saturday afternoon includes rearranging the living room furniture. Unfortunately, that gift passed me by.

Of course, I don't absolutely hate it. Sometimes I change the pillows on my sofa, if that counts.

Change can be uncomfortable, especially change in the workplace. When change comes, take a deep breath. God is still in control. Step back and objectively ask yourself if the change is good. Has it been carefully thought out? Is the goal to help the office function more smoothly? Are your managers supporting it 100 percent? If the answers to some or all of these questions are yes, then it's time to jump on board. If you have concerns, and it's appropriate, voice them. But once the decision has been made, become a team player and make the most of the situation. Your submission and positive attitude will be appreciated by your coworkers and, more importantly, by God.

–GM

POWER PRAYER

Lord, I understand that there is a time and season for every-
thing. Since change is difficult for me, I ask for Your help to be
a positive influence through it.

FEAR NOT

Such love has no fear because perfect love expels all fear.

1 JOHN 4:18 NLT

He smiled a big toothy grin, looking exactly like the Grinch looked when he plotted and planned against *Who*-ville. He may have been my new "team lead," but I thought he was questionable. He had a reputation for "shaking things up" without regard for anyone's feelings, so I was prepared for a battle.

As he talked about the upcoming changes and how they would positively affect our department, I was skeptical. I wanted to "feel this guy out" before offering any help or input. Bottom line? I was being a jerk—a jerk motivated by fear. I was so afraid that he might be as bad as I'd heard, I never gave the guy a chance. And you know what? He ended up being a really nice addition to our department.

Change often comes with an unhealthy dose of fear. And fear causes us to act strangely. If you're in the midst of changes in your workplace and you're walking in fear—stop! Fear is not of God. Ask the Lord to replace that fear with His love. If you get a new boss who seems highly suspicious, pray for him—don't eyeball him. Besides, God is your ultimate boss, and you can always trust Him.

–MMA

POWER PRAYER
Lord, keep my heart full of love, not fear. I trust You during these uncertain times. Amen.

CHANGE IS IN THE AIR

"He changes times and seasons;
he sets up kings and deposes them.
He gives wisdom to the wise
and knowledge to the discerning."

DANIEL 2:21

Change is coming. . . . You can sense it. Perhaps it's a job. A relationship. A volunteer ministry. Something. Anything. And that's exciting! It's as if a beautiful Christmas present has been placed under the tree with your name on it. You're just waiting for the perfect time to unwrap it and peek inside.

The best part about these times is that you are once again reminded that God is working on your behalf. He thinks enough of you to direct you to another job or bring a new relationship into your life. It's one more reminder that you are special to Him.

Of course, until the day arrives when you know exactly what the change is, you have to be patient, consistently doing what you know to do. Then just watch God direct you, and pray for insight. You're not alone. The God of the universe, the Beginning and the End, is right there working in your life. Now isn't that comforting?

–GM

POWER PRAYER
Lord, I feel impressed that You're going to do
something new in my life. I thank You for it in advance
and am ready to see what it is.

A FRESH START

"At that time the Spirit of the LORD
will come upon you with power. . . .
You will be changed into a different person."

1 SAMUEL 10:6 NLT

What an exciting time! It's the beginning of a new year—time for a fresh start, a new beginning, and possibly a new life. If you're at a point where you want to know Jesus, congratulations! You're on a wonderful journey that will change the rest of your life for the better. If you already have a close relationship with the Lord and are committed to continuing and strengthening that relationship, you're an inspiration to others. Through your kindness and faithfulness, you share Jesus' love.

Wherever you are in your faith, this is a great time to think about your relationship with Him. What have you learned? In what area do you want to grow? What is your calling? These are great questions on which to reflect and pray. In time, the Lord will direct and answer you. As you read your Bible, pray, and surround yourself with strong Christian friends, you'll find that your peace, joy, and faith will grow, making you a happier person who lives a more rewarding life for Him!

–GM

POWER PRAYER

Lord, I love You. Thank You for all You've done in my life. I dedicate my life to You and pray that You would change me into the person You want me to be.

WORRY

*"Therefore I tell you,
do not worry about your life."*

MATTHEW 6:25

Layoffs. They happen. And when they happen, it's scary stuff. When my freelance writing contract was up for renewal this year, believe me, I was sweating it, too. We get used to having those paychecks show up every two weeks because they help us pay those bills that show up every month, right? It's only natural to be concerned when people are cleaning out their desks all around you. But don't worry.

Worry never changed a thing. When I was waiting to hear whether I'd be "rehired" by my company, my husband said the most comforting thing to me. He said, "Honey, that company is not your source. God is your source." Such wisdom from such a cutie! He's right.

No matter what is going on all around you; no matter how many people are packing up their offices; no matter what state the economy is in; no matter how many pink slips are circulating; no matter what—God is your source. Philippians 4:19 (NLT) says, "And this same God who takes care of me will supply all your needs from his glorious riches, which have been given to us in Christ Jesus." So don't worry. God is still on the throne, and heaven's economy is just fine!

–MMA

POWER PRAYER
*Lord, I trust You with my career and my finances.
I love You. Amen.*

DISTRACTIONS

Oh, that my ways were steadfast in obeying your decrees!

PSALM 119:5

There are days when I'm set to work. I know just what I need to accomplish. I have everything I need and suddenly. . .the phone rings. In fact, it seems like it continues to ring all day. Between the phone calls, I get several questions from coworkers. Throw in a couple of unexpected—and unproductive—meetings and, voilà, I have a completely wasted day. I've been so distracted that I haven't accomplished anything.

Unfortunately, distractions come in all shapes and sizes. In the office, they're endless phone calls, long meetings, and watercooler banter. In your spiritual life, they may be people, fear, or the business of life. Basically, they're anything that keeps you from focusing on God and spending time with Him.

As you determine to spend time with God in prayer every day, ask Him to help you prioritize your day. As you make this a part of your life, you'll begin to understand true productivity. You'll begin to differentiate the necessary to-do list items in your life from the distractions. In time, you'll have the satisfaction of accomplishing what He's called you to do.

–GM

POWER PRAYER

Dear Lord, thank You for showing me exactly what I need to do today—for You and at work—and help me steer clear of distractions.

DETOURS

"The LORD himself goes before you and will be with you;
he will never leave you nor forsake you."

DEUTERONOMY 31:8

There came a point in my career when I just wanted a change. I had worked in the same field for over eight years, and though I had a great relationship with my boss, there was no longer any challenge in my job. That's when I started looking for something new.

I received a call from an employer in a new field, and I excitedly accepted the position. It wasn't long after I started that I discovered that the job wasn't for me. I didn't care for the duties or corporate structure. Although at first glance it may have appeared to be a false step, I came to see God's hand in the whole process. Through that short detour, I found the courage to do what I really wanted to do. Without that detour, I wouldn't have had the guts to try.

Sometimes situations arise that leave you thinking that you've made a wrong turn. But remember: Although something is hard, it still may be in God's plan. His Word says that He goes before you and will never leave you. With Him, how can you ever really fail?

–GM

POWER PRAYER

Lord, I trust You with every step I take because I know that
You go before me and will never leave me nor forsake me.

SUPERNATURAL PEACE

*May the Lord of peace himself always give you
his peace no matter what happens.
The Lord be with you all.*

2 THESSALONIANS 3:16 NLT

The peace that passeth all understanding. . .yes, that's what I need today. How about you? If your company is in the midst of restructuring, if you've just been switched to a different job with new challenges, if it's time for your annual review, if you're experiencing some trauma at home that is making it impossible to concentrate at work—you need that supernatural peace, too.

Many things come against us in life to steal our peace, but they can't take our peace if we won't let them. You see, the kind of peace I am talking about only comes from our heavenly Father. You can't get His peace from aromatherapy, massage sessions, or relaxing music. His supernatural peace only comes from above.

Even if your life is turned upside down right now and peace seems an impossibility, God's peace is available to you. See, His peace isn't affected by circumstances or any outward distractions. If you aren't experiencing the peace of God today, why not seek it right now? Ask the Lord for His peace and then thank Him for it. Peace out!

–MMA

POWER PRAYER
Lord, I need Your peace today. Thank You for removing my frantic feelings and replacing them with your everlasting peace. Amen.

EFFECTING CHANGE

*[Jesus said to them,] But you shall receive power
(ability, efficiency, and might)
when the Holy Spirit has come upon you,
and you shall be My witnesses in Jerusalem and all Judea
and Samaria and to the ends (the very bounds) of the earth.*

ACTS 1:8 AMP

When many people hear the word *evangelism*, they automatically think about knocking on strangers' doors or going on mission trips. But you are an evangelist everywhere you go—even in the workplace. Though you may be limited by what you can say, you can still share God's goodness and joy through your attitude.

People will see a difference in you. They'll know there is a peace in your life that they're missing. Don't assume that because you're not standing behind a pulpit, you can't minister. Sometimes just by showing kindness you can impact someone's day. And hopefully, one day they'll ask what makes your life different.

You *can* effect change in others just by sharing the goodness that God has shown you. Ask someone to lunch who may need a friend. Bring a cup of coffee to someone who may be stressed. Those little niceties will go a long way in sharing the love of Jesus with the lost.

–GM

POWER PRAYER

*Lord, I lean on the power that Your Holy Spirit has given to
me to be a witness for You in the workplace.*

POSITIVE PERCEPTIONS

*"Why, we even saw the Nephilim giants
(the Anak giants come from the Nephilim).
Alongside them we felt like grasshoppers.
And they looked down on us as if we were grasshoppers."*

NUMBERS 13:33 MSG

How is your perception? Do you have a positive perceiver or a negative perceiver? In Numbers 13, Moses sent out twelve spies to survey the land that God had promised the Israelites. The Bible says that all twelve spies saw the exact same thing—a land flowing with milk and honey; large scrumptious grapes; rich, fertile soil; and some very large giants. Ten of those spies had their negative perceivers on. They came back and reported how impossible it would be to take over the land due to the resident giants. But two of the spies had on their positive perceivers. They came back and said, "Hey, we are well able to conquer those giants and possess the land!"

Basically, ten had faith in the giants and two had faith in God. They all saw the same thing, but only two men saw the situation through faith eyes. Which perceiver do you have on today? Are you looking at your work situation through faith eyes?

Make a decision right now that you're going to use your positive perceiver in all situations, and keep your faith eyes in focus by staying in the Word.

–MMA

POWER PRAYER
*Lord, help me to keep a positive perception no matter what!
Amen.*

STEPPING OUT

*"GOD hasn't quite walked out on us after all!
He still loves us, in bad times as well as good!"*

RUTH 2:20 MSG

Have you ever made a big change in your life? Maybe you've taken a new job or moved to a new city. You don't know what's waiting for you, but you have a peace about your decision, nonetheless. Those can be exciting and scary times. You have to trust that you're doing what God wants you to do.

Ruth was an example of a woman who took a chance and changed her life. She left everything she knew—her culture, home, and family—to follow her mother-in-law back to Bethlehem. She didn't know what awaited them, but she trusted that it was the right thing to do. Thankfully, God was faithful. He led her to the exact place she needed to be.

If you are on the verge of making a big change in your life, or maybe you already have and are just waiting to see how it plays out, continue to trust God. If you believe that He directed you to do something different, trust Him to complete His work. Just like He didn't walk out on Ruth, He won't walk out on you.

–GM

POWER PRAYER

*Lord, thank You for not walking out on me. I'll continue to
follow Your leading and trust that You'll provide for me.*

A NEW WAY

Many are the plans in a man's heart,
but it is the LORD's purpose that prevails.

PROVERBS 19:21

"Well, that's the way we've always done it."

Ever heard that one before? Doesn't it just make you want to run out of the conference room screaming? So many times I've wanted to raise my hand and interrupt the meeting to say, "Just because that's the way you've always done it, doesn't mean it's always been the right way!"

Change, though scary, can be good! Just think. . .if we hadn't embraced computers, we'd still be writing on typewriters and using that "Wite-Out" stuff to erase our mistakes instead of just hitting the BACKSPACE key.

When we become inflexible and stubborn, we hinder growth. Yes, there may be times when "the old way" is still best, but let's not dismiss another idea simply because it's different. If you struggle with change or if new ideas make you nervous, ask God to help you embrace change with hope and a positive attitude. Don't be the office ogre who's known for saying, "But that's the way we've always done it." Instead, be open to new ideas. See change as a chance to grow. God may have all kinds of new and exciting things in store for your office.

–MMA

POWER PRAYER

Lord, help me to be flexible and embrace change with hope—
not fear. Amen.

REACH OUT

Share with God's people who are in need. Practice hospitality.

ROMANS 12:13

We had just moved from Indiana to Texas, and I knew very few people. I wasn't yet very chummy with my coworkers, and I hadn't met many of my neighbors. However, as an author, I was making regular trips to a place called "Max's E-Z Mail" in Lake Worth, Texas, to mail manuscripts. So some of my very first Texas friends were the folks at Max's. From the very beginning, they were hospitable to me. Over the last five years, we've become good friends. You know why? Because they have always made me feel special. In every situation, they've gone the extra mile for me. They weren't just doing their jobs, they were reaching out to a transplanted Hoosier.

Maybe you're the receptionist in your office. If you are, you have the perfect opportunity to welcome people into your office. Or maybe you answer the telephone for your employer. If so, you can "reach out and touch someone" through the phone lines. Whatever your job, make sure you welcome people into your workplace. Go the extra mile of kindness. You may be the only Christian someone encounters all day. If your workplace is inhospitable, be the one to change your environment.

–MMA

POWER PRAYER

Lord, help me to reach out with Your love and kindness to all I encounter at work. Amen.

PASS THE MAYO

And my God will meet all your needs
according to his glorious riches in Christ Jesus.

PHILIPPIANS 4:19

Have you ever been between jobs? It's a scary feeling, isn't it? Those bills just keep coming even though your paychecks don't. But if you're in this situation today, I have good news for you. God can provide for you in a million different ways. Your paycheck isn't your source. God is your source!

Once when we were short on money, I received an unexpected five-hundred-dollar check in the mail. I couldn't believe it! The check came with a letter that said I had won the Hellman's Mayonnaise Essay contest. I had forgotten that I'd even entered! And what's more, I don't even like Hellman's. (No offense to the nice folks at Hellman's.) I'm a Miracle Whip kind of gal. I had entered that contest months before, but God knew when I'd need that five hundred dollars, and it arrived just in time.

God will do whatever it takes to get you what you need. From manna to mayonnaise—He has a way to supplement your income and supply all your needs. You don't have to figure it out. You don't have to sweat it. You just have to trust God and stand in faith.

–MMA

POWER PRAYER
Thank You, Lord, for meeting all my needs. I love You. Amen.

THE CHANGE

Let the peace of Christ rule in your hearts,
since as members of one body you were called to peace.
And be thankful.

COLOSSIANS 3:15

I once worked at an event that catered to a rough crowd. From the outside, these people looked like ex–Hell's Angels (and some of them actually were!). They were big, tough, and rough around the edges. Some were ex-convicts and still others could have been—if they'd ever been caught. But there was something different about them. They were completely sold out for Jesus. I've never quite met a group of people who were so thankful for their salvation. No one had to paint them a picture of hell; they'd seen it. And in their darkness, Jesus had found these men and women and changed their lives.

When I think back to those people, I can't do it without feeling a sense of humility. I have no doubt about the fact that Jesus changed my life and, without Him, I can't imagine where I'd be. Still, the thankfulness that these people had, I sometimes forget. I sometimes take my salvation for granted.

Today, take time to thank Jesus for your salvation. Think about the goodness that He's brought into your life. Remember the change He made. Keeping an attitude of gratefulness will help you keep your eyes on Him no matter where you are.

–GM

POWER PRAYER
Jesus, thank You for dying for me and changing my life.

TOUGH STUFF

Let us fix our eyes on Jesus,
the author and perfecter of our faith,
who for the joy set before him endured the cross,
scorning its shame,
and sat down at the right hand of the throne of God.

HEBREWS 12:2

There are times when we have to make tough decisions. We come to a crossroad and, instead of choosing the easy route, we take the hard way. It could be a change in career or relationships. It may mean going against popular opinion to stand up for morality. We've all had these choices to make, but we have to do what's right.

That's when it's good to remember the choice Jesus made. He knew that in order to restore a relationship between mankind and God, His life would have to be sacrificed. Though it was a tough choice, He made the decision to endure the cross for us. Just because it was right, the lashes and crucifixion weren't any less agonizing.

If you're standing at the crossroad of a tough choice, prayerfully consider your options. If necessary, discuss it with a strong Christian friend or pastor. Though your decision may not be easy, it can be the right one.

–GM

POWER PRAYER
Jesus, thank You for enduring the cross for me. As I make tough choices in my life, help me to make the best one—even if it isn't easy.

THESE CHANGES
ARE MAKING ME CRAZY

Jesus Christ is the same yesterday and today and forever.

HEBREWS 13:8

Have you ever heard the song "Changes" by Three Doors Down? The chorus goes:

> *"Now I'm going through changes, changes. God, I feel so frustrated lately. When I get suffocated, save me. Now I'm going through changes, changes. I'm running, shaking. Bound and breaking. I hope I make it through all these changes."*

Yep, there have been times in my career when that song could've been my anthem. Ever been there? When companies go through "changes," many times they incorporate new policies, new management, and extreme restructuring. I worked for a magazine that restructured three times in three years! I always joked, "If I'm let go over the weekend, please call me so I can bring in a box for my belongings on Monday." But in reality, things were almost that crazy!

When change smacks you in the face, there's only one thing to do—run to God. No matter what kind of craziness is going on where you work, you can rest in this truth—God never changes. So place your future in His hands. It's a good place to be!

–MMA

POWER PRAYER
Lord, I put my future in Your hands. Amen.

A CHANGE OF ATTITUDE

"God is with you in everything you do."

GENESIS 21:22

I absolutely loved my boss. He was gentle. He was kind. He was brilliant. And he was quick to offer assistance. Basically, he was the perfect boss. So when I changed jobs and encountered the exact opposite of my beloved former boss, I panicked. Everything I had respected about my former boss—his dedication to the craft, his backbone, his humor, his willingness to share his gift, his humility—were all lost on my new boss.

I was just about to call my former boss and go crawling back with my tail between my legs, begging for my old position, when I remembered a verse I'd learned in Bible school twenty years before: "God is with you in everything you do." The more I thought about it, the more encouraged I became. I realized that even though I no longer had the perfect boss, I still had God, and He promised to work alongside me in everything I did. That was good enough for me.

See, my situation didn't change for the better, but my attitude did. And that made all the difference. If you're unhappy in your job, change your attitude. Praise God that you have a job, and remember that He is with you today and always.

–MMA

POWER PRAYER

Thank You, Lord, for my job. Please change my attitude that I might honor You in my work. Amen.

STAYING GROUNDED

GOD's Message: "Because of the three great sins of Israel—
make that four—I'm not putting up with them any longer.
They buy and sell upstanding people.
People for them are only things—ways of making money.
They'd sell a poor man for a pair of shoes.
They'd sell their own grandmother!"

AMOS 2:6 MSG

Did you recently get promoted? Or did you just receive a pay increase? Did it change you? Money, fame, and promotion have a way of changing folks. The money and fame aren't necessarily bad, but the attitudes that sometimes accompany those two are destructive.

If the extra income you're now earning has changed you, making you insensitive to people and their feelings, ask God to give you a heart overhaul. Praise Him for your increase, and make sure that your tithe reflects your new financial status. Also ask the Holy Spirit to keep you grounded so that you don't become too pleased with yourself. The Word says that "Pride goeth before a fall," and you don't want to fall on your face.

The Lord loves to give His children blessings, but if He discovers that He can't trust us with promotion and financial breakthrough, then He won't bless us. Let's make sure we pass the test so that we can keep moving up with God.

–MMA

POWER PRAYER
Lord, help me to keep a humble and sensitive heart. Amen.

NEW PEOPLE

*Now to each one the manifestation of the Spirit
is given for the common good.*

1 CORINTHIANS 12:7

I'll never forget the one group of coworkers I loved most. We looked out for each other, encouraged each other, and celebrated each other's successes. We approached problems with unity, trying to find the best solution for everyone. Unfortunately, the bliss was only for a season. Eventually, they took other jobs or went home to spend more time with their families, and I was left behind. When new people arrived, I quickly realized that it wasn't the same. The spirit of the department had changed. It wasn't necessarily bad, just different. It took time for me to adjust, and to be honest, a part of me never did. Some of the joy of doing my job was lost.

As you work, coworkers will come and go. With some, you'll click. With others, you'll coexist. Though they may approach things differently, they aren't necessarily wrong. It could be that God needed new talent in the department or He may be fulfilling someone's calling elsewhere. Regardless, trust Him to help you make the transition. Ask Him to show you how to "gel" with the new people. Though they may be different, you may just be surprised at how well they fit.

–GM

POWER PRAYER

Lord, help me to work well with everyone in my office so I can accomplish all that I need to accomplish.

A FISH OUT OF WATER

The steps of the godly are directed by the LORD.
He delights in every detail of their lives.
Though they stumble, they will not fall,
for the LORD holds them by the hand.

PSALM 37:23–24 NLT

Sometimes when change comes on the scene, we think we're ready for it, but we're not. All of a sudden, we're expected to know skills we don't know, understand concepts we don't understand, meet impossible deadlines, and do it all with grace and wisdom. If recent changes in your life have left you feeling like a fish out of water, don't stress out.

Remember, God has already seen your future, and He will guide you every step of the way. No matter what you need to transition smoothly through the changes in your life, God has it for you. If you need wisdom, just ask Him. Proverbs 1:23 (NLT) says, "Come here and listen to me! I'll pour out the spirit of wisdom upon you and make you wise."

Don't be afraid of change. Embrace it! God will never give you more than you can handle, so you're going to be just fine. In fact, you're going to be better than fine. The Word says that you are more than a conqueror, so confess that today! Change? No problem. Bring it on!

–MMA

POWER PRAYER

Lord, help me to handle the changes in my life with
supernatural grace and wisdom. Amen.

WE'VE COME A LONG WAY, BABY!

GOD's strong name is our help,
the same GOD who made heaven and earth.

PSALM 124:8 MSG

In the last few decades, there has been a huge shift in the way business is handled. Computers are so common that workers can't imagine functioning without them. Just imagine life without e-mail or, at the very least, a DELETE key. Remember when correction tape and Wite-Out were the only way to correct a typo? Or how about carbon paper? Can anyone say, "We've come a long way, baby!"

Even though business has changed and our lives in general have become much more technological, God is still the same. I know there are people in the world who view Christianity as an outdated religion. They're following the "If it feels good (right) to me, do it" approach to life. But if you really pay attention and if you allow God to be active in your life, you'll see how real He is. Whether it's giving you wisdom about handling a situation or helping you save a relationship, He's still there. His fingerprints are everywhere.

As times change, remember that God is still the same. Unlike technology, He will never change.

–GM

POWER PRAYER
Lord, thank You for being real in my life. Help me to see Your fingerprints in everything.

WHERE'D THAT WRENCH COME FROM?

"I command you—be strong and courageous!
Do not be afraid or discouraged.
For the LORD your God is with you wherever you go."

JOSHUA 1:9 NLT

"We need to stop that project to make a change," my manager called as she rushed by my door. "Grab your files and come to my office." Of course, it was five o'clock and I had an appointment, but none of that mattered because a wrench—an unexpected change—had occurred.

After a few minutes (or days) of going through the wrench cycle—disbelief, frustration, and full-blown anger with a dash of self-pity—I picked myself up and started again. Welcome to the business world! I would love for projects to run smoothly from beginning to end, but wrenches happen to the best-laid plans.

If you've been thrown a wrench, don't get discouraged. Changes and disappointments are a part of working with people, but you can rise above them. Stay humble and keep a sense of humor. Focus on God, take a deep breath, and move forward. When the project is completed, you'll have a sense of satisfaction, and in time, you won't even remember the wrenches. You'll only remember the success.

–GM

POWER PRAYER
Lord, help me to have strength and courage when wrenches
come my way and trust You to direct me every day.

SIX-MILLION-DOLLAR ME

*In kindness he takes us firmly by the hand
and leads us into a radical life-change.*

ROMANS 2:4 MSG

We all have times when we want to change something about ourselves. Like the Six-Million-Dollar Woman, we want to become better, stronger, and faster at our jobs. We may want to learn how to communicate more succinctly or boldly or logically. We may want to become more detailed or improve our follow-through. We may want to learn how to be taken more seriously so that our ideas can be heard. We want to make a change.

Of course, there are thousands of books to help us achieve greatness at work, but since God is our creator, doesn't it stand to reason that He can help us change? He can help us become the person, employee, or boss that we desire to be. He can show us how to get the training that we need. All we have to do is turn to Him and obey what He directs us to do. As we follow Him, He will show Himself faithful.

–GM

POWER PRAYER

Heavenly Father, thank You for showing me how to become the best person and employee I can be. I give You all the glory for it.

ONE DAY AT A TIME

"Therefore do not worry about tomorrow,
for tomorrow will worry about itself.
Each day has enough trouble of its own."

MATTHEW 6:34

When change comes, many times it brings worry and fear along with it. In our humanness, we tend to fear the unknown. And since change represents unknown future events, we fear change.

When the company I worked for announced that we would soon undergo a computer system upgrade—my stomach began churning. I started wondering about the switchover. I wondered if I'd be able to learn the new programs. I wondered if the new system would really work like it was supposed to. I wondered if the company would replace me if I didn't learn the new software quickly enough. I wondered myself into a state of worry. Ever been there?

The key to facing change free from fear is to stop fear before it begins. When you have that very first "wondering moment," speak to that situation. Say, "I will not worry about this situation." Instead of allowing your mind to wonder, which leads to worry and fear, find out what the Word says about your situation and speak those words of faith. See, fear is developed by meditating on Satan's lies, while faith is developed by meditating on God's Word. Don't waste your energy worrying. Use that energy to develop your faith!

–MMA

POWER PRAYER
Lord, help me to stop worry and fear in their tracks! Amen.

GET HAPPY

*You were taught, with regard to your former way of life,
to put off your old self. . .
to be made new in the attitude of your minds. . .
created to be like God in true righteousness and holiness.*

EPHESIANS 4:22–24

When I was little, my mother had very little patience for a negative attitude. In fact, whenever I was tempted to have a fit, she would look at me sternly and ask—usually through clenched teeth—"Do you need an attitude adjustment?" That translated to "Do you need a spanking?" For my mother, attitude was everything. I would get in just as much trouble for a bad attitude as I would for disobedience or plain ol' brattiness. Looking back, I'm thankful for her guidance. She taught me at an early age that my attitude was within my control and that I could "get happy" if I put my mind to it. That lesson has served me well.

If you find yourself needing an attitude adjustment, then make the quality decision to make one. Guard against taking your bad moods out on others. God's Word says to "be made new in the attitude of your mind." So let your thoughts and moods display the life that you have in Christ Jesus. With Him, you truly know what it is to "get happy."

–GM

POWER PRAYER
Lord, I pray that my attitude and thoughts would reflect the new life I have in You.

BETTER THAN BEFORE

"Be strong and courageous.
Do not be afraid or terrified because of them,
for the LORD your God goes with you;
he will never leave you nor forsake you."

DEUTERONOMY 31:6

Two of my closest friends have ministered to me in a big, big way. Watching God orchestrate their family's steps is humbling. On two different occasions, I have seen the bottom fall out of their professional lives only to watch God quickly move them into better positions. Watching them handle the changes is amazing. They've truly learned that God—not the company, not the 401(k), not the bank account—is their source.

I often think of them when things aren't perfect in my professional life. Their lives have been tangible reminders that God is working on my behalf and He will never leave me nor forsake me. I'm one of His kids.

And guess what? You're one of His kids, too.

That doesn't mean everything will always be easy. But God doesn't fall off His throne when things go crazy. His Spirit still comforts and His Son still intercedes for us. With all of them working for you, how can you fail?

–GM

POWER PRAYER

Dear Lord, I trust You—regardless of what the situations
around me say. I know that You won't leave me or forsake me
and You're big enough to handle my dilemmas.

BEHIND THE SCENES

For He Himself has said,
"I will never leave you nor forsake you."

HEBREWS 13:5 NKJV

When I first ventured out of the nine-to-five routine to freelance full-time from my home, I had three steady clients. One of those clients had indicated that he'd be using me monthly, paying at least five hundred dollars. So I wasn't worried about losing my regular paycheck.

Well. . .two weeks after I came home to write, one of my clients moved to another state, no longer needing my services. And the other client took a financial hit and let me know that I'd only be needed once a quarter, not once a month. That left me with only one regular client that paid very little. Panic-stricken, I signed up to substitute teach for our local school system. (Who knew 8 a.m. to 3 p.m. could be so long?) The substitute teaching gig didn't pay very much, and I really disliked it. I was unhappy, worried, and discouraged. But just when I was about ready to throw in the towel, God came through with a new client who asked if I could do about five hundred dollars' worth of work every week. (Can you say *ch-ching*?) See, God didn't leave me. He was working behind the scenes on my behalf the whole time. Don't let change worry you. Trust God. His answer is always right on time.

–MMA

POWER PRAYER

Thank You, Lord, for always being right on time with the answer. Amen.

PARDON ME, MAY I USE YOU AS A RUNG?

Love. . .is not self-seeking.

1 CORINTHIANS 13:4–5

Love is not self-seeking. Well, that's a tough one to live in today's workplace, isn't it? I mean, if you don't look out for Number One, nobody else will, right? The world would have you think that you have to push and claw your way to the top—even at the expense of others. But that's not God's way of doing things. God wants to promote you in His way—in His time.

You don't have to "play the game" to climb the corporate ladder. You don't have to step on others to get ahead. You can rest in God, knowing that He has a good plan for your life.

Maybe you've been hurt by a coworker. Maybe someone that you trusted in your company betrayed you to gain placement in the company. It happens, but don't let that situation get you off track. Continue to walk in love, and allow God to open doors for you. He will!

See, God is looking out for you. He wants you to succeed, and He knows the best path for you to follow. You won't miss out on any promotions or successes as long as you follow Him and let love be your guide.

–MMA

POWER PRAYER

Lord, I trust You with my career. I know that You will cause me to succeed. I love You. Amen.

THE GOLDEN RULE OF GETTING AHEAD

*"So in everything, do to others what
you would have them do to you."*

MATTHEW 7:12

Ever worked retail? I worked my way through college as a clerk in a large department store. It wasn't a glamorous job, but it paid the apartment rent and allowed me to buy cool clothes at a discount. That was good.

You know what else was good? I learned what the term "working on commission" really meant—making a sale at any cost to reach your sales quota. This created a friendly (and sometimes not so friendly) competition among coworkers.

We didn't use the "it's your turn" method. Nope, this store's philosophy was simply "move in before your coworkers and make the sale." So that's what I did. But I soon learned that when I made my quota, I didn't make any friends. I was ruthless. I knew I wasn't "doing unto others as I wanted them to do unto me." So I stopped pushing and simply allowed God to open up sales opportunities for me. And He did.

See, God can help you make your sales quota, and you won't have to sacrifice your salvation to do so! Trust Him to help you achieve your goals, and you won't have to step on anyone's head to get ahead.

–MMA

POWER PRAYER
Lord, help me to be sensitive to others as I move up the corporate ladder. Amen.

JESUS' LEADERSHIP STYLE

*"You've observed how godless rulers throw their weight
around, how quickly a little power goes to their heads.
It's not going to be that way with you.
Whoever wants to be great must become a servant."*

MATTHEW 20:25–26 MSG

When some people get a little power, it's scary. Unfortunately, many feel that when they attain power, they'll finally get the respect they deserve or be able to make the changes that they want.

In actuality, leadership and respect aren't one and the same. Surely, you've known bosses, possibly the one you have right now, who didn't have the respect of their subordinates. Given the opportunity, their employees would sell them down the river for a smile and a wink because instead of building up their team, they lead by intimidation.

In Matthew 20:25–26, Jesus responded to a mother's request that her two sons hold powerful positions in heaven by saying, "Whoever wants to be great must become a servant." Regardless of what position you hold, develop an attitude of servanthood. Don't think of yourself more highly than others or look for chances to intimidate people. As you develop Jesus' leadership style, you'll be a leader others will respect and want to follow.

–GM

POWER PRAYER

*Lord, help me to become a godly leader who has an attitude of
serving others. Whatever position I hold, I want to honor You.*

RUN YOUR OWN RACE

*Let us throw off everything that hinders
and the sin that so easily entangles,
and let us run with perseverance the race marked out for us.*

HEBREWS 12:1

Have you ever looked across the conference table, stared your supervisor in the eyes, and wondered, *Just how, may I ask, did you ever advance to that position?* C'mon, be honest. Sometimes it's tough to be respectful when you know the person you call "boss" knows less than you do. It's even more difficult if your boss rose to that position through office politics, nepotism, or via another unfair avenue.

But, hey, that's not your concern.

You shouldn't waste precious time dwelling on such things. Instead, keep your eyes on God. Like the Bible says, run *your* race. Don't worry about anyone else's race. Keep your heart right. Pray for your boss. Then just do your best at your position.

You may have been treated unfairly. You may have been looked over for a promotion you deserved. You may work for a boss who treats you badly. You may have been at the company way longer than your current boss. But don't let it get to you. Just run your race. God already thinks you are a winner.

–MMA

POWER PRAYER

Thank You, Father, for my job. Keep my heart right, Lord, in the midst of nepotism and office politics. Help me to be respectful of those in authority over me. Amen.

HIS WAY

*"Get wisdom, get understanding;
do not forget my words or swerve from them."*

PROVERBS 4:5

In the movie *Legally Blonde 2: Red, White and Blonde*, Elle Woods goes to Washington, D.C., to get some legislation passed that would outlaw animal testing. But this bubbly blond runs into Washington politics at its worst. She tries to play the game, but nothing goes her way. Finally, after several failed attempts, Elle perkily says to her colleague, "You do it the Washington way. . . . I'm going to do it the Elle Woods way." The "Elle Woods way" was the nice, up-front way, and it proved successful.

Have you ever tried to tackle a difficult task in your job "the world's way" only to fall flat on your face? Sure, you might enjoy minimal success doing it the world's way, but God's way is much better. You don't have to play under-handed games to get ahead when you know the Head. You can call on God for wisdom and counsel any time of the day or night. The Word says that we should not lean on our own understanding but in all our ways we should acknowledge Him, and He will direct our paths. Why not get God involved in your business today?

–MMA

POWER PRAYER

*Lord, help me to lean on Your understanding and not my own
so that I might make good decisions today. Amen.*

Not What I Asked For

". . .yet not my will, but yours be done."

LUKE 22:42

Have you ever heard the song "Unanswered Prayers" by Garth Brooks? In the song, Brooks thanks God for not answering his youthful prayer of always loving his high school girlfriend, because he's so thankful for the wife God gave him later in life. It really is a beautiful reminder that God does know best.

There *are* times when it's better *not* to get what you pray for. Sometimes, the promotion or assignment that at first looks so enticing can end up feeling like a death sentence. Or, at the least, it can seem like you jumped from the frying pan into the fire.

If you've prayed for something that didn't happen the way you expected it to happen or God didn't answer your prayer the way you wanted Him to answer it, don't get discouraged. He may have been saving you from a difficult situation or preparing you for something better in the future. Even when it seems that God has "missed it" for you, remember that He's always preparing and protecting you, and He has your best interest at heart.

–GM

POWER PRAYER
Lord, let Your will be done in my life. I know that You only want what's best for me, so I trust You.

HITTING THE MARK

"He will answer them, 'I'm telling the solemn truth:
Whenever you failed to do one of these things to
someone who was being overlooked or ignored,
that was me—you failed to do it to me.'"

MATTHEW 25:45 MSG

I had been freelancing full time for more than a year when I ran into a woman who used to work at the same company where I had been employed. She waved to me from across the room at a local restaurant. I walked over to her table, and we chatted for a few moments. Then she introduced me to her husband. "This is the writer I told you about. . .the one who always took time to talk to me and the rest of the cleaning staff." I smiled and shook his hand. As I walked back to my table, my heart was smiling, too. I miss the mark much of the time, but for once I had hit it. My taking the time to chat with her on the nights I worked late had really meant something to her. And I knew it had meant something to God, as well.

See, we should never let a person's title or position determine how we treat that person. Whether you run into the janitor or the vice president, you should be equally friendly. Love doesn't see titles—only people.

–MMA

POWER PRAYER
Father, help me to see others the same way that You see them.
Amen.

A Cubicle by the Window

Do not think of yourself more highly than you ought,
but rather think of yourself with sober judgment,
in accordance with the measure of faith God has given you.

ROMANS 12:3

Isn't it funny how small things can determine someone's importance? Some revere those who are born to a certain family. Others honor those who have certain possessions. In office society, corner offices or cubicles by the window are coveted. They're given to the chosen, honored few. Everyone wants to be respected. And if you already have respect and honor, don't forget that there was a time when you didn't have the corner office or window view. Once, you were the one desperately trying to prove yourself to the office veterans.

When it comes to respecting others, it's best to follow God's example. He never looks down on you because of what you do or don't have. Instead, He looks at your heart. And even when you were covered with ugly ungodliness, He sent His Son to die for you.

As you go through your day, don't forget to show compassion and kindness for those around you. Value everyone for the people that God made them to be. After all, that's what's truly important.

–GM

Power Prayer

Thank You, Lord, for helping me to value others. Show me how to be an example of Your compassion and kindness to them.

ENCOURAGE DREAMS

*"My mouth speaks what is true,
for my lips detest wickedness."*

PROVERBS 8:7

Did you know that every time you or I say something, we have the ability to inspire or destroy those around us? Our words are a powerful force. We can encourage our coworkers and build one another up, or we can criticize and spew words that hurt.

I once attended a writing seminar called "Writing for Children 101." I had never written for children, but God had put that desire in my heart. So I couldn't wait to hear what the instructor had to say. Unfortunately, she had nothing edifying to share. Her exact words were: "You can't make a living writing children's books. It's very competitive, and the marketplace is already overflowing with new writers."

I wanted to jump up in the middle of class and yell, "You are a dream squasher! Shame on you!" I don't know how many budding children's writers never embarked on their careers because of her speech, but I know if God hadn't already birthed that vision in my heart, I would've said, "Hey, she must know what she's talking about. Forget this. I'll go work at McDonald's."

Be careful of your words. Keep God's Word in your heart, and let His divine words flow through your mouth. Don't be a dream squasher. Be a dream encourager!

–MMA

POWER PRAYER

Father, use my mouth to speak Your words, not mine. Amen.

EMPLOYEE OF THE MONTH

"Be still, and know that I am God."

PSALM 46:10

Don't you hate it when a coworker takes credit for something that you accomplished? It's even worse when a supervisor takes credit for your work. Ever been there?

I once sat in a meeting and listened to my boss read an idea that I'd submitted without ever revealing the source of that idea. When the "big bosses" raved over my idea, my boss was a hero, and I was furious. I couldn't believe that another human being, especially someone I had trusted, could be so deceitful.

I had two choices: Let the big man in the company know about my supervisor's behavior, or let it go and walk away. My flesh wanted to shout from the rooftops that the idea had been mine—all mine. But the Holy Spirit wouldn't let me. Instead, I kept hearing that verse, "Be still and know I'm God." So that's the direction I took, and God honored my obedience. Shortly thereafter, I was named "employee of the month"!

God will cause your ideas to rise to the top. He will make sure that your bosses know you are an asset to the company. After all, He is actually in charge, and He adores you!

–MMA

POWER PRAYER

Lord, I put my career in Your hands. Thank You for bringing my good work to the attention of the powers that be. Amen.

THE DREAM LIST

Write the vision,
and make it plain upon tables,
that he may run that readeth it.

HABAKKUK 2:2 KJV

Years ago, I made a list of things I wanted to do in my lifetime. It included things like sailing around the world, attending the Olympics, going on a cruise, and traveling Europe by train with my husband. I haven't accomplished all of them, and some I no longer have an interest in doing, like skydiving or hang gliding. (Those urges passed with the big hair of the 1980s.) Still, it's fun to review the list and see how many I've accomplished, which I no longer want to do, and others that are yet to be done. And of course, there are always new ones to add.

Writing down a vision—whether personal or professional—is a great way to keep your dreams in front of you. As time passes, it's a great encouragement. During those times when you feel like you're going nowhere, your list can remind you of all that you've accomplished. Then you can thank God for giving you the desires of your heart because He is the author and finisher of your life.

–GM

POWER PRAYER

Lord, thank You for giving me dreams and visions. I dedicate
them and my life to You.

COMPETITIVE OR JEALOUS?

And now these three remain: faith, hope and love.
But the greatest of these is love.

1 CORINTHIANS 13:13

Are you competitive by nature? I am guilty. My husband always teases me because I refuse to let our daughters automatically win whenever we play board games. If I'm playing—I'm playing to win. That competitive nature can work to a person's advantage. It definitely makes me work harder in my chosen career; however, it can also cause a person to act in a ruthless manner. Yes, I'm guilty of that, too. I wasn't aware of it until my supervisor handed me a copy of a small book entitled *Competitive Jealousy* and said, "I just read this book. . . . I think it will also benefit you." Ugh.

Well, like the saying goes, the truth hurts sometimes. If you're struggling with competitive jealousy or a ruthless competitive drive today, don't worry. God created you, and He knows just how to correct that competitive spirit so that it works *for* you and not *against* you. He wants you to succeed—but not at the cost of others.

The Lord prompted me to read 1 Corinthians 13, the Love Chapter, on a regular basis. Why don't you join me? I promise it will take your love walk to a whole new level. Suddenly, winning won't seem nearly as important as winning the lost.

–MMA

POWER PRAYER
Lord, increase my ability to love others. Amen.

FOLLOWING THE LEADER

"When the Spirit of truth comes,
he will guide you into all truth.
He will not be presenting his own ideas;
he will be telling you what he has heard.
He will tell you about the future."

JOHN 16:13 NLT

You want to move up. You want the promotion, but the odds are against you. Maybe you haven't been at your job very long or maybe there is stiff competition, but you know that you could do the job. So, other than working hard and trotting out your accomplishments, how do you go about gaining management's confidence? By listening to the Holy Spirit.

Many assume that God doesn't get involved in business, but if you're involved, He's involved. Ask Him to show you what to do. Don't assume that you can't turn to God and His Holy Spirit for answers. Ask Him to help you put your best foot forward and to give you fresh ideas.

God is interested in your success. So, if you know in your heart that a job is yours, ask Him to give you the direction you need to "wow" your boss. Then trust Him to lead you.

–GM

POWER PRAYER

Lord, I lean on Your Holy Spirit to guide me in all truth.
Please show me what to say and do.

YOUR DREAM JOB

Every good promise which the Lord had made. . .came true.

JOSHUA 21:45 NLV

I have good news for you—there is no such thing as a "glass ceiling" where God is concerned. There are absolutely no limits to how far you can go in your career. There is only one roadblock that can stop you on the path that leads to the dreams God has placed in your heart. No, it's not your boss. No, it's not that nasty coworker who is always sabotaging your work. No, it's not the state of the economy. It's your mouth.

That's right. Only *you* can stop what God has for you. If you speak doubt and unbelief, you tie God's hands. With every negative confession, you move another roadblock smack-dab in the middle of the road. So don't fall into that bad habit. Instead, use your mouth to praise God for all that He has done and all that He is going to do.

Maybe you're not working in your dream job right now. That's okay. God has a plan. Just keep on being faithful and only say what He says about your situation, and pretty soon you'll have that dream position. Begin each day saying, "Thank You, Lord, for my dream job. I know it's on the way." Get excited!

–MMA

POWER PRAYER

Lord, keep a watch over my mouth. Help me to only speak positive things. Amen

FRIENDSHIP OR BUSINESS

*The heartfelt counsel of a friend is
as sweet as perfume and incense.*

PROVERBS 27:9 NLT

I wanted the job, and the manager was desperate to hire a full-time replacement. But there was a catch: My friend Kate was temporarily working in the position. I knew neither woman was happy with the arrangement. Kate felt she hadn't been trained properly, thus set up to fail. The manager, on the other hand, believed that Kate hadn't jumped in to take control of the situation. They just didn't work well together.

So what was I to do? Apply for the position and have Kate feel that I'd stolen her job, or watch it go to someone else? The manager had already decided that Kate wouldn't be hired full-time. A sticky situation to be sure. Well, I applied for the job and got it. Thankfully, my friendship with Kate survived.

When applying for a promotion or new assignment, you may find yourself competing with a friend. Though this can be a pitfall of working with friends, don't avoid workplace friendships. Realize that God brings friends into your life to make you stronger. Sure, you may face tough situations, but together you'll be able to encourage each other through them.

–GM

POWER PRAYER
*Lord, thank You for the friends in my life.
Help me to preserve them.*

ENCOURAGE ONE ANOTHER

My heart overflows with a beautiful thought!
I will recite a lovely poem to the king,
for my tongue is like the pen of a skillful poet.

PSALM 45:1 NLT

Are you a supervisor in your office? Are you rising to the top of your field? Are you on your way to changing the world? That's great! Truly, you should be very proud of yourself. But I bet you didn't do it all on your own, did you? Think back. . . . Weren't there mentors and coworkers who encouraged you along the way? If so, then it's your turn to sow good things into others' lives.

As a successful person, you have the opportunity to speak into the lives of others, so you need to choose your words wisely. You should be writing very skillfully with your mouth—just like this psalm says. Your words could make or break someone.

That's why I love speaking at writers' conferences across the nation. I meet such wonderful people, and we're able to encourage one another. We speak into each other's lives, helping each other realize the dreams that God has put on our hearts. I am thankful for opportunities to use my mouth to write good things on people's hearts. Start using your mouth as a skillful poet today. God has a lot to say to others through you.

–MMA

POWER PRAYER
Lord, use my mouth to encourage others. Amen.

TOUGH CHOICES

*"Whenever they have a dispute, it is brought to me,
and I decide between the parties
and inform them of God's decrees and laws."*

EXODUS 18:16

Do you make tough choices in your work? Maybe you've had to fire someone or go against popular opinion. Good decision making is a vital part of business. Sometimes it means following the facts. Other times it means going with your gut instinct. Though you may be wrong, it's all part of the process.

Finding someone willing to make the tough decisions isn't as easy as it sounds. In scripture, one woman who made tough decisions was Rahab. At great risk to herself and her family, she hid Israel's spies. If she had been discovered, she and her entire family would have been killed for treason. Still, not only did she make the decision to hide them, but she also stood firm. She was courageous. In the end, she and her family were saved for her actions.

If you're in a position that requires you to make tough decisions, rest easy. God and His Holy Spirit are there to help you. Though people may get angry and lash out, be courageous. Remember that it's easy for them to second-guess you when they aren't responsible. God has given you your position, and He's equipped you to do it.

–GM

POWER PRAYER
Lord, help me to follow Your leading and make wise decisions.

ENVY

For where envy and self-seeking exist,
confusion and every evil thing are there.

JAMES 3:16 NKJV

Do you ever find yourself "jockeying for position" in your office? If so, you're not alone. My biggest challenge has been keeping that "go-getter" attitude in balance with the "do unto others as you'd have them do unto you" mandate.

While praying one afternoon, that still, small voice said to me: "Your drive is motivated by fear." I knew immediately what the Lord meant. I had recently been entertaining the thought of applying for an editor's position, yet I really didn't like magazine layout and editing, which this position entailed. I loved to write—period. But I had heard a colleague of mine was applying for the editor's opening, so I thought I would, too. I was afraid of being left behind. Yes, that makes me somewhat of a crudball, because this colleague was a good friend of mine. Why wouldn't I want him to have that job?

I am so thankful we serve a patient and understanding God—a God who loves crudballs. I repented and decided not to apply for that position. If you've been acting like a crudball lately, ask God to help you walk in love. You don't have to jockey for position. Just trust God. He has the perfect position for you.

–MMA

POWER PRAYER
Lord, help me to trust You more and walk in Your love. Amen.

IN FOCUS

So we fix our eyes not on what is seen,
but on what is unseen.
For what is seen is temporary,
but what is unseen is eternal.

2 CORINTHIANS 4:18

Did you know that your situation at work is subject to change? If you're in a terrible work environment right now, that workplace is subject to change. If you are between jobs right now, that, too, is subject to change.

Lakewood Church pastor Joel Osteen shared a story about his mother, Dodie Osteen, that really touched me. Dodie had advanced liver cancer. Weighing only eighty-nine pounds, she was sent home to die. But Dodie didn't focus on her circumstances. She didn't go around murmuring and complaining. Instead, she declared, "I am going to live and not die." Little by little, she got better. Now, more than twenty-two years later, she is perfectly healed and prays for others to be healed.

What if Dodie would have focused on the doctor's bad report? If she had, Dodie probably would have died many years ago. See, she chose to focus on the unseen. You need to make that same decision today. No matter what you're going through at work or at home, it's all subject to change. Fix your eyes on Jesus, and thank Him for turning your negative circumstances around. He can, and He will.

–MMA

POWER PRAYER
Lord, I fix my eyes on You today. Amen.

ALIEN INVASION

*And the peace of God,
which transcends all understanding,
will guard your hearts and your minds in Christ Jesus.*

PHILIPPIANS 4:7

Sooner or later, everyone loses their cool because of pressure and stress, and I'm no different. I've found myself getting irritable at people, worried about assignments, or fearful that things wouldn't be accomplished. It's one of the pitfalls of gaining added responsibilities. There's nothing like a promotion with additional duties, a better title, and a higher salary to give you the chance to "lose it." I've worked with many people whose personalities were altered by work pressures. Their calm rationale is replaced by harsh frenzy, as though some alien creature has taken over their bodies.

The good news is that none of us has to cave in to pressure. In the midst of crazy days when things don't go right and people get on your nerves, you can still have inner peace. You can still have God's perspective on your work and life. It just requires spending time with Him. As you do, you'll be able to bring your emotions, thoughts, and actions back into alignment with Him so that His peace permeates your life.

–GM

POWER PRAYER
Heavenly Father, I pray that Your peace will guard my heart and mind in Jesus Christ.

WORK OF MY HANDS

"But you did not listen to me," declares the LORD, "and you have provoked me with what your hands have made, and you have brought harm to yourselves."

JEREMIAH 25:7

I've always been goal-oriented. It's a trait that I received from my mother. Early on, she taught me the value of setting a goal and working toward it. Though it may take time and patience, I've learned that this brings rewards. In college, I set about studying business with visions of position and money dancing in my head. It wasn't until after I graduated and began working that the Lord redirected my goals. Since then, I've learned the value of following His path for my life. And though money is still an issue—I mean come on, we gotta eat—it's no longer the main one.

God gives us talents and desires that can lead to great things in our work, but more than anything, He wants us to love and serve Him. We have to be careful that our goals are about serving Him and using our abilities to honor Him—regardless of what our jobs are. And though there is nothing wrong with gaining position and money, be careful not to worship your own work. Remember, it is what you do, not who you are.

–GM

POWER PRAYER
Lord, I love and serve You. Direct my work so that it glorifies You.

TORNADO WATCH

*The men were amazed and asked,
"What kind of man is this?
Even the winds and the waves obey him!"*

MATTHEW 8:27

I had walked into a tornado. Excited about my new promotion, I didn't realize what waited for me. What I expected to be an exciting time went out the window. With few staff members, an untested computer system, unrealistic expectations, and lack of training, I was equipped for nothing. It felt like I'd been sucked into a tornado funnel. Around and around I went, and only God knew where I was going to land.

But you know, even through the toughest days, I felt the Lord's presence. It wasn't an easy time in my life, but I learned a lot. I discovered what I could endure and accomplish and what I wanted out of my career. In addition, I gained even more respect for my husband, who supported me through it all.

If you feel that you've been sucked into a tornado funnel, don't give up. God hasn't forgotten about you. He'll give you the wisdom to face it. He may calm the storm, or He may help you come through it. Either way, you'll know He's there with you.

–GM

POWER PRAYER
Lord, I feel like I'm in a storm. Please help me to stay strong as I trust You in every area of my life.

A DOSE OF JOY

Be joyful always.

1 THESSALONIANS 5:16

Before I had a book published, I truly thought that I'd be forever happy when I saw my book on the shelves of a bookstore. And I'll be honest—it was pretty exciting the first time I found my book at our local Barnes & Noble. It was even more thrilling when I did my first book signing. But you know what? That happiness was fleeting. After a few months, I began worrying about my next book contract. I worried I might be a "one-book wonder." I worried that I wasn't doing enough to promote my book. Just like a new toy loses its luster after a few hours on Christmas morning, my shiny new book had lost its appeal. It no longer made me happy.

You can't rely on career accomplishments, material things, or other people to make you happy. True happiness only comes from our heavenly Father. That kind of eternal happiness is actually called joy, and it isn't affected by outside circumstances. See, if you can't be happy cleaning your boss's office, you won't be happy even if you're promoted to boss tomorrow. If you're lacking joy today, turn to Jesus. He has a dose of joy with your name on it, and it won't ever lose its luster.

–MMA

POWER PRAYER

Lord, fill me with Your everlasting joy. Amen.

BOTH FEET ON THE GROUND

*He guides the humble in what is right
and teaches them his way.*

PSALM 25:9

I would love to say that I've remained humble in all situations but, unfortunately, I can't. There have been times when I was wowed by my own accomplishments, like when one of my projects came in looking better than expected, when I accomplished a task that others didn't want to tackle, or when I received a promotion. Those were the times when I sat up a little taller in my seat and gave myself a pat on the back. Of course, there were other times when I made huge mistakes, couldn't figure out a project, or my suggestions were overlooked in a meeting. Those times kept my feet on the ground.

Humility is such an important part of being an example of Christ to others. Face it; if we're so enamored with ourselves, we're not giving Him the recognition for working through us. Instead, we're letting everyone know that we think it all depends on us.

If you've been promoted or received recognition for a job well done, thank God for it. Recognize that your gifts and talents come from Him. As you remain humble, He'll continue to guide you in "what is right" and "teach you His way."

–GM

POWER PRAYER

*Lord, thank You for all I have because I know it comes
from You.*

PLAY NICE

Be kind and compassionate to one another.

EPHESIANS 4:32

I recently saw the movie *Thirteen Going on 30* starring Jennifer Garner. I loved it! Not only was the movie cute, it also had a powerful message. Jennifer's character makes a wish on her thirteenth birthday—she wants to be thirty and flirty. She wants to be one of the popular crowd. Well, she gets her wish. She wakes up a gorgeous thirty-year-old and the managing editor of a successful New York magazine. She has a cute boyfriend who is a professional athlete, a closet full of cool clothes and sensational shoes, and a life she'd only dreamed of. However, she finds out that she attained that life through being a terrible person—a backbiting, overbearing, insensitive player. Over the next sixty minutes, she rectifies the situation, and the movie has a happy ending.

Wouldn't it be great if we could fix our mistakes just as easily? Well, we can't, but God can. If you've stepped over others and made compromises in order to get ahead in your career, ask God to help you rectify those situations. Ask God to keep your heart sensitive to others' feelings. Remember, God doesn't want us to be players. He just wants us to play nice.

–MMA

POWER PRAYER
Lord, help me to treat others as You would have me do. Amen.

MAKING CONTACTS

*Earn a reputation for living well in God's eyes
and the eyes of the people.*

PROVERBS 3:4 MSG

The best business contacts I've ever made came not through
reading about my skills on a piece of paper, but through face-
to-face introductions. They came through networking. People who knew and trusted my work introduced me to their
associates. Or through social settings, people got to know me
and gave me the chance to prove myself.

People know us by our reputation. It's because of how
we handle ourselves that people—business contacts and
friends—come to trust us. Our words, actions, and demeanor
can give us a leg up in business and earn us respect.

In scripture, it says to "earn a reputation for living well
in God's eyes and the eyes of the people." People will know
us by what we say and do. That's why it's important for us
to remember that we represent Jesus all the time. When we
interact with a client, we represent Jesus. When we deal
with an irate customer, we represent Jesus. When we talk to
a coworker, we represent Jesus. So today, as you go about
your work, be the best example of Jesus that you can be.

–GM

POWER PRAYER

Jesus, help me be the best example of You that I can be.

IT ISN'T WHO YOU KNOW

*"Before I shaped you in the womb,
I knew all about you."*

JEREMIAH 1:5 MSG

I began my college career at a small Christian school in Kentucky. Asbury College was small enough that you knew your professors and they knew you. In fact, the college wasn't much larger than my high school. But after my freshman year, I transferred to Indiana University (Go Hoosiers!) in Bloomington, Indiana. IU is a wonderful Big Ten school, but I soon discovered that I was only a number among a sea of other students there. My professors certainly didn't know my name. I was just a social security number to most of them.

Maybe you work in a large company where your boss barely knows your name. Maybe you feel like a number in a sea of employees. Well, that's okay. Your boss doesn't have to know you. Your Creator knows you. The Word says that He knew you before you were even born. He not only knows who you are, but He knows the number of hairs on your head. And what's more, He has a great plan for your life (Jeremiah 29:11). So don't worry if you're not a household name in your field of expertise. God knows your name, and that's all that matters.

–MMA

POWER PRAYER

*Thank You, Lord, for knowing me and loving me so much.
Amen.*

ALL THOSE ISMS

Each of us is now a part of his resurrection body,
refreshed and sustained at one fountain—his Spirit—
where we all come to drink.
The old labels we once used to identify ourselves—
labels like Jew or Greek, slave or free—
are no longer useful.

1 CORINTHIANS 12:13 MSG

It's sad to say that there are still a whole lot of "isms" floating around the workplace—racism, sexism, ageism. Though they're subtly brewing under the surface, if you listen, you'll realize they're still there. I've been in meetings that had several women in attendance and only one or two men, and comments and jokes were made to put down the men. It's a sad commentary on how we don't completely respect each other, and it's counterproductive.

If you want to be productive in the workplace and make the most of your relationships with others, appreciate them—not just their similarities, but also their differences. Put aside the stereotypes and realize that God created all of us. We're all made in His image, and none of us has a higher position in the family of God.

–GM

POWER PRAYER
Lord, help me to appreciate others around me—not just the similarities, but also the differences.

DELIVERING THE MAIL

*If the LORD delights in a man's way,
he makes his steps firm.*

PSALM 37:23

Do you remember the first "career" position you held? Just thinking about mine keeps me *very* humble. After numerous interviews and months of temp work, I finally landed my first professional position as a marketing assistant, responsible for helping the marketing supervisor. Within weeks of my arrival, my new boss, who had never before had an assistant, gained added responsibilities and became a one-woman, Cracker Jack show. She did everything for herself. My days, on the other hand, dragged. My daily highlight became delivering the mail. Sadly, it was the one ten-minute task I had to do.

Thankfully, four months later I was promoted. Because of the things I'd learned, such as the department's procedures and vision, I was prepared to do more. I learned that every step is a preparation for the next.

If you're in a position and you think: *I could do so much more!* don't despair. God hasn't forgotten you; the skills you're learning *will* be put to good use. Until then, be patient and learn all you can. As you trust God, He *will* make your steps firm.

–GM

POWER PRAYER

*Lord, I'm thankful for my job because I know You use it to
meet my needs. As I prepare for promotion, I trust You with
every area of my life.*

NURTURING THE BLOOMS

Lazy hands make a man poor,
but diligent hands bring wealth.

PROVERBS 10:4

One of my favorite hobbies is gardening. I love planning flower beds, choosing plants, and even spending an afternoon in the garden. While I garden, I think about my work and relationships. It's relaxing, yet challenging. I have to imagine what the garden will look like in one to two years. Then, once I do the initial work, I nurture the plants so they can thrive. I have to be diligent if I want to enjoy the benefits of my work.

This is a fast-food world where results are expected quickly and diligence is sorely underdeveloped. But often it takes diligence to see the fruit of your labor. It takes time and effort to excel. A smart boss won't hand over the largest accounts to someone who hasn't proven herself to be a hardworking employee. He wants someone he can trust.

There are some qualities with which people are born, but others—like flowers in a garden—have to be nurtured. Decide to develop the quality of diligence in your life. In the end, you'll enjoy the colorful, lush benefits of your hard work.

GM

POWER PRAYER
Lord, thank You for all that You've given me in my life. I'm thankful for it and I will be diligent in everything I do—my family, my work, and my relationship with You.

THE CONSULTANT ENIGMA

"Now go; I will help you speak and will teach you what to say."

EXODUS 4:12

I remember when my company invited consultants to review our work procedures and make recommendations for how to improve them. In frustration, I listened to them make the same suggestions that the employees had been making for years. "Yes, that's exactly what we need to do!" management cheered, nodding like bobble head characters in a car window.

Of course, bosses aren't the only ones who miss when important things are said. God faces this all the time. He continually speaks to us, showing us how we can work and minister better. He just needs us to listen.

If it's been awhile since you've heard God's voice, then take the time to listen to Him. If you're having trouble getting started, try listening to praise music, closing your eyes, and focusing on the lyrics. Then begin praying—giving thanks, making your requests, and sitting quietly in His presence as you listen to those suggestions and impressions that He speaks to your heart. As you make this a habit, you'll find that you are more peaceful, productive, and in tune with Him than ever.

–GM

POWER PRAYER

Dear Lord, I want to hear Your voice and follow Your will. Help me to develop my prayer time so that I can hear You clearly.

I WANT MY OLD JOB BACK

*In all your ways acknowledge him,
and he will make your paths straight.*

PROVERBS 3:6

I stood waiting in the grocery checkout line when my thoughts were interrupted by a conversation behind me.

"I don't know why that Michelle Adams person has to write all of that garbage in the newspaper," the woman said. "We don't need to know that stuff."

As the two women continued bashing my reporting skills, I tried not to hyperventilate. I paid for my groceries and quickly escaped, wondering why I was being persecuted for simply doing my job—reporting on the school system's scandal.

I had recently been promoted from city government reporter to education reporter, and this was my first big story on that beat. Unfortunately, it wasn't a very flattering story for the community, and I wasn't gaining any popularity points. I suddenly longed for my boring city government beat. It was much safer there.

Change is difficult—even if the change is a promotion! Change comes with situations we've never encountered before. That's why we have to trust God and lean not on our own understanding. We may feel unsure and void of answers, but Jesus is the Answer. So trust Him and He will direct your paths.

–MMA

POWER PRAYER
Lord, help me to trust You no matter what changes I encounter in life. Amen.

LIVIN' FOR THE BELL

But our citizenship is in heaven.
And we eagerly await a Savior from there,
the Lord Jesus Christ.

PHILIPPIANS 3:20

There are days when even the most dedicated employee is "livin' for the bell." You just can't wait until the end of the day or the end of your shift. You may not even consider yourself a clock-watcher, but on the difficult days or when you have something important to do after work, you pack up five minutes early and bolt when the time comes.

As Christians, there is another bell that we should eagerly await: the return of our Lord Jesus Christ. The apostle Paul understood a great truth—his real home was in heaven. And with all that he did, he still wrote that he "eagerly awaited" Jesus' return. Though it can be difficult to imagine Jesus' return in today's world, it isn't any less of a reality, and we shouldn't be any less eager for it.

As you continue going about your business, don't forget to eagerly await the Lord's return. Remember that as important as anything you do here on earth may be, heaven—your true home—awaits.

–GM

POWER PRAYER

Lord, help me to remember You in everything I do. I recognize
Your Lordship in my life and in this world and realize that
this earth is not my true home.

STARS AND STARFISH

"For the battle is the Lord's."

1 SAMUEL 17:47

When I was in seventh-grade biology, our class was divided into pairs and asked to dissect a starfish. Yuck! I had quite a weak stomach, and I knew I'd hurl if I had to touch that stinky starfish. However, I was a fast note taker and a pretty good typist. So my partner and I agreed to work with our strengths—he did the gross stuff, and I did the rest. Our teamwork paid off! We received an "A."

If only every task worked out so well in the real world.

Have you ever been paired with someone in your company who simply wouldn't do any work? It's the worst! You want to rat out your lazy partner, but you're afraid to appear like less than a team player. It's a difficult, yet common, situation.

Maybe you're in that predicament today. If so, hang in there. Just remember that even if your boss never knows how much work you've done (and how little your partner has produced), God knows. Don't become bitter. Simply continue doing your best work. God will cause your actions (and your partner's inaction) to get noticed by those in authority. Soon, you'll be a star and your partner will be a stinky starfish.

–MMA

POWER PRAYER
Lord, help me to keep a right attitude even in bad situations.
Amen.

JUICY FRUITS

*A gossip betrays a confidence;
so avoid a man who talks too much.*

PROVERBS 20:19

"So do you have anything juicy to tell me?" my coworker asked.

I smiled nervously and answered, "No, but I do have some Juicy Fruit gum in my purse."

She rolled her eyes and smiled, hurrying to her desk. I was glad. I had avoided yet another gossip session with a coworker. Since my sister was higher up in the company than I was, she was privileged to information that others were not. Of course, my sister shared some information with me—tidbits that I had promised not to repeat. My coworkers knew this and pumped me for "juicy tidbits" every chance they got.

And to be honest, it was a struggle. I loved being "in the know." But I knew in my heart that I couldn't tell anything that my sister had shared with me in confidence. If I did, I'd be letting her down, and even worse, I'd be letting God down. So I tried my best to avoid those situations.

Maybe you're in an office where gossiping is a problem. If you tend to join in the "gossip fests," ask God to help you in this area. Let your words reflect those of the Father. Those are the only words worth sharing.

–MMA

POWER PRAYER
*Lord, help me to speak only the things You would have me say.
Amen.*

THROUGH HIS EYES

"Man looks at the outward appearance,
but the LORD looks at the heart."

1 SAMUEL 16:7

I remember when I first learned that "Gretta" had been promoted. I almost fainted. Gretta wasn't a very hard worker, and she was always causing strife within the ranks. Her promotion came as a huge surprise to me.

I discovered that my coworkers were also quite dumbfounded by Gretta's move up the ladder. We basically spent one entire lunch hour trashing Gretta. We criticized everything from her educational background to her lack of personality. It felt good at the time, but when I had my devotions that night, the Lord brought it all back to my remembrance. Then He took me to this scripture in 1 Samuel. Although He didn't speak audibly to me, I could hear that still, small voice saying, "You don't know Gretta's heart." He was right. I had judged her unfairly. Maybe she did deserve the promotion, and even if she didn't, I had no right to judge her.

You see, even if the office moocher gets promoted, it's not our job to judge that person's merit or worth. Only God knows that person's heart. He may not be a moocher at all. If you judge others too quickly, ask God to help you see your coworkers through His eyes. His vision is 20/20!

–MMA

POWER PRAYER

Lord, help me to see others the same way You do. Amen.

NAGGING RELAXATION

On the seventh day, having finished his task,
God rested from all his work.

GENESIS 2:2 NLT

I admit it: I'm terrible at relaxing. A multitasker to the core, I try to fill my time—even my days off—with as many projects and chores as possible. At work, if I'm on the phone, I organize my desk at the same time. At home, if I watch a DVD, I simultaneously flip through the magazines that have curiously appeared on my desk. The worst part is that if I don't keep up this frantic pace, I actually feel guilty, as though I'm not taking every opportunity to be productive.

I have to remind myself that relaxation was God's idea. He didn't tell us to take a day off because He wanted to torture us. He did it because He knew that we needed to rest. We need to refill our reserves and declutter our minds once a week. We need a weekly mental health day.

If you're like me and relaxation is a practiced art, start practicing this week. With a refreshed mind and spirit, you'll be able to tackle your job with more efficiency than ever before—minus the guilt.

–GM

POWER PRAYER

Heavenly Father, I know that You want me to take a day for rest. Help me to do that so that I'm more relaxed and productive than ever before.

NO SHORTCUTS
*Everyone has heard about your obedience,
so I am full of joy over you.*

ROMANS 16:19

Everyone wants to be successful. We want to be respected for what we do and rewarded accordingly. And though books and seminars may tell us that the road to success is paved with diligence and perseverance, who would turn down the shortcut—to be plucked out of obscurity and given a pat on the back, a raise, and a more prestigious title? Not many. But the road to success is rarely that simple. We have to be productive, hardworking, and willing to follow our employer's rules to truly be successful.

It's similar in our spiritual life. Though we want God's blessings, we can't casually throw up a prayer and treat God like a benevolent Santa Claus. He wants us to be diligent in our faith, determined in our calling, and obedient to His Word. Only then can He use us mightily. As I heard one minister say, "Don't try to get through prayer what you can get through obedience."

So as you diligently and obediently work to achieve success in your job, be just as diligent and obedient for God's kingdom. Then you'll know true productivity and success.

–GM

POWER PRAYER
Father, I pray that I would be diligent, faithful, and obedient to You and Your Word.

MENTORS

*I always thank God for you because of
his grace given you in Christ Jesus.*

1 CORINTHIANS 1:4

We all have mentors in our career—the people we look up
to in our professions. During my stint as a sportswriter at a
daily newspaper in Indiana, I had such a mentor. Bob was
(and still is) the hardest working newspaperman in the
business. He didn't just go the extra mile. He went the extra
hundred miles. I am so thankful for the time I was allowed
to work with him. Though he'd never discuss it because he's
too modest, Bob has won just about every journalistic
award you can win. I always say, "I earned my journalism
degree from Indiana University, but I learned the craft of
writing from Bob." He worked with me. He coached me.
And, yes, at times he was hard on me. But he made me a
better writer and, in the end, a better person.

In a world of slackers, moochers, and yes-men, it's so
wonderful to have the privilege to work for someone who
gives his all every day. Why not take a moment today and
thank those men and women who have impacted your life
as a working woman? Drop them a note or give them a call.

–MMA

POWER PRAYER

*Thank You, Lord, for placing such marvelous mentors in my
life. Please bless them today. Amen.*

FAITHFULNESS

"The master was full of praise.
'Well done, my good and faithful servant.
You have been faithful in handling this small amount,
so now I will give you many more responsibilities.
Let's celebrate together!'"

MATTHEW 25:21 NLT

Faithfulness—easier said than done, eh? Being faithful means being loyal and consistently doing your best regardless of the circumstances. That means, even if your boss is asking you to accomplish way more than anyone else in your department, you give it your all. That means, even if you've been passed over for promotion time and time again, you still show up for work and do your best. That means, even when your new team lead talks to you like you're a total moron, you work hard to make her look good. That's faithfulness. And God will honor it.

You give God something to work with when you're faithful. In fact, when you're faithful, you put yourself in position to be blessed and promoted. You see, when we're faithful in the little things, we earn God's trust. Once God knows that He can trust us—look out! Promotion is on its way. Rejoice in that fact, and praise God for your job. Praise Him that He is maturing you as you stand faithful. Praise Him for what's to come!

–MMA

POWER PRAYER
Lord, help me to be faithful—no matter what. I am trusting You for promotion. Amen.

ILLUSIONS

*And may the Lord our God show us his approval
and make our efforts successful.*

PSALM 90:17 NLT

A corporate trainer once said, "Time management is an illusion. You can't manage time; you can only manage what you spend your time doing." Instead, he recommended setting limited daily goals and accepting the fact that only so much could be accomplished within a workday. He was right, but at the time, visions of throwing his daily planner out the window filled my mind. The last thing I needed was someone confirming what I already knew: I couldn't get it all done. The best that I could hope for was to keep the engine running—okay, limping—as smoothly as possible.

All of us have limitations, but knowing and accepting them are two different things. Yes, God has called us to be productive, but He doesn't expect us to overload ourselves or constantly beat ourselves up for not accomplishing all that needs to be done.

Accept that God has called you to do your best. Ask Him to show you how you can work more effectively, then trust Him to work through you. Realize that you can only give your best—at work and home. Then ask Him to bless and multiply your efforts.

–GM

POWER PRAYER
*Lord, I dedicate my day to You and ask that You bless my
efforts so that my efforts will be successful.*

LET ME BE HEARD

"I will speak only the messages that God gives me."

NUMBERS 22:38 NLT

Have you ever listened to the difference in the way men and women communicate? As women, our style, though expressive and "full," is generally much more touchy feely.[1] For instance, we are more likely to turn statements into questions, like, "I like the production schedule, don't you?" We add disclaimers to our statements, such as, "Correct me if I'm wrong, but. . ." On the other hand, we are less likely to interrupt others. Regardless of our methods, by communicating effectively, we will get our jobs done and build trust in others.

Of course, the best kind of communication is speaking the things we feel that God has shown us. That doesn't mean that we need to bow our heads before making every statement, but as we follow the leading of the Holy Spirit and pray about our jobs beforehand, we'll be more confident and secure in what we say.

If you're looking for a way to improve your communication skills with your colleagues, take your job to the Lord first. When you have His take on the situation, you'll make even better decisions and be even more productive.

–GM

POWER PRAYER

Lord, help me to speak Your words in every situation.

CHEATING

*"Cursed is the cheat who has an acceptable male
in his flock and vows to give it,
but then sacrifices a blemished animal to the Lord.
For I am a great king," says the LORD Almighty.*

MALACHI 1:14

She had already given her two-week notice. I was sorry she was leaving, so I told her I'd treat her to a good-bye lunch. We laughed and talked and enjoyed one another's conversation. The clock ticked away the minutes too quickly. As our lunch hour came to an end, I just figured we'd walk back to our offices together. Instead, she joined another table of friends. "I'm going to take an extended lunch today. . . . What are they going to do, fire me?" she asked, laughing a bit. She was right. The company couldn't do anything to her. But that was the wrong attitude.

See, when we take a longer lunch break, spend fifteen minutes talking on the phone, or surf the Internet while on the job, we're actually cheating our employers. If they are paying us for an eight-hour day, we ought to give them eight hours of work, right? As Christians, our goal should be to go the extra mile of integrity. If you do, you won't go it alone. God will walk with you.

–MMA

POWER PRAYER
Lord, help me to be a person of integrity in all situations. I love You. Amen.

HAVE MERCY ON ME

*"Shouldn't you have had mercy on your fellow servant
just as I had on you?"*

MATTHEW 18:33

Have you ever made a big mistake at work? Not a little
oops, but a full-blown "oh no" kind of mistake? I have.
Once in the midst of developing a direct mail piece, I left
off a crucial piece of information, a last-minute, special
guest appearance at an international convention. After my
boss's boss called to ask why it wasn't on the final piece, I
dove into my notes only to discover that I had received the
information. I swallowed my pride and admitted my mistake. Oh, that was a painful phone call. She could have
yelled, threatened, fired, or placed a letter of reprimand in
my personnel file. But amazingly, she was merciful. She
began brainstorming about other ways to advertise the
guest appearance. Disaster averted.

If you've ever received mercy, then you can understand
the parable of the unmerciful servant (Matthew 18:21–35).
You know how thankful you are to receive mercy and how
important it is to extend it to others. It's part of the favor
and grace that God, through His Son Jesus, showed to you
and a reflection of the favor and grace that you should show
to others.

–GM

POWER PRAYER

*Dear heavenly Father, thank You for Your mercy, grace, and
forgiveness. Help me to show that same grace to others.*

DON'T STOP YOUR "STUFF"

"But I tell you that anyone who is angry
with his brother will be subject to judgment."

MATTHEW 5:22

You know the type. He comes in late. He doesn't prepare for meetings. He always misses deadlines. His lunch hours are more like two hours. He leaves early almost every day. Yet the bosses love him! (You're thinking of that person right now, aren't you?) Okay, be honest—it makes you angry.

But guess what? As aggravating as he is, that person is not your concern. God wants us to get our eyes off others and back on Him. By harboring ill feelings toward this person, you are only hurting yourself. In other words, you are stopping your stuff. Your anger toward this slacker may be the only thing standing between you and your dreams. So get over it!

Meditate on this verse: "Let us fix our eyes on Jesus, the author and perfecter of our faith" (Hebrews 12:2). If your eyes are fixed on Jesus, they won't be fixed on the guy in the office who is making you so mad. So fix your eyes on Jesus. Give Him your anger and, in return, He will give you love, peace, joy, and so much more! What a deal!

–MMA

POWER PRAYER

Lord, help me to fix my eyes on You and give up my anger once
and for all. Amen.

SHE IS YOU!

She considers a field and buys it;
out of her earnings she plants a vineyard.
She sets about her work vigorously. . . .
She sees that her trading is profitable.

PROVERBS 31:16–18

Have you ever read Proverbs 31? I mean really read it in light of your life? So often people visualize a truly godly woman as a quiet little church mouse, but if you read Proverbs 31, you'll see that she is really a savvy businesswoman. She is frugal, business minded, and hardworking, much like the modern working woman. She cares for her family, buys land, expands her crops, and gets good deals.

Sound familiar? Sure it does.

She's you as you balance your career and family. She's you when you work to make the best sales and meet your employer's goals while serving the Lord with your whole heart.

Don't believe that because you work outside of the home, you will never attain the godly, Proverbs 31 woman's image. The truth is that the gifts and talents you have are God-given, and as you use them, you are honoring Him, which is the true vision of the Proverbs 31 woman.

–GM

POWER PRAYER
Dear Father, thank You for providing for me and for using me to accomplish Your will in my family's lives and in mine. I pray that I would glorify You in all I do.

DON'T BLAME ME

*"And I will put enmity between you and the woman,
and between your offspring and hers;
he will crush your head, and you will strike his heel."*

GENESIS 3:15

Passing the buck is one of the workplace's greatest talents. "It wasn't my fault," people say when a mistake occurs; "I was just doing what so-and-so told me to do." It's funny; more time can be spent trying to pin the offender than correcting the problem. Sure there are times when we need to figure out why something happened, but passing the buck can be counterproductive.

Even in the Garden of Eden, Adam and Eve played the blame game. Adam's response is especially humorous. When asked about why he was disobedient, he responded, "The woman you put here with me." In other words, "God, it's kinda Your fault." Funny, huh? Of course, despite the fact that Adam and Eve disobeyed Him, God immediately implemented a plan to bring mankind back into relationship with Him. In verse 15, He eluded to Jesus when He told Satan that the woman's offspring would crush the serpent's head.

When we do things that are counterproductive to the Word of God, He still tries to protect us. We may try to go our own way, but we are never abandoned. Why? Because God always has a plan.

–GM

POWER PRAYER
Lord, thank You for always having a plan for my life.

A LITTLE HELP

When Moses' hands grew tired,
they took a stone and put it under him and he sat on it.
Aaron and Hur held his hands up—
one on one side, one on the other—
so that his hands remained steady till sunset.

EXODUS 17:12

Remember the story of Moses, Aaron, and Hur? The Amalekites attacked the Israelites at Rephidim. Moses said to Joshua, "Choose some of our men and go out to fight the Amalekites. Tomorrow I will stand on top of the hill with the staff of God in my hands." So Joshua went to battle as instructed, and Moses, Aaron, and Hur went to the top of the hill. As long as Moses held up his hands, the Israelites won, but whenever he lowered his hands, the Amalekites began winning. After a while, Moses' hands became tired, so Aaron and Hur held his hands up—one on one side, one on the other. That way, his hands remained steady until Joshua overcame the Amalekite army.

Together, Moses, Aaron, and Hur were able to keep their side winning. You might say Moses needed a little help from his friends. Let's face it, we can all use a little help from our friends once in a while. Don't try to go it alone. Don't try to be the hero. Together, you and your coworkers can accomplish much!

–MMA

POWER PRAYER
Lord, help me to be willing to assist my coworkers when called upon. Amen.

GOD IS IN THE DETAILS

O GOD, God of Israel, there is no God like you
in the skies above or on the earth below who unswervingly
keeps covenant with his servants and relentlessly loves them
as they sincerely live in obedience to your way.
You kept your word. . . .
You did exactly what you promised—every detail.

1 KINGS 8:23–24 MSG

You know how important paying attention to details is. When drafting a contract, every clause needs to be considered. When counting money or balancing books, every column needs to balance. Even something as simple as a few pennies in the wrong place can wreak havoc. As you are promoted to higher positions and incur more responsibility, the details become even more important.

In fact, in every area of our lives, the details are important. So it's nice to know that God is interested in the details. He doesn't just want the high points, He wants *every* point. And He isn't just interested in your church life or what you do wrong. He's interested in everything about you—home, work, relationships, well-being, health, hopes, disappointments, all of it.

If you've always assumed that God wasn't interested in the details, think again. He wants to be a part of the good and the bad, the beautiful and the ugly of your life.

–GM

POWER PRAYER

Lord, thank You for being a personal God, for being interested
in every part of my life.

KEEP SWINGING

*Watch out, so that you do not lose the prize
for which we have been working so hard.
Be diligent so that you will receive your full reward.*

2 JOHN 8 NLT

I once heard a story about a man who had this huge boulder in his backyard. He couldn't lift it because of its massive size, so he decided he would try to break it into smaller, more manageable pieces. Every day this diligent man would swing at this boulder with a large hammer. Weeks went by, and nothing happened. Then one day that huge rock split right down the middle. The man couldn't believe it! He hadn't swung any harder that particular time, yet the boulder broke into several pieces.

It wasn't that one remarkable hammer hit that destroyed the boulder—it was a cumulative effect. You might say that man's diligence finally paid off. And guess what? Yours will, too. Is there a big boulder that you'd like to destroy in your life? Maybe it's financial debt. Maybe it's past hurt. Maybe your boulder is made up of years of work frustrations. No matter what it is—it's not too big for God. Keep swinging the Word of God at your boulder. Keep being diligent in your prayer life. Keep being faithful in your tithing. Keep doing all that you know to do, and watch that boulder begin to break.

–MMA

POWER PRAYER
Lord, help me to be diligent. Amen.

THE MISSION STATEMENT

He said to them,
"Go into all the world and
preach the good news to all creation."

MARK 16:15

Every company and organization has a big picture, the thing that drives the services they provide. Often it's written in a mission statement so that there's never a mistake about what the company is supposed to be doing.

Often, I've been in meetings with people who had amazing ideas but, unfortunately, they weren't in line with the mission. Of course, missions can change over time, but in general, they're a great way to keep people productively on track.

In our spiritual lives, we have a mission, too. Jesus told the disciples to "Go into all the world and preach the good news to all creation." That is still relevant today. Some get nervous that God will call them to be missionaries in Zimbabwe, but you can actually impact your community right where you are. In your work and your neighborhood, you can fulfill the mission. And for those wanting to take it a step further, you can do a short-term missions trip in a nearby nation. As long as you're doing your part to share the gospel, you're right on track with Jesus' mission statement.

–GM

POWER PRAYER

Jesus, I want to be used to tell others about You. Please show
me how to do that in the best way.

FAITHFUL WITH LITTLE

"And he said unto him,
Well, thou good servant: because thou hast been
faithful in a very little,
have thou authority over ten cities."

LUKE 19:17 KJV

There really is no substitute for hard work. Though sometimes unexpected blessings fall into our laps, it often takes hard work to succeed.

Even in the parable of the ten minas, Jesus spoke of three workers who were entrusted with money. One didn't do anything with it. Another invested it in a mediocre venture, and the wisest of the three earned a 100 percent return. The boss was obviously most impressed by the largest return. His response was, "because thou hast been faithful in a very little, have thou authority over ten cities." In other words, because you've worked hard with a small amount, I know that I can trust you with more.

In our lives, we need to be committed to working hard for Jesus, too. In whatever capacity that He's called us to, we need to be "faithful in very little," so that we can eventually have authority over much more. By giving it our all, we can prove that we're ready and able to be used by God.

–GM

POWER PRAYER
Lord, I am committed to working hard in whatever job or
assignment You want me to do.

GO TO THE SOURCE

I know, LORD, that a person's life is not his own.
No one is able to plan his own course.

JEREMIAH 10:23 NLT

Have you ever worked on a project but had no idea what you were doing? You weren't trained or given the necessary information. You had to figure it out as you went. You felt like a child, playing Marco Polo in the dark. You needed clear communication from your boss.

Similarly, you need clear instruction in your life. You need to know where you're headed and what's expected. On your own, you can feel lost and discouraged. And just like you need direction from your boss for a work project, you need direction from God, your spiritual boss.

I've found that the moments when I begin to feel lost and discouraged in my life are when I've missed talking to God. I've tried to figure things out on my own instead of getting direction from Him.

If you're feeling lost and discouraged, the answers are closer than you think. Reading your Bible and praying are the best ways to discover God's will. By going directly to Him, you won't be left to wander in the dark alone. As you turn to Him, watch as answers come much more quickly.

–GM

POWER PRAYER

Dear Lord, I know that my life is not my own and
I need Your direction. So please direct me; I'm open to hearing
from You.

A PLACE FOR EVERYTHING

"And now about prayer.
When you pray, don't be like the hypocrites who
love to pray publicly on street corners and in the synagogues
where everyone can see them. I assure you,
that is all the reward they will ever get."

MATTHEW 6:5 NLT

You know her. . .Connie Crusader. She spends her workday reading God's Word instead of doing her work. She lays hands on people in the copy room. She goes out on the office balcony to pray on her lunch hour (And she'll position herself so you can see her praying, too.)

The problem is this—her witness isn't a good one! If you're like "Connie Crusader," reading your Bible when you should be reading reports or testifying when you should be typing, you're out of whack. God wants us to be bold for Him, but God is a God of order. There is a time and place for reading God's Word, praying for others, and testifying, but it's usually not during company work hours.

As Christians, we want to make God look good, and if we're slacking on the job, that's not going to get it. Unsaved coworkers resent Connie Crusaders and, in turn, they resent the God they represent. We must be very careful as we live out our Christian lives. Ask God to help you be a good representative for Him.

–MMA

POWER PRAYER
Lord, help me to be the kind of witness that will draw my colleagues to You. Amen.

GIVE IT YOUR ALL—
NO MATTER WHAT

*"I know, my God, that you test the heart
and are pleased with integrity."*

1 CHRONICLES 29:17

Be honest. Do you work a little harder when you know your
boss is looking over your shoulder? Do you slack off a bit
when you know the boss is on vacation?

If you answered "yes" to either of those questions, I'd
say you're not alone. It's a natural instinct to work a little
harder in order to impress those in authority over us; yet,
God wants us to do our best even when nobody is watching. God wants us to walk in the utmost integrity.

That means even if your coworkers are surfing the Internet when they're supposed to be working, you resist that
temptation and do your assignments instead. That means
even if every person around you steals office supplies, you
leave those paper clips and notepads in your office. That
means you give 110 percent whether your boss is in the office
or out of town.

Do your best every single day, and watch God work.
Sow integrity, hard work, and loyalty and reap a great harvest. God will cause your hard work and your integrity to
gain your boss's attention. And you can rest assured that
your Boss in heaven is taking note, too.

–MMA

POWER PRAYER

*Lord, help me to work to the best of my ability—no matter
what. I love You. Amen.*

MULTIPLY MY TIME

*Man shall not live by bread alone,
but by every word that proceedeth out of the mouth of God.*

MATTHEW 4:4 KJV

On the days when I have more work in my "inbox" than I have hours in the day, I start to feel overwhelmed and out of breath. I am definitely a "Type A" person with way too many irons in the fire, so this feeling of being overwhelmed is a familiar one. Can you relate?

But I have discovered something that makes no sense in the natural realm, yet it's absolutely true. When I give God my time—spending time in prayer and Bible study—He multiplies it back to me. It's when I neglect my time with God that I get into trouble.

I even pray, "Father, I thank You that You are disciplining me to stay committed to this Bible study and prayer time, and I ask You, Lord, to multiply my time back to me so that I may accomplish all that is on my plate today."

God is no respecter of persons, so what He does for me, He will do for you. Go on. . .try it! Spend time with Him today, and you'll discover that your work passes from your inbox to your outbox a lot more efficiently when you include God in your workday.

–MMA

POWER PRAYER
*Lord, help me to make time for Your Word every single day—
no matter what. Amen.*

IT'S HIS BATTLE

"No weapon forged against you will prevail."

ISAIAH 54:17

Do you have a supervisor who has about as much backbone as the marshmallow monster in the movie *Ghostbusters*? You know the type. He tells you and your comrades, "Oh, yeah. We're not going to put up with this latest corporate ruling. It's not fair to you guys. Don't worry. I'll fight for you. I'll make corporate understand what this new ruling is doing to our department." But when push comes to shove, he cowers out of his boss's office saying, "Yes, sir. Yes, sir," all the way down the hall.

Sure, it's frustrating. But don't resent your spineless boss. Instead, pray for him. You can bet that he probably feels worse about the situation than you do. Besides, you don't need your boss to fight your battles. God says in His Word, "The battle is mine!" He also says that "No weapon forged against you will prevail." Confess those verses over your work situation. Whenever corporate comes up with an idea that won't benefit you or your coworkers, pray that God enlightens the decision makers. Pray for favor. Pray that God might deliver you from that job. Just pray. Griping never changed a single thing, but prayer—especially Word-based, faith-filled prayer—changes much!

–MMA

POWER PRAYER

Lord, help my boss to walk in love, not fear. And Lord, help me to trust You more. Amen.

SHAVING OFF YEARS

*"I'll set honest judges and wise counselors among you
just like it was back in the beginning."*

ISAIAH 1:26 MSG

Do you have a mentor in your work? Not just a teacher, but
someone from whom you've learned how to be productive
and efficient? You can learn a lot from observing people
who have vast experience. It's a great way to shave years off
of your learning curve, and it's not a new concept.

In the Bible, there are several examples of mentors. In
the Old Testament, you can study about Abraham, Isaac,
and Jacob. Each learned from the one before them. Or
think of Moses and Aaron. Or Elijah and Elisha. Naomi
and Ruth. Then in the New Testament, there was the
greatest mentor of all—Jesus.

If you're looking for a way to boost your wisdom and
improve your productivity, pray for God to help you find a
godly mentor. In fact, you may want to find several to help
you in all the areas of your life—work, faith, and/or family.
These are people that God can place in your life to help you
develop a wise and mature approach to living.

–GM

POWER PRAYER

*Lord, thank You for the people You've brought into my life.
Help me to learn from them.*

WHAT ARE YOU SOWING?

Remember this—
a farmer who plants only a few seeds will get a small crop.
But the one who plants generously will get a generous crop.

2 CORINTHIANS 9:6 NLT

Have you ever heard the expression, "You reap exactly what you sow"? That's scriptural, you know. If you are arriving late to work every day, taking long lunches, leaving early, passing your work on to someone else, and spending hours playing on the Internet during the workday, you're sowing some bad seed. And you're giving God very little to work with.

God desires to bless His children, but if we show a lack of integrity on the job, we tie His hands. "But," you say, "Michelle, you don't understand. My company treats every employee badly. They don't pay me enough for what I do anyway, so I'm just going to take advantage of them." Well, maybe that's true, but you don't want to sow bad seed to get back at your company. You know why? Because you don't want to reap that kind of negative harvest.

No matter how badly your company treats you, give it your all every day. Do your work unto the Lord. Truly earn your paycheck, and give God something to work with. Pretty soon, you'll enjoy a harvest of promotions, raises, new jobs, favor, vacation days, and so on. Your blessing crop can't be far off!

–MMA

POWER PRAYER
Lord, I do my work unto You. Amen.

PRESS TOWARD THE MARK

I press toward the mark for the prize of
the high calling of God in Christ Jesus.
Let us therefore, as many as be perfect, be thus minded.

PHILIPPIANS 3:14–15 KJV

Motivating others is one of the greatest gifts someone can have. I've worked for bosses and with other coworkers who were flat-out inspiring. They could rally any group to follow them. People wanted to help them and loved being around them. This generally made them much more productive than the taskmasters, who tried to motivate out of fear.

In scripture, you'll find that the apostle Paul was a motivator. His epistles corrected the churches, but they also reminded the Christians of what they were really doing. He inspired them to "press toward the mark for the prize of the high calling of God in Christ Jesus." He said that it was what he did and it was what he hoped others did, too.

If you're looking for a way to be more productive and have a positive, inspiring influence on those around you, become a motivator. As you do, you'll share the joy that Jesus has placed in your life with those around you.

–GM

POWER PRAYER
Lord, I want to inspire others to "press toward the mark" of Jesus, too. Please show me how to become a motivator for You.

GUESS WHAT I LEARNED AT THE WATERCOOLER

*Do not let any unwholesome talk come out of your mouths,
but only what is helpful for building others up according to
their needs, that it may benefit those who listen.*

EPHESIANS 4:29

"He is such a moron," your coworker whispers over lunch.

"No kidding. How did he get to be boss?" your other friend chimes in. "He is so incompetent. And is he ever a lousy dresser! What is with that tie today?"

"I know. He is such a loser!" you add, forming the "L" sign with your right hand.

Ahh. . .lunchtime chatter. It's all harmless, right? Well, not exactly. According to Ephesians 4:29, we aren't supposed to let *any* unwholesome talk come out of our mouths.

Take your mother's advice: If you can't say something nice, don't say anything at all. Remember, your words are powerful. They can be building blocks or wrecking balls, so use them wisely. Don't bad-mouth your boss with your coworkers. Instead, find positive comments and observations to make. Be the positive force in your office.

This will take practice. You may have to bite your tongue really hard to keep from participating in the next boss-bashing session, but God will help you. Ask the Holy Spirit to keep a watch over your words. He will. And soon your words will create a better work environment.

–MMA

POWER PRAYER
Lord, help me to only speak words that build up. Amen.

HELP! I'M SURROUNDED
BY YES-MEN

"God is with you in everything you do."

GENESIS 21:22

Do you work in a company where you're surrounded by yes-men? You know the type. The boss says, "I think it would be a good idea if we all get our hair cut in Mohawks." And suddenly every person in the room says, "Absolutely. I've always wanted a Mohawk—it's my favorite hairstyle! Mohawks rule! Why didn't I think of that?"

Ahh! It makes you want to run out of the conference room screaming, doesn't it?

Every time it happens, the rebel spirit in me wants to stand up and say the exact opposite—even if I agree with the popular consensus. It's even more upsetting if you know in your heart of hearts that the yes-men are enthusiastically backing a wrong decision.

Let's face it. Working in the midst of brownnosers and yes-men is never easy. It's hard to stand up for what you believe—especially when you're the only one willing to have an opinion that differs from the boss. But don't despair. You don't have to go it alone. God will be your ally. And even if it's just you and Him against the world, that's all you'll ever need.

–MMA

POWER PRAYER

Lord, help me to have the courage to speak my mind, and help me to do so with respect and tact. Amen.

SURVIVING THE BOYS' CLUB

Refrain from anger and turn from wrath.

PSALM 37:8

Have you ever heard the saying "A woman has to be twice as good as a man to receive half as much credit"? I don't believe this is true in all situations, but I do believe that in some offices there is still a stigma against women. A woman can say the same thing that a man says, but the man's opinion carries more weight.

Though some women are bitter about this, as Christians, we need to guard against the bitterness. And we can take comfort that the tide is changing; not all male coworkers and bosses can be lumped into the boys' club mentality. Yes, it may still exist, but getting spiteful won't solve anything.

Only through sharpening your skills and praying will you succeed in a "boys' club" business. Learn from the successful women in your organization or industry. Trust God to show you how to be effective, then rest in the knowledge that you're doing all that He's told you to do. Yes, it may still be a man's business world, but with perseverance and faith, you can succeed.

–GM

POWER PRAYER

Lord, help me to be the best employee that I can possibly be. I want to be successful in the position that You've given me, and I trust that You'll show me the steps to take in order to do so.

PAINFUL PUNCTUALITY

There is a time for everything,
and a season for every activity under heaven.

ECCLESIASTES 3:1

Punctuality. Just writing the word is painful to me. I've never been very good at being on time. It's not that I don't give myself ample time to get ready. It's just that I try to do too much before I leave the house. For instance, I'll get ready and head for the door, and then I'll remember that I need to switch the laundry. Next thing I know, I'm off to another late start.

I once worked in an optometry office for a very kind doctor. He never yelled about my 8:05–8:10 arrival. Instead, he pulled me aside one day and said, "Listen, I don't care if you're a little late. But some of the other employees are upset about it. So just try to be on time." As they say in Texas, I felt lower than a snake's belly. I realized that my tardiness was creating stress for my wonderful boss, and it was ruining my Christian witness. I asked God to help me change that very day.

If you're challenged with punctuality, ask God to help you. He wants to be involved in every part of your life. Go ahead and talk to Him. He's got the time.

–MMA

POWER PRAYER
Lord, help me to be on time. I want to be a good witness for You. Amen.

ROUND AND ROUND IT GOES

The words of a gossip are like choice morsels;
they go down to a man's inmost parts.

PROVERBS 26:22

A few years ago, my company underwent a restructure. During that time, several important people were reassigned or dismissed. It was a difficult time for everyone. But even worse than what happened was listening to the rumor mill churn. Every day there were more and more theories tossed around about who was leaving and how jobs were going to be reorganized. Just listening to the churning caused people to become anxious—regardless of whether the rumors were true or not.

I have a friend who is brilliant at avoiding the rumor mill. She will change the subject or quietly walk away from conversations. I'll admit that I strive to be more like her 100 percent of the time. Unfortunately, sometimes I fail.

Imagine if everyone determined to avoid the rumor mill, making the decision to change the subject or walk away from hurtful conversations. Perhaps the next helpless victim would be saved and there'd be less anxiety in the workplace. You never know, it could just be the first step in winning your office for Jesus.

–GM

POWER PRAYER

Lord, please help me to stand strong against the office rumor mill so that I don't hurt others. Let me be a part of the rumor mill solution.

RUBIES, GOLD, AND SHORT SKIRTS

Charm is deceptive, and beauty is fleeting;
but a woman who fears the LORD is to be praised.

PROVERBS 31:30

Recently, I watched a reality TV show where several young professional women were competing for a promotion. They were trying to land accounts and increase sales. Sadly, they were relying on their sexuality to be successful, flirting with potential clients. They were trying to get ahead based on something other than their talents.

It made me wonder if I had ever tried to get ahead with cheap tricks rather than the talents God has given me. Had I flirted with manipulation or not telling the "whole" truth to make my way to the top? I hope I haven't, but it made me think: How easy is it in the workplace to resort to bending the rules of integrity rather than using the talents God has given us?

As God's daughter, you don't have to rely on cheap tricks to get ahead. You can rest knowing that God has given you every talent and ability you need to succeed. You can keep His standard of holiness and be "a woman who fears the Lord."

–GM

POWER PRAYER

Lord, thank You for loving me. I accept Your love,
and I desire to be a woman who fears and loves You.

THE BALANCING ACT

Fight the good fight of the faith.

1 TIMOTHY 6:12

Balancing your commitment to your faith and your work can sometimes be difficult. At times, your bosses or clients may question your commitment to your job, or they may honor your coworkers for achieving success even though it meant lowering their ethics or living for their jobs.

I've experienced this and struggled against the pull to be more like my peers. Though I was committed to my job, I was more committed to my convictions and my family's time. Unfortunately, those traits aren't always honored in business, but in the end, I appreciated the peace of mind that my faith gave me. For me, the trade-off was worth it.

If you're finding it difficult to balance your convictions and your job, don't let yourself get frustrated. Don't doubt yourself. Follow the truth, fighting the good fight of faith that you know is right—the truth and peace of mind that only Jesus gives. Then trust Him to promote you and give you favor. You won't be disappointed.

–GM

POWER PRAYER

Lord, thank You for giving me this job. I commit to following You with all my heart, regardless of the pressures others try to place on me. Help me to see the value in the stand I take and not doubt Your truth.

THAT NASTY NEPOTISM

You too, be patient and stand firm.

JAMES 5:8

Okay, so he went from delivering the mail to your manager in no time flat. Is he qualified for a managerial position? No. Is he knowledgeable about the area he now manages? No. Is he a relative of the big boss? Bingo!

As aggravating as it is when nepotism runs rampant, you still have to honor your manager. In actuality, it's not his fault that he was shown such favor. He probably knows he isn't qualified and is feeling a bit threatened right now. The worst thing you can do, professionally and spiritually, is challenge his authority. Instead, find ways to honor him. Look for ways to help him succeed. Don't give in to your flesh that's saying, "Let's undermine him and make him look really bad." Be an asset to him.

Even if you feel that position should've been yours, let it go. If you keep your heart right and walk in love, a promotion will be in your future, too. God honors those who honor Him, and by honoring your boss (even though you really don't want to), you're honoring your heavenly Father. You may not be related to anyone who can pull some strings for you in your company, but you're in really good with the Creator of the Universe. And that's a connection you just can't beat!

–MMA

POWER PRAYER

Father, help me to always honor my superiors. Amen.

AN HONEST DAY'S WORK

*Moses inspected the work and saw that they had done it
just as the LORD had commanded.
So Moses blessed them.*

EXODUS 39:43

"Knock. Knock. Can I come in?" she asked, peeking her head into my office.

"Uh. . .sure," I said, hesitantly.

It was her—Tammy Talker. Once she entered your office, you could count on at least a 15-minute distraction.

I'm sure you know Tammy—every office has a Tammy Talker. You know, the coworker who keeps you from getting your work done.

While it seems harmless enough, talking at length with others during the workday is the same as stealing time from your company. As Christians, we should go the extra mile when it comes to integrity. We should make sure that we give an honest day's work for an honest day's dollar. We should have the courage to say, "I'd love to talk with you after work, Tammy, but right now I need to get back to my assignment."

Granted, this response may not make you the most popular gal at work, but sometimes you have to be willing to ruffle a few feathers in order to do the right thing. It is possible to walk in love and integrity at the same time. And rest assured, God will be pleased with those steps.

–MMA

POWER PRAYER
*Lord, help me to stand up for what I believe—even if it's not
the most popular thing to do. Amen.*

DID YOU HEAR THAT?

I will listen to what God the LORD will say.

PSALM 85:8

Preacher Billye Brim said something I'll never forget. She said, "There's an 'ear' in the middle of your heart." Then she circled the "ear" in the word *heart*. There's a lot of truth in that observation.

In the midst of office craziness, training seminars, and watercooler gossip, it's hard to hear God's voice, isn't it? But it's not impossible. Jesus says in the scriptures: "My sheep know my voice" (John 10:27 CEV). Well, if we're born again, we're His sheep. So we should know His voice. But in order to hear His voice, we have to make time to listen. We need to quiet ourselves before Him every day and simply listen for His voice.

The Lord's voice can be drowned out by many distractions in the office and the home, but don't allow it. You can't be the best version of you—at work or home—if you don't spend time hearing from God on a daily basis. He has all the answers. He knows the future. He has all the wisdom you'll ever need. So tune out the world and tune in to Him. And don't just listen with your ears; listen with the "ear" in your heart. That's where you'll hear that still, small voice.

–MMA

POWER PRAYER

Lord, help me to hear You more clearly. I long to know You more. Amen.

TRANSLATE THIS

If any of you lacks wisdom, let him ask of God,
who gives to all liberally and without reproach,
and it will be given to him.

JAMES 1:5 NKJV

Sitting across from my new boss, Karen, I listened as she gave me promising points about the position that I had just accepted. She rattled off how successful I would be as her newest manager. Unfortunately, what she said and what reality was were miles apart. *Sign me up*, I thought at the time. It was only later that I discovered the truth.

When she said, "You're staff is set for growth," I discovered that she actually meant, "All but two employees have quit." And when she said, "Your sales goals are on track," she meant, "Last week was the first time in eighteen months that we've even come close." Not quite the translation that I'm used to. . .

There are times in the workplace that you'll be misled. It's just a fact. When it happens, turn to God for wisdom. His Word says that when you ask for wisdom, He'll give it to you liberally.

Many times, I've thrown myself on God's mercy, begging for wisdom. And thankfully, I've received it, and you will, too. He'll show you what to do and say, leading you in wisdom the whole way.

–GM

POWER PRAYER
Lord, I need Your wisdom for my situation. Please show me
what to do and say.

TAKE THE HIGH ROAD

*"Do not seek revenge or bear a grudge
against one of your people,
but love your neighbor as yourself. I am the LORD."*

LEVITICUS 19:18

Okay, it doesn't happen often in the publishing business, but it does happen. Once in a while, another writer will knowingly steal your ideas. Gena, my friend and coauthor of this book, and I wrote another book together before this one. During that time, we discussed our book with two other writers who were very enthusiastic about our project. We thought they were just being supportive, but now we know they were pumping us for information. Just a few months later, the two of them embarked on a *very* similar book.

When Gena and I found out, we felt betrayed, violated, and aggravated. "How could they do this to us?" I asked. I wanted God to zap them or something.

But you know what? Gena and I had to totally give that situation to God. We couldn't let our ill feelings toward them stop our stuff. In other words, we weren't willing to stop our blessing flow from heaven by staying mad at them—even though we felt justified in our anger. As Christians, God expects us to take the high road in every situation—even the situations that hurt our feelings. If you're feeling betrayed today, take the high road.

–MMA

POWER PRAYER

Lord, help me to always take the high road. Amen.

FOR SUCH A TIME AS THIS

*"And who knows but that you have come
to royal position for such a time as this?"*

ESTHER 4:14

Esther was a risk taker. A strong, faithful woman, she stood for what she believed, though it could have cost her life. Maybe it would have been easier to remain silent, but she knew that silence wouldn't save her from danger. Eventually, it would have arrived at her door, so she persevered.

Standing for what you believe in or what is honorable can cost you a lot. You run the risk of losing your job or being banished from the company's inner circle. You may even find that future promotions are unavailable. Are these worthwhile risks? Only you can decide, but living with integrity comes with a price. Unlike some of your coworkers, you have a moral code that surpasses anything written in a policy manual.

The good news is that God blesses obedience. Deuteronomy 28:1 says, "If you fully obey the LORD your God and carefully follow all his commands I give you today, the LORD your God will set you high above all the nations on earth." So don't fear your bosses or coworkers, because when you stand for God's commands, God stands for you.

–GM

POWER PRAYER

*Lord, I trust You to show me how to follow Your commands
with integrity and to stand for what is honorable.*

I'm Not Listening

*"But I tell you that men will have to give account
on the day of judgment for
every careless word they have spoken."*

MATTHEW 12:36

The office gossip. Yep, every workplace has one. Isn't it amazing how quickly she can move her lips? Of course, she can go through stories pretty quickly since she only tells half-truths. I have a good friend who was greatly hurt by one such gossiper. The office gossip started a rumor that my friend was seeing another coworker outside of work, even though both were married to other people. It simply wasn't true! I knew it. My friend knew it. I think even the office gossip knew it, but she didn't care because it made for good storytelling. Thankfully, my friend's husband believed her, and their marriage survived the vicious rumor, but it was a challenging time.

Gossiping, whether you are the one telling the lies or the one listening to them, is flat-out wrong. Don't participate in office gossip. Don't fan the office gossip's flame by showing any interest in her words whatsoever. Ask God to help you keep your lips and ears closed whenever you encounter the office gossip. Here's an idea: Why not tell her about Jesus and give her something really worth talking about?

–MMA

POWER PRAYER
Father, protect me from the rumor mill, and help me to never participate in office gossip. Amen.

HOLY ROLLERS UNITE

*"Blessed are those who are persecuted because of righteousness,
for theirs is the kingdom of heaven."*

MATTHEW 5:10

In our day and age, many of us don't think much about being persecuted for our faith. Living in countries that protect religious freedom, we don't face life-and-death persecution. But that doesn't mean that we don't face a type of persecution. If you work with coworkers who top off their workweeks by partying or flirting with immorality, you could be perceived as a Holy Roller because you refuse to participate. If you walk away from gossip or refuse to join the occasional bashing of an absent coworker, you may be labeled as self-righteous. These are types of persecution.

You are living by the standards of your Christian integrity. Others will see it and try to bring you down. But stand strong. Don't allow the allure of pleasing others make you lower your standards. Understand that persecution is part of living the Christian life. In 2 Timothy 3:12, it says that "everyone who wants to live a godly life in Christ Jesus will be persecuted" and the above scripture calls those who are persecuted "blessed." So take heart, knowing that God is on your side.

–GM

POWER PRAYER

*Lord, I will stand for You regardless of what others say. Thank
You for Your blessings in my life.*

COMPROMISE

*I refuse to take a second look at
corrupting people and degrading things.*

PSALM 101:3 MSG

Do you ever compromise your faith in order to fit in with the workplace crowd? Do you occasionally tell a dirty joke? Or do you join in the "gossipfest" and add your little tidbit of information once in a while?

It's difficult to live a holy life, isn't it? Especially when you are the only Christian in the workplace. But you don't have to go it alone. God will help you. You can also help yourself by filling yourself with God's Word instead of filling yourself with things that are contrary to the Bible.

I once heard a preacher say that we need to be careful what goes in and out of the "gates" that allow entrance into our spirits—the eargate and the eyegate. That's good advice. If you're watching movies that contain lots of cursing, off-color remarks, and sexual scenes, you're filling yourself with the wrong stuff. So when the opportunity to join in corrupt conversation occurs, you won't have any Word in you to stand strong. Instead, you'll have corrupt stuff to add to the conversation. So fill up on the Word, and you'll be able to withstand any office peer pressure. Ask God to guard "your gates" today.

–MMA

POWER PRAYER
Father, help me to fill myself with Your Word and nothing contrary to it. Amen.

RULES AND DRESS CODES

*Your obedience will give you a
long life on the soil that GOD promised
to give your ancestors and their children,
a land flowing with milk and honey.*

DEUTERONOMY 11:9 MSG

Do you have a problem with authority? I'll be honest—I sometimes do. I once worked for a company that had a very strict dress code. Women were expected to wear hosiery year-round. Okay, summers in Texas are insane. It's nothing to have an entire month of 100-plus days. And you know how hot hosiery can be, right? So I used self-tanner on my cleanly shaven legs and went to work without stockings. Needless to say, I was written up before noon. I protested, stating it was too hot to wear hosiery. Besides, my dress was very long. You could only see about four inches of calves! But you know what? All of my reasons (though they were good) weren't good enough, because I had directly disobeyed my supervisor by ignoring the dress code.

God doesn't want us to obey *some* of the time. He wants us to obey *all* the time. He doesn't want our obedience just when we agree with Him. He wants our obedience no matter how we feel about it. He also wants us to honor those who are in authority over us. So if you're a bit of a rebel like me, ask God to help you follow the rules—all of them.

–MMA

POWER PRAYER
*Father, help me to walk in obedience to You and those in
authority over me. Amen.*

WHAT'S DIFFERENT?

*"You will be his witness to all men
of what you have seen and heard."*

ACTS 22:15

Thomas Payne said, "Reputation is what men and women think of us; character is what God and the angels know of us." In other words, people see our actions and words, whereas God sees our hearts. It's through our actions and words that the people around us will see the truth of our faith and know the difference that knowing Jesus makes.

When we make the decision to live for Jesus, we become His hands and feet in the world. People can either be drawn to Him or repelled from Him because of our actions. They may not even realize what it is, but they'll know something is different. They'll know that we have more hope and peace in our life than they've known. In time, hopefully, they'll ask us about it and we'll have the opportunity to invite them to church, pray for them, or encourage them.

Just because you're at work doesn't mean that you're not a witness for Jesus. Through your thoughtful actions, kind words, and graceful integrity, you can be a witness to everyone of what you have seen and heard and the difference He's made in your life.

–GM

POWER PRAYER

Lord, let me be a witness for You so that others will want to know You.

THE DOWNFALL

Pride only breeds quarrels,
but wisdom is found in those who take advice.

PROVERBS 13:10

If there is one quality that I've seen eventually lead to some-one's downfall, it's pride. Some talented people I've known have fallen into pride's trap. They didn't make unpardon-able mistakes; they just didn't believe they *could* make mis-takes. In their eyes, they were always right, and everyone else—all us other poor, unenlightened souls—were wrong.

Pride can come from many sources. Some people get puffed up because of a spiritual gift like discernment. Because they have a gift for reading situations and people, they set themselves up as the judge of everyone. Or because someone is talented at their job, they see themselves as the standard and look down on everyone else. None of us is immune, and of course, all of us want to be valued for our talents; but we have to be careful to keep pride out of our lives. We need to be open to others' ideas and realize that our own talents are God-given.

By remaining humble and keeping pride out of your life, you allow God to work through you and use you for His glory.

–GM

POWER PRAYER

Lord, thank You for the gifts and talents that You've given to
me. Help me to keep pride out of my life and remain humble in
everything I do.

A GOOD WITNESS

*Be imitators of God. . .
and live a life of love.*

EPHESIANS 5:1–2

I once sat across from an editor at a writers' conference who flatly said, "Before you start your little book proposal pitch, my answer is already no. It's your responsibility to change my mind to yes." Well, as you might imagine, that just made me want to jump right into my presentation. (Go back and read that line with a hint of sarcasm for the full effect!) He was a tough guy with a stern look, and my energetic, somewhat peppy personality didn't exactly make me his favorite person. However, by the time I was done with my peppy pitch, he actually cracked a small smile, and he asked me to send him my book. Yay!

You know, I think our coworkers feel much like the book editor I described above. I think they've seen too many Christians behave badly, and they've already decided that their answer to Christianity is 'no' unless you can convince them otherwise. I don't mean they want us to shove scriptures down their throats every day in the office. I mean, they are watching us very closely. If they see something in us that they like. . .if they see Jesus in us. . .they'll crack a smile, too. Be a good witness today!

–MMA

POWER PRAYER

Father, help me to be a good witness for You day in and day out. Amen.

FRUITS?

*But when the Holy Spirit controls our lives,
he will produce this kind of fruit in us:
love, joy, peace, patience, kindness, goodness,
faithfulness, gentleness, and self-control.*

GALATIANS 5:22–23 NLT

When it comes to the fruit of the Spirit, have you ever noticed that we try to split them up? We think: *Well, I've got love covered, but now patience and self-control still need some work.* I know I have. Just ask me after I've inhaled a big bowl of pasta with cream sauce and followed it with a hot fudge brownie sundae. That's when I think I need to work on my self-control!

But notice that the above verse doesn't say *fruits*; it says *fruit*. So we can't just develop love, joy, or peace and not develop kindness, faithfulness, and self-control, too. They're all part of the same package.

If you're struggling to develop the fruit of the Spirit in your life, ask God to show you how to do it. You could even make it a joint study that you do with a friend so that you can keep each other accountable. Though none of us is perfect, through prayer, the leading of the Holy Spirit, and diligence, we can develop this fruit so that others will see the difference Jesus makes in our lives.

–GM

POWER PRAYER

Lord, thank You for Your Holy Spirit. Please help me to develop the fruit of the Spirit so that others are drawn to You by my example.

LOYALTY

But Ruth replied,
"Don't urge me to leave you or to turn back from you.
Where you go I will go, and where you stay I will stay.
Your people will be my people and your God my God."

RUTH 1:16

I love the story of Ruth and Naomi. Naomi's husband had died, and so had her two sons, leaving her with only two daughters-in-law, Ruth and Orpah. Because there was a famine in the land, Naomi decided to return to Judah and urged Ruth and Orpah to return to their own homeland. Naomi wished the best for her daughters-in-law, telling them that they should go and find new husbands. Orpah kissed Naomi good-bye and did as Naomi had instructed, but Ruth wouldn't budge. She basically said, "I'm with you 'til the end." Her loyalty to Naomi was so precious.

You know, loyalty is hard to come by these days—especially in the workplace. People trade company secrets like baseball cards. Coworkers backbite and maneuver their way up the corporate ladder. But you don't have to participate in any of those activities. If you'll trust God with your career, He will take good care of you—just like He did Ruth. She ended up with a life she'd only dreamed of. You will, too!

–MMA

POWER PRAYER

Father, help me to be loyal to You, to my family, to my friends, and to my coworkers and employers. Amen.

IT'S JUST MY PERSONALITY

As you come to him, the living Stone. . .
you also, like living stones,
are being built into a spiritual house to be a holy priesthood,
offering spiritual sacrifices acceptable to God
through Jesus Christ.

1 PETER 2:4–5

I admit it; personality tests make me nervous. Though they've given me great insight into myself, I've seen people use them to one-up each other. Instead of valuing each other for their strengths and differences, they automatically assume that certain personality types are better. They say, "Well, I'm a choleric"—or *lion* or some other test's label—"and that's why I'm strong-willed." Or "I'm an otter"—or *sanguine*, etc.—"and that's why I'm a social butterfly." I've even heard it taken to the extreme of excusing bad behavior because, "Well, that's just my personality."

When we become children of God, we're called to a higher standard than just our natural inclinations. He wants us to be "living stones" so that we become "spiritual houses" and "a holy priesthood" and "offer spiritual sacrifices acceptable to God." Yes, He made each of us different, with dissimilar attributes and tastes. Through those beautiful differences, we can grow spiritually stronger and become examples of godly integrity for Him.

–GM

POWER PRAYER

Lord, thank You for allowing me to come to You. Please help me to become a spiritual house for You.

THE ROAD MAP

*"My people are ruined because
they don't know what's right or true."*

HOSEA 4:6 MSG

Be honest. How often do you read your Bible? Do you
meditate on the scriptures so that they become written on
your heart? While it's difficult to find time to read God's
Word, it's so important. We need so much Word on the inside of us that there's not room for anything else.

This verse in Hosea really says a lot. See, if we don't
know what we believe. . .if we don't know what is right and
wrong. . .how will we ever be able to live a Christian life?
When you're faced with an ethical dilemma at work, you
need the Word to illuminate the way you should go. You
need God's guidance in your life. His Word is full of wisdom and guidance, but if you don't know it, it doesn't do
you a lot of good. Neglecting the Word of God is like having a road map to where you're going and never bothering
to look at it for direction.

So get out your road map to life and dive into God's
Word today and every day. He will help you make the best
decisions at home and at work. He not only knows the way,
He is the Way.

–MMA

POWER PRAYER

*Father, help me to crave Your Word and Your ways above all
else. Amen.*

GOD'S INTEGRITY

Surely he hath borne our griefs, and carried our sorrows:
yet we did esteem him stricken, smitten of God, and afflicted.
But he was wounded for our transgressions,
he was bruised for our iniquities:
the chastisement of our peace was upon him;
and with his stripes we are healed.

ISAIAH 53:4–5 KJV

During this season, as we ponder the sacrifice that Jesus made on the cross, we must remember that it wasn't an accident or coincidence. His life's purpose culminated in His death and resurrection. Because of Him, we know our heavenly Father as a personal God. Jesus *is* our example of integrity and godly living.

In this scripture, Isaiah prophesied of Jesus years before Jesus' birth, death, or resurrection. Through Isaiah, God made a promise to His people. He assured them that there was hope and that He had a plan to save them from spiritual death. Through Jesus, He kept His word.

As you go about your workday, remember that God *always* keeps His word. If you believe you have a promise from God, don't let it go. Whether it's salvation for a loved one, healing, restitution, promotion, or wisdom, don't let go. Continue to trust Him and take Him at His word.

–GM

POWER PRAYER

Lord, thank You for keeping Your word. I trust You to do what
You've promised to do.

YOU CAN COUNT ON IT

*Strong God, I'm watching you do it,
I can always count on you.*

PSALM 59:9 MSG

Don't you love people whom you can count on? These are special people that you know that are always true to their word and stand by you. They really are the best kind of friends.

Did you know that you have another friend that you can count on? That's right; God is that friend. He keeps His word even when it's difficult. When studying Israel's history, you see how strong God's word is. He promised Abraham that he would be the father of many nations and that his people would be God's people. Then if you follow history, you see how Israel turned its back on Him. Many times, the people abandoned their faith and worshiped other gods, yet God never gave up on them. He always remained faithful to His word and the covenant He made.

In our lives, God is just as faithful. He extended His mercy to us long before we accepted it. He loved us first, regardless of whether we returned the sentiment. Today, thank God for His faithfulness to His word. Make time to study the Bible so that you can better understand the promises He's given you. Then take a stand for those promises, knowing that He is true to His word.

–GM

POWER PRAYER
Lord, thank You for Your faithfulness and for always being true to Your word.

ON MY HONOR

Obey them [your masters] not only to win their favor
when their eye is on you,
but like slaves of Christ,
doing the will of God from your heart.

EPHESIANS 6:6

During my on-the-job training, I learned a lot more than
how to turn on the computer. In between technical instruction, my trainer shared company gossip and little tidbits of
information she thought would prove useful. For instance,
she warned: "When you're surfing the Internet, make sure
you don't stay on very long all at once. They monitor us.
Just be smart about it." Then she proceeded to tell me how
to "outsmart" the watchdogs so I could still slack off at
work and not get in trouble. Wow!

It's a pretty sad day for us when we have to figure out
ways to outsmart our bosses so that we can get paid and not
do any work, isn't it? God expects us to do an honest day's
work for an honest day's pay. Even if you're the only one
following company rules, keep doing the right thing. God
will honor you for honoring your superiors. Do your best
when you're being watched and even when you're not. God
has called us to be excellent, so let's do it!

–MMA

POWER PRAYER

Father, help me to walk in the utmost of integrity every day.
Amen.

WHEN NO ONE'S LOOKING

*"GOD, God-of-Heaven, the great and awesome God,
loyal to his covenant and faithful to those who love him
and obey his commands. . ."*

NEHEMIAH 1:5 MSG

Isn't it obvious when the boss is out on vacation? The atmosphere becomes a little more relaxed. Some people like to treat it like a mini vacation for themselves—kicking back, doing only what is necessary to squeak by, and basically taking an eight-hour coffee break. It's sad, and it's certainly a lack of integrity.

When our bosses are out of the office, we should be working just as hard as if they were there, not just because we are trying to please them, but because we are doing what needs to be done and taking pride in our work.

Imagine if God took a break from us whenever we weren't deep in prayer, if He was there when we were on our knees, but the moment we got up, He sat back and took a Starbucks break. It would never happen. Why? Because God is diligent and faithful in everything. He never goes on vacation and He's never out of the office. He's working on our behalf even when we don't realize it. His angels are protecting us and His Holy Spirit is directing us. Even when no one is looking, God is still on the job.

–GM

POWER PRAYER

*Heavenly Father, thank You for Your faithfulness and
for continuing to work in my life even when I don't see it.*

LITTLE WHITE LIES

*"For out of the heart come evil thoughts,
murder, adultery, sexual immorality,
theft, false testimony, slander."*

MATTHEW 15:19

Little white lies. . . Do you ever tell them? You know. . .
you're running late for work so you fudge a bit and tell your
boss that there was a major wreck that had traffic stopped
for fifteen minutes! Or you are out of vacation days, so you
call in "sick" so you can have a day off? Or you left the office unlocked last night, but you swear you weren't the last
one to leave. . . .

While describing these untruths as "little white lies"
certainly sounds better than calling them "big, whopping
dirty lies," they're still lies. And what's more, they are sin.
Notice in Matthew 15:19 that God puts lying (giving false
testimony) in the same sinful categories as murder, adultery,
sexual immorality, theft, and slander. Whoa! Those are
some big ones, eh?

Lying compromises our integrity, and it opens the door
to the devil. Don't give Satan any entrance in your life. Ask
God to help you be honest in every situation—even when
you're backed against a wall. While it's not always easy to
tell the truth, it's even more difficult to keep track of the
lies you've told. So walk in integrity. God will help you.
And that's no lie!

–MMA

POWER PRAYER

*Father, help me to live a life of integrity, free from telling
lies—white or otherwise. Amen.*

OKAY, I ADMIT IT

Praise the LORD, O my soul,
and forget not all his benefits—who
forgives all your sins and heals all your diseases.

PSALM 103:2–3

Don't you hate making mistakes? Some are relatively small, but others are life changing. Of course, none of us wants to be wrong. We want to believe that we have the best ideas and know the best way to work and live, but unfortunately, even the best of us make mistakes.

Even David, the man after God's own heart, made mistakes. In fact, he made a doozy. Most people know the story of David and Bathsheba. Bathsheba was someone else's wife, but David wanted her. After getting her pregnant, he tried to cover his mistake by sending her husband to the front lines of battle to be killed. But even after a series of bad choices, he eventually came to the tough place of admitting it. He came back to God and served Him with his whole heart.

When we make mistakes, we need to come back to God, too. Instead of trying to justify poor decisions, we need to run back to Him, knowing that His mercy and grace are always waiting.

–GM

POWER PRAYER
Father, I'm sorry for making a mistake and I thank You for Your forgiveness.

OUT OF BALANCE

By the seventh day
God had finished the work he had been doing;
so on the seventh day he rested from all his work.

GENESIS 2:2

When Friday night rolls around, are you exhausted? Have you given so much at work during the week that you have nothing left to give to your family and friends? If you answered yes to either question, you might be a workaholic.

While you should give your company 110 percent when you're on the job, if you take mounds of work home or you're constantly on your cell phone fielding questions from clients, you've crossed over into the land of workaholics.

It's a tough call. You want to be the "go-to gal" when your boss is looking for someone to promote. So if that means taking work home, you're willing to do it—but at what expense? If your job is stealing time away from your family, your friends, and your God, then you're out of balance. And you know what happens when we're out of balance? We fall on our hind ends.

So take time today and ask God to help you get your life in balance. He will! He is the great prioritizer. Follow His example. He worked hard for six days and rested on the seventh. We should do the same.

–MMA

POWER PRAYER

Lord, I'm asking You to put my life in balance. I love You and
trust You. Amen.

THERE'S NOT ENOUGH OF ME TO GO AROUND

I can do everything through him who gives me strength.

PHILIPPIANS 4:13

Did you ever walk on a balance beam when you were a child? I loved gymnastics when I was growing up, but I was never very good on the balance beam. I'd topple off to one side quite often. You know what's ironic? I'm still having trouble with that whole balancing concept. Only now I'm having trouble balancing my personal and professional life. How about you? Maybe you're an employee, a wife, a mom, a friend, a daughter, a sister, an aunt, a church volunteer, etc.; and you're not sure how to be all of those things at one time. If you are, welcome to the Sisterhood—the "Sisterhood of There's Not Enough of Me to Go Around."

There are days when I wonder how I am supposed to accomplish everything that is on my plate. But you know what? *I'm* not! God never intended me to do this by myself, and He never intended for you to go it alone, either. The Word tells us that we can do all things through Christ who gives us strength. *All* means *all*, right? So no matter how many roles you're fulfilling today, don't sweat it! God will help you.

–MMA

POWER PRAYER

Thank You, Lord, for giving me the strength and wisdom to stay on the balance beam of life. I know I can do all things through You. Amen.

TWISTED WORDS

*"For God so loved the world
that he gave his one and only Son."*

JOHN 3:16

I once oversaw a project that turned out to be a disappoint-ment. Because I understood the challenges with it, I had taken a *c'est la vie* approach to the results. When I showed it to a coworker who had worked on it, I explained what had happened. She wasn't so understanding and decided to confront a manager in another department about it. Dur-ing her rampage, she told the manager that I was "very upset." As you can imagine, things escalated, and it took two meetings and several weeks to repair the damage that she'd created—all because she'd twisted my words.

It got me thinking that sometimes we do this to God, too. We take His Word out of context. Instead of accepting that He loves us just as we are, we think: *If only I change this or do that, then God will love me.* The truth is that God accepts us just the way we are. He may want to perfect something in our lives, but He still loves us—wholly and without reserva-tion. So the next time you start to view yourself differently than God's Word says, remind yourself what His words *say*—truthfully and untwisted.

–GM

POWER PRAYER

Thank You, Lord, for loving me just as I am. I will look to Your Word for the truth about who I am in Your eyes.

READJUSTING THE COMPASS

The steps of a good man are ordered by the LORD:
and he delighteth in his way.

PSALM 37:23 KJV

My friends will sometimes ask me, "Are you still working as much or are you taking time off to relax?" I usually just laugh and shrug because, to me, it's just life as usual. I'm like most women: I work, play, socialize, and worship—sometimes all at the same time.

But every so often, I have to readjust my schedule. It's as though the needle on my internal compass has to be readjusted to point north again. I take a deep breath, put aside some time for myself, and get before the Lord for a heart-to-heart. This isn't a quick five-minute appointment. It's a several-day journey where I reevaluate my priorities and ask God to nix anything that isn't necessary to help me refocus.

If you're feeling like you're low on energy and have no time for yourself, take time to have a heart-to-heart with God. Ask Him to readjust your compass and show you where to focus your energies. With a renewed sense of purpose and direction, you'll have the energy to do what you really need to be doing.

–GM

POWER PRAYER

Lord, I am so busy that I can't even decipher what things on my to-do list are truly necessary. Help me to reprioritize and focus on what You want me to do.

NOT JUST A WORKER BEE

From him the whole body,
joined and held together by every supporting ligament,
grows and builds itself up in love,
as each part does its work.

EPHESIANS 4:16

In a meeting that my husband once attended, an executive referred to the attending staff as "worker bees." He said they were not to set the vision, only carry out the project. They weren't to have any ownership, but be mere drones. Of course this fell flat—way flat. On that day, my husband and I both determined that we were more than mere worker bees. And I hope that you make that same determination for yourself.

You may have a position to carry out others' plans, but that doesn't make you a drone who mindlessly works without adding to or taking pride in your job. God has placed gifts and talents in you, some of which you don't even understand yet. He's using you to provide for your family, help others, and be His example. That's not mindless droning. So the next time you feel like a drone, remember: You are more than a worker bee. You are a chosen, called, and gifted child of God!

–GM

POWER PRAYER

Thank You, Father, for calling me by name and giving me
every gift and talent that I have. I pray that You would help
me to diligently use them to bless You and others.

THE FLU

I will lie down and sleep in peace,
for you alone, O LORD,
make me dwell in safety.

PSALM 4:8

It was the first day off that I'd had in two weeks. Lying on my couch, I felt like I'd been run over by a truck. Exhausted, I could barely move. I ached all over, and I didn't want to eat. Though I didn't have a fever or an upset stomach, I felt sick. At the time, I didn't understand my symptoms, but later, I came across a newspaper article that enlightened me. It talked about a common illness found among Americans. The symptoms likened themselves to the flu and were caused by stress-induced fatigue. "Well, at least I'm not alone," I consoled myself, secretly wondering how long I could keep up the pace.

You don't have to live a stressed-out life. You can have peace. Turn to God and allow Him to help you. He may lead you—like He did me—to leave your position. Or He may show you how to delegate or prioritize better. Or He may give you peace to endure your job. Just know that you are not alone. God is ready to help you.

–GM

POWER PRAYER

Lord, thank You for Your peace, which surpasses all under-
standing. I pray that it would continue to guard my heart and
mind as You show me how to live in it all the time.

TEMPLE MAINTENANCE

Do you not know that your body is
a temple of the Holy Spirit,
who is in you, whom you have received from God?
You are not your own.

1 CORINTHIANS 6:19

Do you ever just make time for yourself? When is the last time that you took time out for a facial or a massage? If Boy George was topping the music charts the last time you spent a whole day taking care of you—it's time to take a "personal day."

If you don't occasionally make time for you, you'll burn out faster than a shooting star. God wants you to take care of yourself. If you don't, you won't have the energy, enthusiasm, or will to take care of business or your family.

The Word says that our bodies are the temples of God, so we need to do some temple maintenance once in a while. And in between those special pampering days, we should start taking better care of ourselves. Drink more water. Get eight hours of sleep. Find time for fitness. Make time for Bible study and prayer. Take time to have fun with family and friends. In short, we should enjoy the journey—especially the rest stops!

–MMA

POWER PRAYER

Lord, help me to find time in my busy schedule to take care of
me. Help me to make good choices for my spirit, body, and soul.
Amen.

SOMEBODY STOP THIS MERRY-GO-ROUND!

*"But seek first his kingdom and his righteousness,
and all these things will be given to you as well."*

MATTHEW 6:33

There are days when I feel as though I am on a merry-go-round, and it is spinning about 100 mph. In addition to work responsibilities, I have to take my children to their appropriate after-school endeavors, help them with their homework, pick up the dry cleaning, do a few loads of laundry, do some light housework, and so on. Then, if I'm really ambitious, I'll work out and shower before my husband comes traipsing in from his long workday. By bedtime, I'm spent. Yet that's the time I've reserved for God.

Many times I find myself falling asleep before I've even read an entire passage in the Bible. Or I'll finish my Bible study and snooze all through prayer time. A few months ago, the Lord began dealing with me on this issue. That's when it dawned on me—I should be giving God the *best* minutes of my day, not the leftovers. So that's my daily goal. And you know what? I've discovered that God actually multiplies my time. When I put Him first, He gets involved in the rest of my day. So give God your best minutes today, and He will bless the rest of your day. That's just the kind of God He is!

–MMA

POWER PRAYER
Lord, I give You my best minutes today. Amen.

TIME FOR STRENGTH

*So you must remain faithful to what
you have been taught from the beginning.
If you do, you will continue to live in fellowship
with the Son and with the Father.*

1 JOHN 2:24 NLT

Have you ever caught yourself treating the time you spend with the Lord like an obligation, a task to cross off your daily list, instead of an honor? I have, but recently I was reminded that it is so much more.

Sitting in a church service, a minister talked about his trip to Israel. Out of all the sites he'd visited, he found the Garden of Gethsemane the most touching. He said that it was where Jesus, during His private time with God, found the strength to endure the cross. I felt duly convicted.

If you're like me and sometimes you struggle to prioritize the things in your life, decide to take time out for God. Trust me; it'll make a *huge* difference. Spend some quiet time praying and worshipping Him. Let Him soothe your mind and arrange your day. When you do, you'll find your time with Him so much more satisfying and your day so much less overwhelming.

–GM

POWER PRAYER

Heavenly Father, I want to spend time with You today, not out of obligation but because I consider it an honor. Let Your will be done in my life and work.

WORKING FOR JESUS

*If I were still trying to please men,
I would not be a servant of Christ.*

GALATIANS 1:10

Don't you love to receive compliments? I do. It's nice to hear things like: "I know I can count on you." And it *really* means something when it comes from someone who doesn't give them very often.

A friend once worked for a boss who was hard on her. Sometimes during a trying time, she would escape to my office. During those moments, she would shake her head and say, "I work for Jesus, not her." At the time, I didn't completely understand what she was saying, but now I do.

Compliments, though nice to receive, aren't why we should do our jobs well. If we can feel good because of a compliment, then we can feel just as bad when we're insulted. In truth, our self-worth should only be dependent on God. That doesn't mean we shouldn't enjoy a compliment, but we should perceive ourselves the same regardless of what someone else says.

So the next time you receive a compliment or an insult, keep it in perspective. Ultimately, you work for Jesus, not man.

–GM

POWER PRAYER

Lord, thank You for loving me just as I am. Help me to see myself through Your eyes and not be bound to what others think of me.

ONLY ONE THING

"Martha, Martha," the Lord answered,
"you are worried and upset about many things,
but only one thing is needed.
Mary has chosen what is better,
and it will not be taken away from her."

LUKE 10:41–42

In today's world, women are expected to bring home the bacon, fry it up in the pan, then find time to run on the treadmill to burn off those bacon calories. Seriously, there are a lot of demands on us, aren't there?

If you're like me, you don't do anything halfway. I am a classic Type A personality, taking on way more than one person can handle, then working crazy hours to accomplish everything. Then, of course, I feel guilty for neglecting my family, so I'll spend quality time with them, sacrificing sleep, "girl time," and time with God. Sound familiar?

Well, like Martha in the Bible, we are worried and upset about many things when only one thing is needed—spending time at the feet of Jesus. I desire to become more like Mary, but my nature is very Martha-like. So it's a constant battle. But guess what? When I actually spend quality time at the feet of Jesus, everything else in my life is much better. So go ahead. Do the "bacon thing," but don't neglect your time with God.

–MMA

POWER PRAYER
Lord, help me to become more like Mary and less like Martha.
I love You. Amen.

WHAT'S RIGHT, NOT WHAT'S WRONG

*"Indeed, the very hairs of your head are all numbered. . . .
You are worth more than many sparrows."*

LUKE 12:7

Recently I watched an interview with a famous makeup artist. The interviewer asked the makeup artist for her number-one beauty tip. The artist said that her best tip wasn't about makeup at all. "When you look in the mirror, see what's right about yourself," she said, "not what's wrong."

Her comment struck me. As women, we can be very critical of ourselves. We don't think we're thin enough or attractive enough or we don't dress well enough. In the workplace, we even berate ourselves for things like making mistakes or not speaking up or not making the best decisions. We constantly beat ourselves down without anyone ever saying a word.

If you constantly think about what's wrong with yourself instead of what's right, remember that you are one of God's lovely creations. He doesn't see you as anything other than His precious child. He gave you attributes and talents, and He loves you just the way you are.

–GM

POWER PRAYER

Lord, thank You for loving me just as I am. Help me to see myself through Your eyes and to stop being so critical of myself.

AN ALL-NIGHTER WITH GOD

*My help comes from the LORD,
the Maker of heaven and earth.
He will not let your foot slip—
he who watches over you will not slumber.*

PSALM 121:2–3

Ever pull an all-nighter? In college, I basically lived on No-Doz and Diet Mountain Dew in order to stay up and study. Now that I'm in my thirties, staying up all night is much harder. (And it takes a whole lot more concealer to camouflage my dark circles.) But sometimes an all-nighter is the only option.

I had to stay up all night just recently to turn around a magazine article for an editor friend of mine. Another writer had suffered some personal tragedy and couldn't finish the piece. They were in a bind. So while the entire Adams family slept (even our miniature dachshunds were passed out on the bed), I typed away. I felt very alone.

As I prayed for direction about writing the lead to that article, it hit me—God is awake! Somehow, that made staying up all night much easier. It was like having "a study Partner." Isn't it comforting to know that God is always there for us? No matter how much work you have on your plate today, God can help you accomplish it. You don't need Diet Mountain Dew or No-Doz—all you need is Him.

–MMA

POWER PRAYER
Thank You, Lord, for being on call, day and night. Amen.

FAITH EYES

The seventh time the servant reported,
"A cloud as small as a man's hand is rising from the sea."
So Elijah said, "Go and tell Ahab,
'Hitch up your chariot and go down before the rain stops you.'"

1 KINGS 18:44

Remember the story of Elijah and the small cloud? There was a terrible drought in the land, and God told Elijah to present himself to evil King Ahab, and He would send rain. Elijah did as God instructed. Still, there wasn't a cloud in the sky. Elijah kept praying and sent his servant out to look toward the sea for signs of rain. Elijah sent him out seven times, and the seventh report came back: "A cloud as small as a man's hand is rising from the sea." Elijah knew it was God and basically said, "Tell Ahab to get ready for a toad strangler!" Elijah had his faith eyes on.

When you get ready for work each day, do you remember to put on your "faith eyes"? No, I'm not talking about some new miracle cream that diminishes wrinkles. (But if you have any of that, bring it on!) I'm talking about a state of mind—a faith-way of thinking. It's one of the most important things you can "put on" each day. Like that famous credit card advertisement says: "Don't leave home without it."

–MMA

POWER PRAYER
Lord, help me to keep my "faith eyes" in focus. Amen.

STANDING AT THE CROSS

Near the cross of Jesus stood his mother, his mother's sister,
Mary the wife of Clopas, and Mary Magdalene.

JOHN 19:25

Women are a resilient bunch. I mean, come on; we endure childbirth, which in itself is an award-winning feat. But even in everyday life, many balance families, friendships, and work, all while keeping a cool head. At home, they can cook dinner, talk on the phone, and balance a baby on one hip. At work, they can juggle multiple projects, referee opposing sides, and still find the energy to work out with a friend during lunch. They do what needs to be done.

That's why it comes as no surprise that women remained at the foot of Jesus' cross. They were devoted to Him and ready to remain until the end. Even in the midst of brutality and the impending loss of someone they admired and loved, these women kept their eyes on Jesus and remained.

When challenges—whether unexpected or the everyday variety—come, keep your eyes on Jesus. Place yourself at His feet and ask Him to show you the big picture. Let Him give meaning to what you're facing. Remember, you have a God-given strength and resiliency to handle whatever comes your way.

–GM

POWER PRAYER

Lord, help me to remain at Your feet and to keep my eyes on
You through any challenge.

IF I'M WONDER WOMAN,
WHERE'S MY INVISIBLE JET?

*He gives strength to the weary
and increases the power of the weak.*

ISAIAH 40:29

"Michelle, I'm going to need you to work late again to-night," my boss says, poking his head into my office.

I grimace.

"Is that going to be a problem?" he asks, eyebrows raised.

"No, sir," I answer, dialing my husband to see if he can pick up the children from day care.

Is this a familiar scenario? If so, I feel for you. It's tough to juggle all of the balls that are thrown at you daily, isn't it? There are some days when I just want to yell, "Calgon, take me away!" But in reality, I'd have to bring my wireless laptop computer into the tub with me if I were to squeeze a relaxing bath into my schedule. Life is busy—especially for the working woman. We're expected to bring home the bacon, fry it up in a pan, serve it, clean up the dishes, work out so the bacon doesn't deposit on our thighs, and do it all again the next day.

If you're feeling weary today, turn to God. No matter what you are facing. No matter how overwhelming it seems. No matter how tired you feel. God can help you. He will give you strength. Just ask.

–MMA

POWER PRAYER
Lord, renew my strength. Help me to accomplish all that is on my plate. I love You. Amen.

EUREKA!

[Jesus said,] "I came down from heaven
not to follow my own whim but
to accomplish the will of the One who sent me."

JOHN 6:38 MSG

Many of us have things that make our lives rewarding: family, work, or other personal achievements. If we don't keep these priorities in mind, we may wake up years from now far from where we want to be.

I discovered myself in this position a few years ago while attending a Dale Carnegie seminar. The speaker asked us to list the ten most important things in our lives. I rattled them off the top of my head: God, family, health, friends, et cetera. Then he asked us to rank them. Suddenly I realized that my priorities were out of whack. Certain priorities were at the top of my list, but they weren't the things on which I spent most of my time. I believe it was a divinely appointed "eureka."

If you are unclear whether your priorities are straight, make a list of the ten most important aspects of your life. Then rank them from one to ten. If you aren't spending your time on important things, ask God to help you rearrange your schedule so that you can accomplish what He's called you to do.

–GM

POWER PRAYER

Lord, help me to accomplish Your will. You know the things
that are the most important to me; please help me to make time
for them.

LAUGHTER AND HAIRPINS

*He will yet fill your mouth with laughter
and your lips with shouts of joy.*

JOB 8:21

Like most women, I like to look my best when I leave the
house. So when I received the worst haircut of my life a few
years ago, I was panicked! I had a mullet. To improve my
hairstyle during the growing out process, I bought some
faux hair that matched my natural hair. It sort of clipped in
my natural hair, but it took me awhile to get the hang of it.

Imagine this. . .I'm in the office of a coworker, dis-
cussing the outcome of a meeting we'd just had in the conference room, and as I went over a point very passionately,
I flipped my hair. In fact, I flipped it right off my head. My
faux hair landed on the ground, near my coworker's feet.
She jumped and screamed a bit. (I think she thought it was
a gopher or something.) We both laughed until our stom-
achs hurt.

I learned a valuable lesson that day—well, two actually.
First off, it's good to laugh at yourself. And second, always
use a lot of bobby pins when securing faux hair.

Laughing together and showing your vulnerability can
be very bonding. Don't be afraid to be imperfect with your
coworkers and God. They'll love you—mullet and all.

–MMA

POWER PRAYER
Lord, help me to be able to laugh at myself. Amen.

IDENTITY CRISIS

*And we were in our own sight as grasshoppers,
and so we were in their sight.*

NUMBERS 13:33 KJV

I love what I do. I truly enjoy writing inspirational books a...
magazine articles. But as much as I love it, I have learned th...
my identity comes from the Lord—not my career.

When I gave birth to our second child, my husba...
and I prayerfully decided that it would be best for me
stay home with the girls. So I quit my daily news repor...
position and went home to write and be a mom. While I
loved being a stay-at-home mom, I have to admit that...
missed "the position" I'd held at the newspaper.

After a few months of being home, Jeff and I were...
vited to a community function. As we socialized with
important folks in town, I realized just how much my id...
tity was rooted in my career. When asked "What do
do?" I'd mumble, "I'm a stay-at-home mom, but I use...
be a journalist for the local newspaper." I wanted the...
know that I could talk about more than diapers. That n...
I realized that I defined who I was by what I did and H...
others viewed my career. Maybe you're in that same boa...
so, jump ship! Your career doesn't define who you are...
God can do that.

—M...

POWER PRA...
Lord, help me to find my identity in You.

CELEBRATE WOMEN

*Dear friends, since God so loved us,
we also ought to love one another.*

1 JOHN 4:11

I admit it. I admire strong women. I admire them for their lively conversations, devoted friendships, headstrong determination, and humorous observations about life. They work hard, love intensely, and keep their senses of humor through it all. Even through the tough times, they never give up believing that, with God's guidance, they'll be okay. They're the ones who have shaped my life, and I hope that you've had a few of them in your life, too.

During this season, take time to honor the women who have meant so much to you: your mother, grandmother, aunt, neighbor, mentor, friend, coworker, boss. Don't miss the opportunity to give back to them—whether a gift or a note of appreciation. Let them know how special they are. These women have taught you so much through their example and friendship. They are gifts from God, people He brought into your life to teach you, love you, and be your friend, so honor them today. Because of them, you're who you are.

–GM

POWER PRAYER

Dear Lord, I pray that You would bless the women who have meant so much to my life. Let them sense Your presence today.

SAVOR THE SUCCESS

That's exactly what Jesus did.
He didn't make it easy for himself by avoiding people's troubles,
but waded right in and helped out.

ROMANS 15:3 MSG

There is a satisfaction that comes from having earned everything you have, isn't there? If you are one of the many who didn't come from wealth or had to overcome great opposition, you know what I mean. Maybe you put yourself through college. Or maybe you're a single parent who has alone provided for your children. Maybe you've survived an abusive past or destructive habit. Regardless, you savor every success.

But even as you savor your success, remember Jesus. Think back to when you got the job that turned your life around or the person who helped you. Remember the close calls when things could have gone wrong but didn't. These memories should remind you that you didn't make it alone. Jesus was there. Whether you realized it or not, He began drawing you to Him. Take time to thank Him for your salvation—and not just the moment you made the commitment—but the path that got you there. He was there, and He's still here, partaking in your every success.

–GM

POWER PRAYER

Dear Jesus, You're so merciful. Even when I didn't realize You
were there, I know that You were with me. Thank You!

SUPER WEAKNESS

But he said to me,
"My grace is sufficient for you,
for my power is made perfect in weakness."
Therefore I will boast all the more gladly about my weaknesses,
so that Christ's power may rest on me.

2 CORINTHIANS 12:9

I used to love to watch the superhero cartoons when I was a little girl. My absolute favorite superhero has always been Wonder Woman, with her awesome invisible jet and her cool magic lasso. I dreamed of growing up and looking just like Linda Carter. (I think I am about as tall as one of her legs.)

You know what I learned from watching years of superhero cartoons? Even superheroes have a weakness. For example, Superman's weakness is kryptonite. So why should *we* expect to operate free from weakness?

I have many weaknesses—some more evident than others. How about you? Driven any invisible jets lately? Well, I have good news! God's power is made perfect in our weaknesses. When we are weak, that's when God can really show Himself strong. So even our weaknesses aren't liabilities when we've got God—our secret weapon. When we are at our weakest point, God is at His strongest. Leave that invisible jet in the garage, and call on God today. He is the only superhero you'll ever need!

–MMA

POWER PRAYER
Thank You, Lord, for showing Yourself strong when I am weak. Amen.

I HAVE A QUESTION

*So we fasted and petitioned our God about this,
and he answered our prayer.*

EZRA 8:23

Have you ever wanted to question God about something
but wasn't sure if it was appropriate? It could have been
about a life-changing event, an accepted teaching in your
church, or whether or not you were doing what He wanted
you to do—even if it seemed good and godly. These are the
kinds of questions that we sometimes don't ask. We assume
that it's unnecessary or ungodly to question God, but usually He's the only one with the answer.

For me, one of the most freeing statements that a minister ever said was, "God is bigger than all your questions."
I'd never considered that. I assumed that it was wrong to
question God and that some topics were just off-limits. It
wasn't until that moment that I saw she was right. God *is*
bigger.

If you're struggling with a question that only God can
answer, go ahead and ask. You may not always understand
or even like the answer, but it's good to know that nothing
is off-limits with Him.

–GM

POWER PRAYER

*Lord, thank You for always hearing my prayers and questions.
I know that You are bigger than anything I bring Your way.*

CREDIBLE WITNESS

*"A good man out of the good treasure
of his heart brings forth good;
and an evil man out of the evil treasure
of his heart brings forth evil.
For out of the abundance of the heart his mouth speaks."*

LUKE 6:45 NKJV

When people think of you, what sort of person do you suppose comes to mind? A positive person? A negative person? A complainer? An encourager? As a Christian, you should have more positive days than negative ones. Of course, we're all allowed a bad day now and then, but if you're claiming to be a Christian yet you're constantly complaining and acting depressed, your witness is way off. If you struggle with down days and depression, you should get up every day and say, "No more down days! I have the joy of the Lord in my heart." Don't just accept gloomy days as a way of life. Obliterate them with the Word of God!

We should live our lives as walking witnesses of God's goodness and favor. In other words, we should be living, breathing billboards for the Lord. Trust me, people are watching you, just waiting to see how you'll react in every situation. They want to see if you really walk the walk or if you're all talk. So put a little joy in your walk and talk today!

–MMA

POWER PRAYER

Lord, help me to be a good witness for You. Amen.

OUT OF TIME

There is a time for everything,
and a season for every activity under heaven.

ECCLESIASTES 3:1

I've read a lot of interviews with people who are dying. I've even conducted a few of those deathbed interviews. When people are faced with death, they get pretty philosophical about life. But you know what? Not even one interview that I've read ever included this comment from the dying person, "Well, I just wish I'd worked a little more overtime in life. That's my biggest regret." No, usually regrets include things like: "I wish I'd laughed more and enjoyed each moment for what it was." Or "I wish I could've spent more time with my precious family." Or "I wish I could've made a difference." Work rarely comes up.

Yet, some of us work way too many hours, sacrificing time with our family, our friends, even our Lord. If you fit into this workaholic category, ask yourself why you do it. Are you working overtime because you desperately need the money? If so, ask God to provide additional financial provision through some other means. He has a million ways He can get money to you. Are you working more hours to prove something to yourself or someone else? You don't need to prove yourself. God already approved you before you were born. Whatever your reason, God has a better way. Just ask Him.

–MMA

POWER PRAYER
Lord, prioritize my life. Amen.

BOUGHT AND PAID FOR

*You were bought with a price
[purchased with a preciousness and paid for by Christ].*

1 CORINTHIANS 7:23 AMP

Though many people have bowed their knees to Christ and committed to follow Him for the rest of their lives, they still feel unworthy of His love. They're thankful that their sins have been washed away, but they still don't think of themselves as joint-heirs with Him. They still think of themselves as part of the lost world.

In this verse, you can see that you no longer belong to this world. Though you live in it, you are no longer a part of it. Jesus Christ paid for you. As the perfect sacrifice for all of mankind, He went to hell so that you wouldn't have to endure it. Once you committed to follow Him, anything you did in your past doesn't exist.

Whenever you begin to feel worthless or remember things you've done or the person you once were before Jesus became your Lord, remember that you were bought and paid for. You no longer belong to the world; you belong to Him. So your identity is no longer dependent on what you did in the past. It's based on to whom you belong today.

–GM

POWER PRAYER
Jesus, thank You for paying for me and my sin so that I could belong to You.

NO MORE SPINNING WHEELS

*"But seek first his kingdom and his righteousness,
and all these things will be given to you as well."*

MATTHEW 6:33

We live in a busy, busy world, and our lives are super busy, too. Making time to do everything that we need to be doing—working, playing, eating properly, exercising, worshipping, relaxing, sleeping—can seem overwhelming. I mean, how did we ever get along without daily planners or computers to remind us of where we need to be and when? But in all of our busyness, there is one priority that must be at the top of the list—our relationship with Jesus.

Everything else depends on it.

We can't hope to find happiness and fulfillment in our homes, work, or relationships without it. And without the peace and direction that a dedicated life brings, we're spinning our wheels.

If you find yourself so caught up in doing everything else that you can't seem to find time to pursue Jesus, then you're too busy and it's time to rearrange your priorities. Nothing else will do. When you put that priority first—above *everything* else—you'll find the peace and purpose that you desire.

–GM

POWER PRAYER

*Jesus, I am committed to following Your kingdom first.
I love You and want You to be the most important priority
in my life.*

MAKING THE B LIST

*Your love, O LORD, reaches to the heavens,
your faithfulness to the skies.*

PSALM 36:5

Every once in a while something unexpected comes across my desk that makes me chuckle for the rest of the day. On one day in particular, it came in the form of an e-mail invitation to a friend's farewell party. After perusing it, I noticed something that made me stop. It wasn't addressed to me or the other twenty-plus people beside my name. We were in the "CC," or carbon copy, address section. The "To" section was reserved for about six company bigwigs. Though the slight was unintentional, I'm pretty sure it was the equivalent of being asked to use the service entrance as opposed to the front door at a party.

I wasn't offended by it. In fact, I couldn't stop laughing. Unfortunately, my halo hadn't been polished that day and I called the e-mail's sender. Through snickers, I asked if I was "invited" or simply "informed" about the party. I was being ornery.

Isn't it nice to know that you are always on God's "To" list, and never, even when your halos are in desperate need of scrubbing, on his "CC," a.k.a. B list? Regardless of where you are on the company ladder, you will always be on God's A list.

–GM

POWER PRAYER

Lord, thank You for choosing and loving me just as I am.

THE SQUIGYS IN OUR LIVES

He has made everything beautiful in its time.

ECCLESIASTES 3:11

Close to my home is a small park with winding trails and a small creek. It's a slice of the country right in the middle of the city, and I love to walk through it. Along the way, I count the animals I come across—raccoons, snakes, birds, frogs, and my personal favorites: turtles. There is one small turtle in particular that I look for each time. I've affectionately named him Squigy.

Often, as I search for him, other park-goers have rushed past me, oblivious to anything else. It makes me wonder: How often have I rushed by God's handiwork because I was too hurried to appreciate it? As busy as we are in our lives, it's easy to miss God's beauty—spring wildflowers, giggling children, and yes, even small turtles.

Today, take time to appreciate the beauty around you—in nature and in people. There will always be a project due or meeting to attend, but a year from now, will you really remember it? Don't be so focused on your work that you lose sight of the Squigys. In the end, the small beauties—the Squigys—will probably be what you remember most.

–GM

POWER PRAYER

*Lord, thank You for the beauty that You've placed around me.
Help me to appreciate those beauties every day.*

THE REAL WORLD

I can do everything through him who gives me strength.

PHILIPPIANS 4:13

Okay, so your house doesn't look like a home decorating diva lives there. When you throw a party, you don't bake a cake, you buy one from the discount market. Your house definitely isn't passing "the white glove test." And you've been known to buy a new package of underwear simply to avoid doing the laundry. Yep, we live in the real world.

It's difficult to juggle work, a family, a home, church commitments, friends, and more. But hey, "difficult" is a piece of cake for God. He says in His Word, "When you are weak, I am strong." If He was able to create the world and everything in it in less than a week, He can certainly help you keep your life straight. But you have to ask Him to get involved in every aspect of your day.

Before your feet even hit the floor, say out loud, "Father, this is the day that You have made. I will rejoice and be glad in it. Order my steps, Lord, all day long. Help me to do exactly what You want me to do today." Talk to God throughout the day, and include Him in all of it!

–MMA

POWER PRAYER

Thank You, Lord, for being strong when I am weak. And thank You, Lord, for ordering my steps every single day. Amen.

YES OR NO

*Let your "Yes" be yes,
and your "No," no, or you will be condemned.*

JAMES 5:12

Do you have trouble saying no? I do. That's why a woman at my church gave me a book called *Boundaries*, but I let someone borrow it before I ever had the chance to read it. Do you know why? Because when she asked to borrow it, I couldn't say no! Isn't that ridiculous?

As women, we need to learn that saying no isn't a bad thing. Actually, it's a healthy thing. If you're like me, you've said yes to so many things that your time is not your own. I even do this in the professional realm. Last year, I said yes to two book contracts that had my final copy due on the same day. That's nuts! But guess what? I didn't want to make anyone mad, so I said, "Sure, I can do that," and I practically killed myself getting those manuscripts done.

God is teaching me in this area. He's showing me that I don't have to be pressured into yeses that I'll later regret. And neither do you! Ask God to help you only say yes to things He has planned for you. He will get involved in every aspect of your daily life, if you'll only ask Him. So ask Him today. He will say, "Yes." I promise!

–MMA

POWER PRAYER
Lord, I say yes to You! Amen.

NO-MAN'S-LAND

I will say of the LORD,
"He is my refuge and my fortress,
my God, in whom I trust."

PSALM 91:2

Once upon a time, I worked with two managers who feuded constantly. I don't know what started the feuding, but I do know that it made for a *challenging* working environment. It was a no-man's land, a place where no one wins and even the simplest tasks become major battles.

Unfortunately, this isn't unusual. Even in the Bible, Jonathan lived in a "no-man's land" between his father, Saul, and his blood brother, David. His father wanted to kill David while David raced around the countryside trying to understand why (1 Samuel 20). Fortunately, God's plan won out.

In the same way, God has a plan for you. It doesn't mean that you won't face uncomfortable situations, but it does mean that God can give you the grace to handle them. He may lead you to another position or direct you to be an example of peaceful professionalism. Regardless, keep praying. Don't get dragged into office gossip. Instead, focus on your work and pray. More than any anger, fear, or distrust, your prayers will be the real force.

–GM

POWER PRAYER

Lord, You know the situation even better than I do. I pray that You'll show me how to pray for the people involved and be an example of peaceful professionalism.

YOU CAN'T WIN 'EM ALL

*"But I tell you: Love your enemies
and pray for those who persecute you."*

MATTHEW 5:44

I was a senior in college, working in the Misses Designer Clothing section at a large department store. I needed the job to pay for college expenses. I was young and full of enthusiasm, high ideals, and big dreams—all of which really irritated my thirty-something boss. Just when I thought I'd won her over, I found out differently. I was in one of the stalls in the ladies' room when my boss and another department head came in to fix their lipstick.

"I have to figure out a way to get rid of Michelle," my boss whispered. "She drives me crazy. She's just so bright-eyed and bushy-tailed. Maybe I can transfer her to Men's Accessories."

I was the only Michelle in her department. I was crushed. I stayed in the stall until they left, had a good cry, and took my post back at the cash register. I learned a hard lesson that day—not everyone in the workforce is going to like you—no matter how hard you try. If you're dealing with persecution at work, begin praying for those who are deliberately being mean to you, and watch God change your situation. He will.

–MMA

POWER PRAYER

Lord, I pray for those workers who are being mean to me right now. And I thank You for vindication and favor. Amen.

I THINK I CAN TAKE 'EM

"You will not have to fight this battle. . . .
Stand firm and see the deliverance the LORD will give you."

2 CHRONICLES 20:17

Do you work with someone who is absolutely impossible? Are there days when you dream about jumping across the conference table and throttling that person? C'mon, be honest. It's tough to get along with every coworker. Some folks are just downright rude. But that doesn't give you the right to return their rudeness.

I used to work with a guy who said crude remarks every time he saw me. One day, he smarted off about my IQ and the size of my chest, and I wanted to deck him. I didn't care if I lost my job over the incident, I was ready to face the consequences. But on my way to his cubicle, the Lord stopped me. I distinctly heard His voice: "The battle isn't yours." Oh, but I wanted it to be mine. Still, I knew I had to follow God's leading, so I returned to my office.

A month later, that nasty individual moved—never to be heard from again. God took care of the situation, and I didn't have to lose my job over it. See, the battle wasn't mine. It was God's, and He had it under control. Give your battle to God today!

–MMA

POWER PRAYER

Lord, I give all of my battles to You. Thanks for taking care of me. Amen.

OUT FOR BLOOD

"Love your enemies, do good to those who hate you,
bless those who curse you,
pray for those who mistreat you."

LUKE 6:27–28

Janet was very unhappy in her job, and I had to work with her. She disagreed with management and thought she knew how the office should be run. Though she was angry with management, she decided to take her hostility out on me.

Wherever I turned, her accusations followed. Several times, she questioned my integrity. Unfortunately, whenever I tried to defend myself, people looked at me as though I were guilty. Eventually, months later, she left the company, but it was still a bad situation. I felt like I was one of Cinderella's evil stepsisters in a parallel universe.

It would be wonderful if everyone played by the same rules, but some people are just out for blood. Maybe you stand between them and a promotion. Maybe you have favor with management, or maybe you're just the nearest victim. Whatever the reason, situations like that don't usually go away by themselves.

If you have a coworker who is out for blood, pray for her. Be wise and follow God's advice to "bless" her. Eventually the truth will rise to the surface.

–GM

POWER PRAYER

Lord, You know the truth about this situation. I am deter-
mined to bless this person and ask for Your wisdom as I deal
with her.

LOVE THEM ANYWAY

"A new command I give you:
Love one another.
As I have loved you,
so you must love one another."

JOHN 13:34

It was happening again. The company needed a scapegoat, and my friend was the latest victim. While heating up my lunch in the company microwave, I overheard my boss's plan to fire my friend. As my boss discussed the particulars with another department head, I felt sick inside. I wanted to stand up on top of the lunch table and say, "Liar, liar. Pants on fire." Everything they were saying about my friend was untrue. Still, she received the pink slip the next Friday.

After witnessing that fiasco, I had absolutely no respect for my boss. My flesh wanted to talk about her with my coworkers. I wanted to tell them how she'd sold out to protect her own job. But the Lord reminded me that she was still in authority over me and I had to honor her. And because I was a Christian, I had to love her. Ugh! That was a tough one.

Maybe you have a boss who is hard to respect. If you're struggling today, ask God to let you see your boss through His eyes. You don't have to like your boss, but you do have to love your boss. Why not start today?

–MMA

POWER PRAYER

Lord, help me to love my boss the way that You do. Amen.

GETTING ZINGED

"Bless those who curse you,
pray for those who mistreat you."

LUKE 6:28

Let's be honest; we've all been zinged. You know, those comments that are said so sweetly that it isn't until you walk away that you realize you were insulted, like "I *love* your hair. It looks like something from the forties." Yeah, I loved hearing that one.

As an individual who is blessed to breathe air, you're sure to have received a zinger. And as women, we've been blessed with long memories that allow us to relive those comments over and over again.

When the zingers come—and they *will* come—you have two choices. You can respond emotionally, leaving godly grace at the door, or you can respond in love—either by remaining silent or by *gently* responding to the comment. The choice is yours.

However, if you're listening to the Holy Spirit, you know that He won't let you get away with responding with a verbal assault. No, it's much better to respond in love. And the next time you see the "zingee," follow the advice found in Luke 6:28 and pray for God's blessing in her life. As you do, God promises that "your reward will be great" (Luke 6:35) and you will become more and more like Him.

–GM

POWER PRAYER

Lord, I ask that You help me to be an example of Your love and
grace in everything I do.

GIVE THEM YOUR DUE

The entire law is summed up in a single command:
"Love your neighbor as yourself."

GALATIANS 5:14

Do you feel like you're always going the extra mile and being taken advantage of? I imagine Abraham felt the same way when Lot chose the best piece of land. Remember that story?

Abraham followed God's leading and gathered all of his family, traveling for months before finally arriving at the new land. But after being there only a short while, they discovered there wasn't enough land and water to support all of the people and flocks. So Abraham told Lot, "We're going to have to separate. Choose whichever piece of land you want, and I'll take whatever is left over." Lot looked around and chose the beautiful, green, lush valley, leaving Abraham an old, dry field.

Don't you imagine that Abraham felt used and unappreciated? But that's not where the story ends. See, God told Abraham to climb the highest mountain and look in every direction. Then He said, "As far as you can see, I'll give it all to you." That's the kind of God we serve.

When you're good to people, God will make sure you come out on top. God sees you preferring other people. Nothing that you do goes unnoticed by Almighty God. Honor others and God will honor you.

–MMA

POWER PRAYER
Lord, help me to treat others as You would have me do. Amen.

GO THE EXTRA MILE

A man's wisdom gives him patience;
it is to his glory to overlook an offense.

PROVERBS 19:11

Sometimes when working with difficult people, I've imagined that I could pull a big lever and make them disappear through the floor. Nice, huh? This usually crosses my mind when someone is either giving me 1,001 excuses or playing devil's advocate. So when I came across Luke 9:52–56, I realized I wasn't the only one to have felt this way. In this passage, Jesus and His disciples had entered a Samaritan village but hadn't received a warm welcome. In response, the disciples asked if they should "call fire down from heaven to destroy them."

Don't you understand their frustration? Surely you've wanted to call down fire from heaven on someone who was making your life hard. Thankfully, Jesus wasn't as easily offended because He corrected His disciples. He knew the Samaritans were acting out of ignorance and needed His patience. In the same way, we need to have patience with others. More than judgment, those who irritate us need our patience.

The next time you're tempted to grab the imaginary lever or call down fire from heaven, take a moment—and a deep breath—to pray for patience. You may just be the first to show that person mercy.

–GM

POWER PRAYER

Lord, help me to have patience and overlook offenses.

PATIENCE, PLEASE

Be patient, bearing with one another in love.

EPHESIANS 4:2

How do you react when one of your coworkers acts ugly to you? Before you get too aggravated, put yourself in his or her shoes, and see that person through the eyes of Jesus.

I heard Pastor Joel Osteen tell about his encounter with a woman who manned the phones at a local pizza place. He shared that he frequently called that establishment to order pizzas, and the first thing they always asked him was his telephone number. So Joel knew the routine, and simply gave his phone number as soon as the woman answered. She said, "Sir, I didn't ask you for your phone number. I'm not ready for it, and when I get ready for it, I'll let you know." Joel said that she had spoken so ugly to him that he wanted to order about twenty fake pizzas and cause her to make dry delivery runs all over the city. Instead, he chose to respond in love. By the end of their conversation, she was throwing in hot wings and two-liter sodas and coupons for free pizza. He had won her over through the love of Jesus.

Why not follow Joel's example? Go that extra mile and respond in love. God will reward you, and He gives even better gifts than free hot wings.

–MMA

POWER PRAYER
Lord, help me to always respond in love. Amen.

BIG PLANS

"For I know the plans I have for you," says the LORD.
"They are plans for good and not for disaster,
to give you a future and a hope."

JEREMIAH 29:11 NLT

Being in a meeting with her was pure torture because I knew she was going to take her best shot at making me look bad before the meeting was over. She used words like darts—shooting all who might come between her and the boss's ultimate approval.

One day I saw her sitting in the boss's office, chatting it up, and an eerie feeling shot down my spine. "She's setting somebody up," I thought. I worried all day that it might be me. By that night, my stomach was in knots. As I went into my prayer time, I heard the Holy Spirit say, "She can't keep you from My plan for your life—only you can do that with your doubt and unbelief."

I felt ashamed. I had my eyes on her, not on God. I was so worried that she might sabotage my position, I never once figured in the "God factor." No one can stop God's plan for your life—not even that coworker who is always making you look bad. So get your eyes off her and back on God. He's got big plans for you!

–MMA

POWER PRAYER
Lord, help me to keep my eyes on You. Amen.

DUCK!

Answer me when I call to you,
O my righteous God. Give me relief from my distress;
be merciful to me and hear my prayer.

PSALM 4:1

I once worked for a very difficult boss. Molly's favor was
rarely bestowed, and her comments were biting. Tough on
her staff, she demanded excellence of herself and everyone
around her. Though I was fortunate enough to never directly receive her unleashed wrath, I was aware that I was
only one incident away from receiving the honor.

Molly's administrative assistants usually caught the
brunt of it. One actually crawled into Molly's office on her
knees to admit that she'd made a mistake, eager to disarm
Molly with a bit of humor. Another would come out of her
office, gently close the door, and grab her heart, feigning
that she'd been shot. These were not overly dramatic women
or incompetent workers. They were just dealing with the
situation as best they could.

If you're working for a boss who is beyond difficult, the
kind who has everyone ducking to miss her angry arrows,
pray. It's not easy and you may never see a difference in her,
but pray. Avoid complaining, and pray. Prayer is the only
thing that will give you insight into her personality, teach
you how to communicate with her, and show you how to
gain her favor. It may not be easy, but it's your best defense.

–GM

POWER PRAYER
Lord, I need Your help. Please show me how to have favor
with my boss.

BETWEEN A ROCK AND A HARD PLACE

My mouth will speak words of wisdom;
the utterance from my heart will give understanding.

PSALM 49:3

There was bound to be trouble. My relatively new boss, Jarrod, was out of the office. Though he came with a long history of experience, his personality and work style didn't gel with the office's culture. He just wasn't fitting in.

While he was gone, his boss—my *big* boss—began calling each of Jarrod's employees, asking about his performance. How was he doing? Did he follow through with things? Was he helping or hindering the office? I had a bad feeling about it and tried to be fair in my assessment without launching a full-out assault. Some of the employees were diplomatic; others were not.

When it comes to speaking out against someone—even a questionable coworker or boss—be very careful. Though you may tell the truth, you could find yourself on the short end of retribution. It's good to heed this scripture: "My mouth will speak words of wisdom; the utterance from my heart will give understanding." Notice that the verse talks about "words of wisdom." Do yourself a favor; speak the truth *wisely*. This will protect you from steamrolling over others or being perceived as launching your own full-out assault.

–GM

POWER PRAYER

Lord, help me to speak words of wisdom and to have
understanding when I do speak.

BITE MY TONGUE

Do everything without complaining or arguing.

PHILIPPIANS 2:14

Have you ever worked for an incompetent boss? I don't mean a boss who occasionally makes bad decisions, but ones that leave you shaking your head every time you deal with them. When they give their opinion, you think: *That's the most ridiculous (or wrong or dim-witted) thing I've ever heard.* And meetings are really fun because you get to cringe the moment they start bestowing their vast wisdom on others.

I've had the unfortunate privilege of working for one of these bosses. It actually got so bad that my coworkers and I made a pact not to complain about him, which we had elevated to an art form. When he pulled out his bag of absurd tricks, we bit our tongues.

Incompetent bosses often prevent you from performing at your best, but the best decision you can make is to refuse to complain about him. Though it won't change his incompetence, it will actually make work more bearable because you won't relive every situation. Complaining can only make a difficult situation worse, so determine to work without complaining. It will help you make the most out of difficult situations.

–GM

POWER PRAYER
Lord, forgive me for complaining about the things I can't change. Teach me how to stay quiet even in crazy situations.

DISCERNER MALFUNCTION

Evil words destroy one's friends;
wise discernment rescues the godly.

PROVERBS 11:9 NLT

I thought she was my friend. We had shared several long phone conversations while working on the same project. We had even prayed for one another. When questioned about her integrity and work ethic, I went to bat for her, putting in a good word with the vice president of the company. She seemed like such a nice person. Whoa, was my discerner off!

She turned out not to be such a nice person. In fact, once she attained her new position, she acted really ugly to me and tried to weaken my credibility as a writer within the company. Wow! I *so* didn't see that one coming.

Have you ever been blindsided by someone? Did a coworker that you trusted turn out to be a rat fink? Yep, we've all been there. It hurts. And sometimes it hurts for a while. But God is the healer of all hurts, and He cares about you. So if you're hurting today, give it to God. Allow Him to mend your broken heart. And ask Him to give you better discernment in the future. Don't trust your "gut instinct." It's faulty. Only trust your "God instinct." It works every time!

–MMA

POWER PRAYER

Lord, please give me better discernment and heal my hurting
heart. Amen.

GROWING FRUIT

*But the fruit of the Spirit is
love, joy, peace, patience, kindness, goodness,
faithfulness, gentleness and self-control.*

GALATIANS 5:22–23

Of course you're not going to automatically get along with every coworker in your office. It's going to take some real effort on your part. I mean, even the disciples had problems with each other.

In Acts 15, we learn that Paul and Barnabas had a fight about another "coworker," John (who was also called Mark). It seems that Paul didn't want to take Mark along on a ministry journey because Mark had previously abandoned them in Pamphylia, but Barnabas insisted he come along. So Paul and Barnabas parted ways. Paul took Silas to Syria and Cilicia, while Barnabas took Mark to Cyprus. Interesting, isn't it? Both Paul and Barnabas were godly men. They were committed to doing God's work. They were part of the chosen group, yet they had strong differing opinions at times.

Strife happens. Maybe it's happening at your workplace. If so, don't join in the strife-fest. Instead, walk away. Turn to God and ask Him to help you be the peacemaker of the group. See these strife-filled times as a chance to grow in the fruit of the Spirit. God will use this time in your life to take you to a higher place with Him.

–MMA

POWER PRAYER
Lord, help me to grow in the fruit of the Spirit and walk in peace. Amen.

DADDY

*"I will be a Father to you,
and you will be my sons and daughters,
says the Lord Almighty."*

2 CORINTHIANS 6:18

When people work together, there is always the temptation or forbearance to hold some at arm's length. You quickly learn that there are some you can trust and others you have to watch. You know they'll sell you down the river if the opportunity arises. It isn't necessarily malicious; it's just business.

So it's comforting to know that we can trust the Lord. In 2 Corinthians 6:18, God says "I will be a Father to you, and you will be my sons and daughters." Through Jesus' sacrifice, we were accepted as members into the family of God. That's not a trivial thing. Before Jesus, worshippers didn't talk directly to God nor He to them. Once a year, a priest—at his own peril—entered the inner sanctuary to offer amends for everyone's sins. But today you and I can "approach the throne of grace with confidence" (Hebrews 4:16).

If you find yourself surrounded by people that you distrust, remember that God isn't one of them. He is a faithful Father who sent His Son to die for you. And He did it because you mean the world to Him.

–GM

POWER PRAYER

Heavenly Father, thank You for making me Your daughter and allowing me to approach Your throne with confidence.

THE BEST IMITATION

Be imitators of God. . .and live a life of love.

EPHESIANS 5:1–2

I finally had an office of my own. I couldn't wait to decorate it. Since I didn't have a bulletin board, I simply taped a few family pictures on the back of my door. That way, I could look at my loved ones throughout the day. Well, in the midst of my gleeful decorating, my supervisor poked her head into my office.

"No, I'm sorry. You can't do that," she barked. "We don't allow the use of tape on our walls or doors."

"Oh, is that all?" I said, smiling. "The personnel office supplied me with 'office friendly tape,' guaranteed not to damage anything."

"Still, it looks unprofessional," she added.

"But they are on the back of my door," I reasoned. "No one will see them but me."

"I want them down by morning," she ordered and walked off.

I had a decision to make. I could follow her instruction with a Christlike attitude, or I could give her the raspberries. In the end, I removed the pictures and even forced a smile when I saw her the next morning.

If you're feeling mistreated today, I want to encourage you to follow after Christ's example. Don't give your difficult supervisor the raspberries; give her the love of Jesus instead. God will honor your Christlike attitude.

–MMA

POWER PRAYER

Lord, help me to walk in love every day. Amen.

THE REAL STRUGGLE

*For we are not fighting against people
made of flesh and blood,
but against the evil rulers and authorities
of the unseen world.*

EPHESIANS 6:12 NLT

"The spiritual world is more real than the physical," I once heard someone say, and I've tried to remember that. Often, workplace struggles are chalked up to differences of opinions or personalities. Everyone assumes that the parties simply view things differently, but there are times when the struggles are more spiritual than physical.

In 2 Kings 6, the prophet Elisha, who was targeted by the Aramean army, stood his ground. When his servant asked, "Oh, my lord, what shall we do?" Elisha replied, "Those who are with us are more than those who are with them." He then prayed for his servant's eyes to be opened so that he could see that they were protected by horses and chariots of fire.

Of course, that doesn't mean spiritual forces are involved in every difficult situation, but you can watch and pray to know the difference. Pray for sensitivity and wisdom. Pray for the truth, and pray for the person's peace of mind and salvation. Through prayer and sensitivity, you can be more tuned in to what's going on around you.

–GM

POWER PRAYER

Lord, help me to see the truth about the struggles I face each day—whether they're spiritual or physical. Then give me the wisdom to deal with them.

LIGHT FOR JESUS

"If you love those who love you, what reward will you get?
Are not even the tax collectors doing that?
And if you greet only your brothers,
what are you doing more than others?
Do not even pagans do that?"

MATTHEW 5:46–47

I once heard a preacher say, "Hurting people do hurtful things." For some reason, that has really stuck with me. Now, every time I encounter a rude person in the business world, I'll think, "I wonder what that person is going through right now. I bet she is really hurting inside." When you think that way, it's impossible to retaliate. Your flesh will cry out, "Return rudeness for rudeness. If she zings you, go ahead and zing her back." But your spirit will be filled with compassion and love for those who are hurting.

If you find yourself ready to "zing back" at a moment's notice, it might be time for a compassion checkup. Ask the Great Physician in the sky to fill you with His love and compassion for people.

When you return rudeness with love, you totally change the atmosphere. You don't give that rude person anywhere to go except to the Father. I always tell my children, "Be a light for Jesus today." That's good advice for all of us. Let your light of love brighten every situation.

–MMA

POWER PRAYER
Lord, help me to love Your people like You do. Amen.

HURFUL WORDS

*"But I tell you anyone who is angry with his brother
will be subject to judgment."*

MATTHEW 5:22

Are you the queen at zingers? Are you able to retaliate with
a witty, cutting remark when someone else hurts you? I'm
not like that. Instead, I cry a lot and think about what I
should've said. Oh yeah, I can really tell somebody off like
two hours later.

Although I'm not very good with one-on-one con-
frontations, I'm quite skilled at firing off some wicked e-
mails. I can compose a scathing, tell-somebody-off e-mail
like nobody's business. This, of course, is a very bad thing.
It's so easy to hit that SEND key and walk away satisfied. But
later, when I go back to my computer and reread my hurtful
e-mail, I feel sick right in the pit of my stomach. By that
time, the Holy Spirit has had time to deal with my heart,
and I wish I'd never sent the e-mail. Ever been there?

Words, whether uttered or written, can wound a person. Even if you're simply reacting to a hurtful remark
hurled at you, you have no right to react and return a hurtful comment. Go ahead, hit the DELETE key. The only
thing we should be sending is our love.

–MMA

POWER PRAYER

*Lord, help me to remember it's better to think before speaking
(or writing) than spend my life regretting. Amen.*

THE HIGH ROAD

Therefore, as God's chosen people,
holy and dearly loved, clothe yourselves with compassion,
kindness, humility, gentleness and patience.

COLOSSIANS 3:12

Wouldn't it be nice if everyone treated each other with
kindness? Happily, most of my coworkers have been pleasant, but every so often, I've come up against Cruella De
Ville's mean sister. Once, after I moved to a new position,
a coworker decided that I was her enemy. For two weeks, I
endured her belligerence.

Though I'd love to say that I was the picture of calm
rationale, the truth is I wanted to be just as catty to her.
Fortunately, two things stopped me. First, she knew that I
was a Christian and I didn't want to ruin my witness. Second, a pastor friend encouraged me to "take the high road."
Though I wanted to get just as rude with her, I was determined to walk out of the situation with no regrets.

None of us is perfect. We all have weak moments when
we want to hurt others the same way they've hurt us, but as
Christians, we must act like God's chosen people. We must
be clothed with compassion, kindness, humility, gentleness,
and patience. In short, we must take the high road.

–GM

POWER PRAYER
Lord, thank You for choosing me. Help me to clothe myself in
compassion, kindness, humility, gentleness, and patience so that
my actions are pleasing to You.

COMING UP ROSES

"No weapon that is formed against you will prosper;
And every tongue that accuses you
in judgment you will condemn.
This is the heritage of the servants of the LORD,
And their vindication is from Me," declares the LORD.

ISAIAH 54:17 NASB

Have you ever had something happen at work that left you feeling persecuted and victimized? We've all been there. Isn't your first instinct to defend yourself? I know that's usually how I react. I want to move into "lawyer mode" and present my side of the story, fact by fact, in my defense. But that's almost never the right way to handle the situation. See, the more you defend yourself, the guiltier you appear— even if you are innocent.

My good friend Gena always says, "Don't worry. It will all come out in the wash." She's right. No matter what kind of craziness is going on in your office, the truth will eventually be known. So don't sweat it. Just trust in the Lord and allow Him to be your defender. Memorize Isaiah 54:17 and say it every morning. Remember, God's Word says that no weapon formed against you shall prosper. That means you'll come through this smelling like a rose no matter how many weeds are coming up all around you.

–MMA

POWER PRAYER
Lord, I am trusting You to be my ultimate defender. Thank
You for watching over me. Amen.

BRING ON THE BLONDE

Love is patient, love is kind. . . .
It is not rude, it is not self-seeking,
it is not easily angered, it keeps no record of wrongs.

1 CORINTHIANS 13:4–5

Believe it or not, I actually learned a spiritual lesson from the movie *Legally Blonde*. For those who haven't seen it, it's a comedy about a Beverly Hills ditz who decides to follow the man she loves to Harvard law school. Because she doesn't quite fit into the East Coast Harvard persona, people don't accept her. In fact, she has to earn their respect in her own unique way. Even though people treated her badly, she never held it against them. She never wrote them off or tried to get even. Some might argue that she wasn't bright enough to think that far ahead, but to me, it just wasn't in her character. Even when they were catty, she responded with kindness.

I came out of the movie thinking, "Lord, I want to be more like that." I want to come to a place where I don't even acknowledge or realize that people are being rude so that I can always give them the benefit of the doubt. Some may think it's an unrealistic goal, but to me, it would make loving people—even the difficult ones—so much easier.

–GM

POWER PRAYER

Lord, help me to always be kind and never keep a record of wrongs.

BAGGAGE

*"Forgive us our debts,
as we also have forgiven our debtors."*

MATTHEW 6:12

Have you taken any business trips lately? I have been racking up the frequent flyer miles over the past year, speaking at various conferences and going to lots of book signings. So you'd think I'd be a skilled packer, right? Not a chance. I always pack way too much. Since you're only allowed to check two bags these days, I end up taking as many carry-on pieces as the airline will allow. While that seems like a good plan, all of that extra carry-on baggage is difficult to maneuver. I usually end up dropping a bag and fumbling them throughout the airport. I am always so relieved when I reach my destination and can unload all of those bags.

You know, handling too many emotional carry-on bags is a bad thing, too. Can you just imagine walking through your office, juggling four or five small bags? It would be difficult, wouldn't it? Well, if you're carrying around past hurts and resentments, you are doing just that—day in and day out. You'll never be able to climb that ladder of success with all of that extra baggage, so get rid of it. God made you more than a conqueror—not a bag lady!

–MMA

POWER PRAYER

Father, I give You all of my baggage. Replace it with Your everlasting love. Amen.

AN AFFAIR TO AVOID

"You shall not commit adultery."

EXODUS 20:14

Did you know that workplace affairs account for 80 percent of all marital infidelity? That's a startling statistic, isn't it? Most affairs start off very harmless. A man and a woman become friends because they are coworkers. Soon they begin to have lunch together—alone. The woman begins confiding in her male coworker. In turn, he also shares intimate details with her. Suddenly, they become quite attracted to one another. Soon the two are emotionally involved. This, of course, leads to the physical relationship. Eventually, they both leave their spouses and children—tearing up two families. And it all started with a few harmless lunches. Amazing, isn't it?

Unfortunately, the above scenario is far too common. There may be an office affair going on where you work right now. You may even be taking part in one. If you are involved in an office romance, nip it in the bud. Run away from your coadulterer and into God's arms. God will forgive you.

If you are happily married and thinking, "I would never do such a thing," just heed this warning: Be careful. Don't be flirtatious at work. Don't have lunch alone with a male coworker. Ask God to make you sensitive to dangerous situations. Let your conscience (Holy Spirit) be your guide.

–MMA

POWER PRAYER

Lord, help me to be sensitive to actions that might promote an office affair. Amen.

ALWAYS THE SAME

Jesus Christ is the same yesterday and today and forever.

HEBREWS 13:8

Have you ever had a friend become mean once she was promoted? Up to that point, she was wonderful—smart, fun, encouraging, and dedicated—but once she got the new title, she became harsh, withdrawn, and overly serious. It's one of the strange effects of management. Of course, we have to admit that she's facing new challenges and expectations, some of which may be difficult to handle. Other coworkers and managers may be constantly pulling at her, and if we're ever in a similar position, we'd want our friends to continue to support us. So we have to give her a break and a prayer.

Isn't it reassuring to know that Jesus never changes? He won't suddenly turn harsh and distant when new challenges come His way. No, He's the Son of God, our Savior, and He knows exactly what to do. The Bible says that He's "the same yesterday and today and forever." He never changes. He still redeems the lost. He still forgives the sinful. He still aids the weak. He still sits at the right hand of God, interceding for us. Thankfully, He's still the same Jesus.

–GM

POWER PRAYER

Dear Jesus, thank You for changing my life and for always being my Savior.

TALK, TALK, TALK

If you listen obediently to the Voice of GOD. . .
your God, will place you on high,
high above all the nations of the world.

DEUTERONOMY 28:1 MSG

Do you work with someone who always has to be the center of attention? In meetings, he hogs the floor and talks incessantly about nothing. When you try to pin him down—desperate to figure out what he's saying—he evades you with high-minded, vague concepts. Or he doles out all the responsibility for his plans, while trying to only retain the authority. Please tell me I'm not the only one to have sat through these *long, tedious, confusing* meetings.

I have to admit there have been times when I've caught myself talking incessantly to God without listening to what He has to say, too. I'll talk, talk, talk about something that concerns me and give Him all the reasons why my way is the best way or why I'm justified in my feelings. But if I stop to listen, many times He'll speak something very simple and piercing to my heart, clearing up any confusion and getting me back on track.

If you find yourself talk, talk, talking to God during your prayer time and not listening, then start listening. It's through listening to His voice that you'll receive your answers.

–GM

POWER PRAYER

Lord, I trust You with my life and am ready to hear from You.

DO WHAT?

Love your enemies, bless them that curse you,
do good to them that hate you,
and pray for them which despitefully use you,
and persecute you.

MATTHEW 5:44 KJV

I'll never forget that Sunday morning. I was so distraught. I wanted to quit my job because my boss was impossible. She took great joy in humiliating her staff, and I had been her latest victim. I was hurt and confused, so I went forward for prayer. The prayer minister smiled and nodded empathetically as I replayed the events from the prior work week. Then I asked through tears, "What should I do?" I was expecting him to say, "Quit! God has something better for you." But that's not what he said. Instead, he whispered, "Pray for her. In fact, you might even give her a small gift—just to let her know you're thinking of her."

Huh? I looked at him dumbfounded—like a cow at a new gate! Praying for her and buying her gifts were not what I had in mind. In fact, I was hoping he would call down fire from heaven to consume her or something along those lines. But against my fleshly will, I did exactly what he said. My boss didn't change, but it set me free. Do you need freedom today? Pray for your enemies—even if you have to do it through gritted teeth.

–MMA

POWER PRAYER
Father, I pray for those who have hurt me. Bless them today.
Amen.

GOD SEES

*Search me, O God, and know my heart;
test me and know my anxious thoughts.*

PSALM 139:23

You can see them coming. As soon as the boss enters the room, they smile as big as ever and schmooze their way into better assignments. They have the boss's ear on a whole host of matters from new policies to other coworkers. As they weave their magic, their eyes are usually set on the big fish: promotion. They are the yes-men who live among us. God bless them.

As Christians, we know that God sees our hearts. Regardless of what we do or say, God sees what's inside us. He knows if our motives are pure or impure. Now some might feel nervous about God being able to see everything they think and feel, but actually, it's refreshing. We don't have to try to live up to some perfect image with Him. He sees that even when we fall short, we're still trying. He sees what we mean, even if others assume the worst. God sees.

Instead of trying to shut God out of the corners of your heart, go ahead and let Him in. He loves you. There's no flattering God; He sees it all.

–GM

POWER PRAYER

Lord, search my heart. I try to hide nothing from You because I know that You know my deepest thoughts and concerns.

DISTRACTIONS

All the ways of the LORD are loving
and faithful for those who
keep the demands of his covenant.

PSALM 25:10

I have worked near some loud coworkers. I'm not talking about the sporadically noisy person, I'm talking about the "my inside voice rivals most baseball game announcers" voice. In fact, I kept a pair of ear plugs in my desk drawer for the times when it became too much and I couldn't drown her out with my low-volume CD player. She distracted me, no matter how hard I tried to ignore her, making it hard to focus.

Likewise, in your relationship with God, there are lots of distractions that could keep you from focusing on Him. Just like you have to find ways to overcome the distractions of a loud coworker, you have to find ways to overcome the distractions that would keep you from pursuing your relationship with God. You may set your alarm a few minutes early or sit in your car during lunch or leave work at an appropriate time in order to pray or attend church. Whatever you have to do, it will be worth it. Keeping life's loudness from distracting you from God will allow you to enjoy a more fulfilling relationship with Him.

–GM

POWER PRAYER

Lord, thank You for knowing me and always making time
for me. Help me to protect my relationship with You from
distractions.

MY PINTO VERSUS YOUR LEXUS

*"What have I accomplished compared to you?
Aren't the gleanings of Ephraim's grapes better than
the full grape harvest of Abiezer?"*

JUDGES 8:2

She was everything I wanted to be. I looked across the newsroom at her, and I wondered how she was able to write award-winning stories, parent such wonderful children, and remain a size 4. I admired her, and yes, at times I was jealous of her—especially when I started playing the comparison game.

Ever played that game?

At first, it seems quite harmless. You simply admire a coworker. But if you take it a step further, you'll be sorry. That's when you start wondering, "Why can't I do my job as well as she does hers? How does she afford such wonderful suits?" From there, it's a downward spiral. By the time you hit the bottom, you dislike your coworker and you can't stand yourself.

I've got three words for you—*don't go there!* The next time the devil whispers in your ear, "See Carol over there? She earns ten thousand dollars more a year than you, and she is two sizes smaller!" tell him to back off. Begin praising God for who you are through Him, and thank Him for the plans He has for your life. They are awesome—just as awesome as Carol's. I promise!

–MMA

POWER PRAYER
Lord, help me to stop comparing myself to others and become happy with who I am in You. Amen.

LIGHTEN UP

For God hath not given us the spirit of fear;
but of power, and of love, and of a sound mind.

2 TIMOTHY 1:7 KJV

Are you way too hard on yourself? If you are, you're not alone. As working women, we expect a lot out of ourselves. We have to if we want to stay in the game, right? But many times, we put such unrealistic expectations on ourselves that we're in a constant state of panic—afraid of failure.

That's no way to live, sister. The Bible says that we have not been given a spirit of fear but of power, love, and a sound mind. Yet we go around biting our freshly manicured fingernails, worrying about a missed opportunity or a less-than-stellar job review. Take a deep breath, and stop worrying. Of course, we're going to drop the ball once in a while. But don't beat yourself up. Accept your mistakes, learn from them, and move on.

Don't waste your time worrying (which is a sneaky form of fear) about what could've, should've, or might've been. God wants you to live free from fear. Remember, the Word also says that when we are weak, He is strong. That means, even when you miss it, God has your back!

–MMA

POWER PRAYER

Lord, I give all of my fears to You today. Help me to stop
setting unrealistic goals. I only want what You want for me.
Amen.

BRING YOUR OWN PAPER CLIPS

*Cast your cares on the LORD
and he will sustain you.*

PSALM 55:22

Ever felt persecuted at work? Ever felt like everyone else was treated better than you? Once when I was working as a writer for a magazine, I requested a box of paper clips on the office order sheet. I didn't ask for a display phone, which all of the other writers had. (My phone was so old, it didn't ring. It sort of moaned!) No, all I requested was a box of paper clips. I never dreamed my request would be denied.

That afternoon, my supervisor poked her head into my office and said, "You'll need to bring paper clips from home. We're only purchasing the absolutely necessary items." I could not believe it! I thought, *Do you mean I work my guts out for this company and I'm not even worth a thirty-nine-cent box of paper clips?* Then I started noticing how many other "office items" my cowriters had that I did not have. The more I made mental notes about my "have-not" situation, the worse I felt and the worse I acted.

Ever been there? Maybe you are getting the short end of the stick in your workplace, but don't dwell on it. Give your situation to Him. God cares about everything that affects you—even a paper clip shortage!

–MMA

POWER PRAYER
Lord, help me to keep my heart right in the midst of this mistreatment. Amen.

LOOKING OUT FOR NUMBER ONE

At that time the disciples came to Jesus and asked,
"Who is the greatest in the kingdom of heaven?"
He called a little child and had him stand among them.
And he said: ". . .whoever humbles himself like this child
is the greatest in the kingdom of heaven."

MATTHEW 18:1–4

I find this passage really interesting. Here the disciples were walking with Jesus, and they were more concerned about themselves than the job at hand. I'm sure Jesus' response really took them aback. He gently held up a child as a standard of faith and humility. Though it sounds simple, I'm sure if I had been standing there, I would have been tempted to ask, "Yeah, but what are the three steps to being Number One?"

I can be a bit stubborn sometimes.

So how can you be the greatest you can be with God? Well, if you love and serve Him with childlike faith and humility, you already are. Take comfort in that and continue to be faithful to Him. Loving Him with your whole heart will bring you more satisfaction than any other position you'll ever hold.

–GM

POWER PRAYER

Lord, thank You for loving me and calling me to be Your child.
I commit to serving You with childlike faith and humility. You
are an awesome God, and I love You.

FOLLOW THE LEADER

*"Anyone who intends to come with me has to let me lead.
You're not in the driver's seat; I am."*

MATTHEW 16:24 MSG

The workplace is an interesting and comical place to play
Follow the Leader. I once had a beautiful, talented boss
who was successful in many areas. She was a visionary at
work and a wonder-woman wife and mother. Many wanted
to be like her. If she changed her hairstyle, women changed
theirs, too. If she wore a certain brand-name clothes, others followed. People followed her diets, exercise regimens,
and even changed to use her OB/GYN doctor. Because obviously hers was better, right?

There will always be talented people you admire. They'll
teach you how to succeed, and it would be foolish not to learn
from them; but ultimately Jesus is the best role model you
could ever have. His is the greatest example of love, compassion, leadership, hard work, and humility. His life is the one
you want to emulate. So play Follow the Leader with Jesus,
allowing His ways to become your ways. Put Him in the driver's seat of your life, realizing that He is your ultimate role
model. As you do, you'll become more and more like Him.

–GM

POWER PRAYER

*Lord, thank You for being in the driver's seat in my life. I fol-
low You first and pray that Your ways become my ways.*

THE GREEN-EYED MONSTER

*Anger is cruel and fury overwhelming,
but who can stand before jealousy?*

PROVERBS 27:4

Wouldn't it be great if adults could avoid jealousy, if they could celebrate each other regardless of looks, style, talents, money, or position? Unfortunately, that's not the case. One such situation included two dear friends. Melissa was a vivacious, beautiful, talented woman. Kendra was also a beautiful and talented woman, but whenever Melissa's name was mentioned, she tensed. I couldn't figure out the problem. Then one day in an angry fit, Kendra exploded over something small and yelled, "Who does she think she is?" Aha, a lightbulb went on; Kendra was jealous.

Everyone has weaknesses and strengths, but it's unfortunate when someone else's strengths are threatening. Jealousy stops you from appreciating God-given gifts in others. It hinders you from doing your best work because your view is altered. Don't let jealousy take hold of you. Pray for the wisdom to see the truth in someone and take time to get to know her. Many times, if you'll put your insecurities aside, you'll find something endearing about that person. Then celebrate the gifts that God has given to her, realizing that they're not better, just different from your own.

–GM

POWER PRAYER

*Lord, help me to celebrate the gifts You've given to others and
to avoid jealousy.*

ACHIEVEMENT

Let us not become conceited,
provoking and envying each other.

GALATIANS 5:26

When your coworker gets a new Lexus, do you celebrate with her? When she loses ten pounds, do you congratulate her? Okay, here's the really tough one. When she gets the promotion that you thought you would get, are you genuinely happy for her?

If you find it difficult to rejoice with others when they experience victories in their lives, you'll never have any victory in your life. Harsh as that seems, it's true. I speak from experience. About six years ago, before I had any books published, my friend sold a book to a well-known publisher. When she sent me a signed copy of her book, I didn't want to celebrate. I wanted to burn it. Yep, I had an attack of the green eyed monster. I had to take those ugly feelings to the Lord and ask for His forgiveness. I truly believe that if I hadn't repented for my envy, I would never have sold my first book that next spring.

See, God can't bless us if our hearts aren't right. If you're struggling with feelings of envy today, ask God to replace those feelings with His love. And remember, God has enough blessings to go around. He hasn't forgotten about you.

–MMA

POWER PRAYER

Father, help me to celebrate with my coworkers when they achieve great things. Amen.

COMPARISONS

*Be sure to do what you should,
for then you will enjoy the personal satisfaction
of having done your work well,
and you won't need to compare yourself to anyone else.*

GALATIANS 6:4 NLT

Okay, let's have a "Dr. Phil moment." Step outside of yourself and take a good look. . . . Are you really doing the very best you can every day on the job? Are you reaching the goals you set for yourself? Are you meeting and exceeding your job requirements? If you are, celebrate with me, sister! Maybe you don't have a corner office (or even a corner cubicle), but if you are giving it your all, you are more than all right!

So why is it that so many of us feel badly about ourselves? I'll tell you why—we fall into the comparison trap. And we fall short when we compare ourselves to others. The result? Feelings of inadequacy, incompetence, and insecurity follow, and none of those feelings is from God.

I once read a cute plaque that said, "God isn't interested in your ability—He is interested in your availability." You should always strive to do your best, then feel good about your efforts. God isn't comparing you to others, so you shouldn't be, either. Your best is plenty good enough for God.

–MMA

POWER PRAYER

*Father, help me to feel good about my good work, and help me
to stop comparing myself with others. Amen.*

DANCE OF JOY

Oh, visit the earth, ask her to join the dance!
Deck her out in spring showers, fill the God—
River with living water. Paint the wheat fields golden.
Creation was made for this!

PSALM 65:9 MSG

Do you remember the 1980s sitcom *Perfect Strangers*? The premise of the show was simple. Two distant cousins lived together in Chicago. Larry was an uptight American; Balki was an ex-sheep herder from the Isle of Mypos. Together, they got into all sorts of jams. One of the things I remember most was Balki's "Dance of Joy." Whenever something exciting happened, Balki would grab Cousin Larry and begin a festive shuffle that included kicking out their legs to each side in sync.

Though this may not seem like the most spiritual application in the world, I do think that everyone needs a Dance of Joy kind of friend, someone who will get excited when something good happens. When a friend or coworker has good news, get excited for her. Instead of comparing your successes to hers and silently questioning, *Why her?*, celebrate the fact that something exciting has happened. That kind of selflessness is part of encouraging others in the blessings God has given them. And what He's done for them, He'll do for you, too. . .because there's always enough joy to go around.

–GM

POWER PRAYER

Lord, thank You for Your blessings. Let me be an
encouragement to others.

AH, YOUTH!

*Aim for perfection, listen to my appeal,
be of one mind, live in peace.*

2 CORINTHIANS 13:11

Growing up, my older brother and I had this bad habit of keeping tallies of who-did-what. If my father asked me to do something, I added it to my "I've done more than you" list. So the next time I was asked to do something, I gleefully responded, "I did it last time." Ah, youth. . .

It's funny, though, because this same type of "who-did-what" exists in the workplace. If someone has to work harder, she grumbles about picking up the slack, similar to Martha in the Bible. Now, Martha usually gets a bad rap for working while Mary sat at Jesus' feet (Luke 10:38–42), but she was a hard worker. She welcomed Jesus into her home and probably wanted to prepare a special dinner for Him. So her hard work wasn't a problem, but her attitude was. Instead of listening to Jesus, she became consumed with doing things and compared her work to Mary's.

Working hard is important. In fact, Proverbs 14:23 says, "All hard work brings a profit," but don't get caught up in comparing your work with someone else's. It's better to work harmoniously with others than to demand equality.

–GM

POWER PRAYER

Lord, help me to live in peace and be of one mind with my coworkers.

TATTLING

But the Pharisees and the teachers of the law
who belonged to their sect complained to his disciples,
"Why do you eat and drink with tax collectors and 'sinners'?"

LUKE 5:30

Remember when you were in elementary school and some-one would tattle on another student? The teacher would say, "Why don't you just worry about yourself, and I'll han-dle the other classroom concerns!" I was in fifth grade with a guy who thought it was his job to report the wrongdoings of every child in the school. Needless to say, he didn't have many friends.

Well, unfortunately, little tattletales grow up to be big tattletales. Maybe one of them works in your office! Young or old, there's no excuse for complaining and tattling about somebody else. It certainly doesn't create a very positive workplace environment.

If you're a complainer/tattler by nature, ask God to change you today. After all, who are we to judge someone else's actions? We can only see snippets of life, while God sees the big picture. Whenever I begin to look at someone else's faults, I am reminded of the whole "speck in his eye, board in my eye" verse (Matthew 7:3). And I don't know about you, but I have enough specks in my eyes to keep me busy for years!

–MMA

POWER PRAYER

Lord, help me to focus on Your work in my life, not on others'
faults. Amen.

PORK CHOPS

*"Do not throw your pearls to pigs.
If you do, they may trample them under their feet,
and then turn and tear you to pieces."*

MATTHEW 7:6

Has God shown you a glimpse of your future? Has He placed big dreams in your heart? Isn't it exciting? I know the first time I really heard God's voice concerning my career was during praise and worship at church. He told me (in that still, small voice) that I'd someday have books published and that I'd be teaching at writers' conferences around the world. At the time, that seemed absolutely ridiculous. I was a magazine journalist who knew nothing about writing books, and I had attended a few writers' conferences, but speak at them? Are you kidding? Still, I held those words dear. I wrote them in my journal and shared them with my family. I should've stopped there.

Instead, I was so excited about what God had shown me that I told a coworker, too. Can I just share that she wasn't nearly as excited? In fact, she spent our entire lunch hour telling me how difficult it would be to ever make it in the book business. So be careful. Don't share your dreams with Miss Piggy. She might give you a karate chop. *Hi-ya!*

–MMA

POWER PRAYER

*Thank You for my dreams, Lord. Help me to keep them quiet
until You're ready for me to share. Amen.*

A SHORT ROAD

"Do not hate your brother in your heart."

LEVITICUS 19:17

There is an Italian proverb that says, "Short is the road that leads from fear to hate." In the workplace, there are many chances for becoming afraid. There is the fear that another employee will influence the boss or take over our jobs. These fears can quickly lead to hate—from fearing that someone to hating everything they do and everything about them. It really is a short road.

That's why it's so important to reconcile that we are doing our very best, that God is in control of our futures, and that we work for God's approval more than man's. It's only then that we won't get caught up in comparing our place in the office with others. Only then will we protect ourselves from traveling the short road to hate.

If you've found yourself drifting toward fear, jealousy, or hate, take time to ask forgiveness from God and possibly that person. Don't let those feelings become roadblocks in your professional or spiritual life. Remember that God directs your every step and there is nothing that person can do against you that will have eternal effects. God is your ultimate employer, and He will take care of you.

–GM

POWER PRAYER

Lord, help me to love others the way You do and trust You with everything in my life.

MOLDS

*There are different kinds of gifts,
but the same Spirit.*

1 CORINTHIANS 12:4

Have you ever been on someone's bad side but couldn't figure out why? You've worked as hard as you can to do a good job, but your work was met with skepticism. Even when you went above the call, you were still treated badly.

Over the years I've talked to friends about this. We've each had situations that left us wondering, "What did I do?" We try to recall where we missed it. We compare our work to those around us and wonder if we've just overestimated our talent. We tried to fit into the mold but couldn't.

If that's you, remember John the Baptist. As special as he was, he didn't quite fit the mold of the day. Here was this wild man who came out of the wilderness, wearing camel's hair and eating locusts and wild honey. He was different, but he was also anointed for what he was called to do.

If you don't fit into someone else's mold, don't second-guess or hold yourself to an unreasonable comparison. If after praying, you believe that you've given your best by trying to accomplish the tasks at hand, then relax. You may not fit someone else's mold, but you do fit God's.

–GM

POWER PRAYER

*Lord, I know that You've given me different gifts. Help me to
use them so that others value them.*

COMPARISON TRAP

It is good to give thanks to the LORD,
to sing praises to the Most High.

PSALM 92:1 NLT

Do you love to attend home shows? My coauthor, Gena, and I love to go. It's so fun to tour the finest homes in Fort Worth. There's just one problem. After an afternoon of seeing the finest furnishings and the finest flooring and the most divine accessories, it's hard to go home. Suddenly, everything in my house makes me want to go, "Yuck!" I look at my walls, and I wish I had more artwork. I look at my carpeting, and I wish I had new rugs. I look at my countertops, and I desire granite. Get the idea?

You know what? It's the same way in the workplace. The minute you start comparing the size of your office to your coworker's office, you're in a heap of trouble. One comparison leads to another, and before you know it, you're unhappy, ungrateful, and unmotivated.

Instead of comparing, start praising. Be thankful that you have an office instead of a cube. Be thankful that you have a job. Bottom line—be thankful. As Psalm 92:1 says, it is good to give thanks to the Lord. It will immediately lift your spirits, and God appreciates it, too!

–MMA

POWER PRAYER

Lord, help me to be content in my job and stop comparing myself to my coworkers. Amen.

PEARLS AND SWINE

"Do not throw your pearls to pigs.
If you do, they may trample them under their feet,
and then turn and tear you to pieces."

MATTHEW 7:6

You have happy news. You just received a promotion with a raise. Finally, you'll receive recognition for all your hard work. Gleefully, you tell your coworkers all the exciting details—how it's a dream come true, what you want to change in the position. On and on you go. But instead of encouragement, you receive plastic grins.

When happy news happens, we want to shout it to the world. We're excited and hope that others will be just as excited for us. Unfortunately, that's not always the case. Instead, they could be comparing your success to their own or assuming that you're gloating.

That's why you need discernment. In the above verse, Jesus warned His disciples about the insincerity of the religious leaders of the day. He wanted them to have discernment when sharing their good news. He knew that instead of hearing the truth, the leaders would turn on the disciples. Unfortunately, it's the same with all good news. Instead of saying everything that's on your heart, trust the Holy Spirit to show you what you can share. With this sensitivity, you're more likely to receive the response you desire.

–GM

POWER PRAYER

Lord, help me to have discernment when I speak, regardless of
what I'm sharing.

STINKIN' THINKIN'

I can do everything through him who gives me strength.

PHILIPPIANS 4:13

I love to read. I especially love to read children's books, which is good because I also write books for children. However, once in a while the devil will use that simple activity to make me feel inferior. It usually goes something like this: I pick up a really great children's book. I devour it because it's so wonderful. Then I sit around wondering things like, "Why would God call me to write books for children when there are so many other more talented authors?" Of course, this wondering activity leads into the whole "feeling sorry for myself" syndrome, and it usually goes downhill from there.

Pretty pathetic, isn't it? It's not only pathetic but also self-destructive. And what's more, God doesn't appreciate it, either. Are you also guilty of this kind of wondering? If you find yourself participating in this negative thought process— stop! It doesn't matter if you're not the very best in your chosen profession. God didn't call you to be the best. He just called you to be the best version of yourself. Comparing yourself and your work to others is never a good idea. Instead, use that energy to meditate on God's promises, such as: "I can do everything through him who gives me strength." Now that's something worth thinking about!

–MMA

POWER PRAYER
Lord, help me to stop my negative thinking. Amen.

APPROVAL

*Before I formed you in the womb
I knew [and] approved of you.*

JEREMIAH 1:5 AMP

I had never felt so intimidated. I looked around the room at all the other writers' conference speakers, and I thought, *What am I doing on staff? I am not worthy to sit next to most of these authors. I mean, they write life-changing books—books that sell millions of copies. Maybe if I slip out the side door, no one will notice. . . .*

It was my first year to teach at a writers' conference. I'd gone from conferee to staff member in two years, and I wasn't sure God had promoted the right person.

Comparing ourselves with others is a dangerous activity. I'm convinced that we fall into this comparison trap because deep down, we don't like ourselves very much. We feel flawed in some way, so we compare ourselves with others to confirm what we already know—we don't measure up. That, sister, is wrong thinking.

If you're in this comparison mode, stop the cycle of self-abuse. If you get nothing else from this book, I want you to realize one thing—God adores you. He has already approved you. You don't have to prove anything to anyone. God made you exactly the way you are—flaws and all. So you need to accept yourself. God already has.

–MMA

POWER PRAYER
Lord, help me to love myself the way that You love me. Amen.

THANK THE LORD, I'M FREE!

Now the Lord is the Spirit,
and where the Spirit of the Lord is,
there is liberty (emancipation from bondage, freedom).

2 CORINTHIANS 3:17 AMP

The month of July is a great time to consider our freedom—freedom from past mistakes, freedom from spiritual and physical slavery, freedom to choose how and where to live, freedom from living up to others' unrealistic expectations, freedom from trying to keep up with the Joneses, freedom from anything that would separate us from Jesus. For those of us who live in a Western country, we sometimes take freedom for granted, but our brothers and sisters who live in other parts of the world know how precious freedom really is. It's something to be treasured.

As you go through your day, thank Jesus for the freedom He provided for you. Thank Him that loving and serving Him are the only requirements for a fulfilling life and eternal salvation. Thank Him that He paid the price for your freedom so that you wouldn't have to. Remember that it's because of Him that you have the kind of freedom that can never be taken away.

–GM

POWER PRAYER

Jesus, thank You for making me free—free from anything that would try to separate me from You.

BIRTHDAY EXTRAVAGANZA

For we know, brothers loved by God,
that he has chosen you.

1 THESSALONIANS 1:4

At my workplace, there was a long-standing tradition of extravagant birthday celebrations. After exchanging names, each birthday host was responsible for planning the celebration. Everyone else was expected to cough up $10 so that the birthday person would receive a $50 gift. As the department grew, so did the donations. Some months it was possible to give $20–$30 within a few weeks, and when it was your turn to host, the party could cost $30–$40. Now, this may not sound like much, but trust me, I felt like the Salvation Army Santa stood outside my office door ringing his trusty bell at rock concert decibels. But to speak out against the birthday tradition was discouraged. It would immediately kick you out of the "in crowd."

Isn't it nice to know that you are always part of God's in crowd? You don't have to buy your way into His acceptance; we're accepted wholly and completely. If you're struggling to try to earn God's favor by measuring up to some imaginary standard, take a moment to reflect. Remember, there is nothing you can do to make Him love you more or less. You're already part of His crowd.

–GM

POWER PRAYER

Lord, thank You for loving me just as I am.

RESPECT

*"By this all men will know that you are my disciples,
if you love one another."*

JOHN 13:35

When I was growing up in the seventies and eighties, I remember hearing this expression on more than one occasion, "You're so stuck-up that if it rained, you'd drown." It took me a few days to figure out exactly what that meant, but when I realized the person who said that to me thought I had my nose in the air, I was horrified! I really didn't think I was better than anyone else. In fact, most of the time, I felt quite inferior.

Do you ever accidentally give off the wrong impression? When your coworkers compare you to others, would they say that you're stuck-up? Would they say you think better of yourself than those around you? As Christians, we need to be keenly aware that we are under constant scrutiny. That's why the Word of God says, "They will know we are Christians by our love."

Be sure that you treat your coworkers with respect. Go the extra mile. Ask God to make you sensitive to their feelings. Read over 1 Corinthians 13 on a regular basis, and ask the Lord to develop the fruit of the Spirit in your life. Soon you'll be known for His love and nothing else!

–MMA

POWER PRAYER
Lord, help me to treat others with respect and love. Amen.

APPLES AND ORANGES

But in fact God has arranged the parts in the body,
every one of them, just as he wanted them to be.
If they were all one part, where would the body be?
As it is, there are many parts, but one body.

1 CORINTHIANS 12:18–20

Have you ever heard the expression, "You can't compare apples to oranges"? While apples and oranges are both types of fruit, are very, very different. They have different peels. They have different textures. They are different colors. And they certainly have different tastes.

As Christian working women, we also have different areas of expertise, different strengths, different callings, different talents, and more. So why do we compare ourselves with each other? It's like comparing apples to oranges. See, the devil would love to get us to focus on our shortcomings instead of our strengths. He'd love to convince us that we have nothing to offer compared to the other talented women we know. He wants us to get our eyes off of Jesus and onto our inabilities. But don't go there!

Instead, ask God to help you focus on your strengths and your abilities. Ask God to help you see yourself as He sees you. Maybe you've always wanted to be an apple, yet you were born to be an orange. Take heart! You're the apple of God's eye!

–MMA

POWER PRAYER
Lord, help me to see myself as You see me. Amen.

NO COMPARISON

For who in the skies above can compare with the LORD?

PSALM 89:6

We serve an amazing God. He is the creator of the heavens and earth, the beginning and the end. He has always existed and will always exist. Those should be reasons enough to worship Him.

For those of us who serve Him, it gets even better. He knows everything about us and He still loves us. From the moment of mankind's first betrayal, He set a plan in motion to bring us back into relationship to Him. He sent His innocent Son to die so that we could live. And in our lives, He is a personal God. We now have access to come directly to Him in prayer. His Holy Spirit is with us constantly, allowing us to live a holy and righteous life.

Though you know all of these things, sometimes it's just good to remind yourself of whom you serve. No other god compares to Him. He alone is worthy of your praise. So take a few minutes to praise Him today. Thank Him for what He's done in your life and for bringing you into His family. He really is a faithful God. "Who in the skies above can compare with the LORD?"

−GM

POWER PRAYER

Heavenly Father, You alone are worthy of all praise. No other god compares to You.

MARVELOUS

I will praise thee;
for I am fearfully and wonderfully made:
marvellous are thy works;
and that my soul knoweth right well.

PSALM 139:14 KJV

Do you ever dream of being somebody else? Maybe a movie star? A famous singer? A millionaire? Growing up, I always dreamed of being Doris Day. To me, she had it all—beauty, class, talent, intelligence, money, and then some. (Plus, she got to costar with James Garner, Cary Grant, and Rock Hudson! Wow!)

While it's fun to daydream about being somebody else or having someone else's life, it's also quite dangerous. The Lord doesn't want us to waste our energies dreaming of being somebody else, because He already thinks we're awesome. Meditate on that a moment—the Creator of the Universe thinks you are awesome!

Do you feel inferior today? Do you feel like you just don't measure up compared to those around you? Well, I've got news for you. God created you just the way you are, and He doesn't care if your middle toe is longer than your big toe. He doesn't mind that your manicure is chipped. And He's fine with the fact that you have trouble balancing your checkbook. God loves us—flaws and all. So quit dreaming about being somebody else and celebrate being you!

–MMA

POWER PRAYER
Lord, help me to be content with who I am. Amen.

IF I DO SAY SO MYSELF

*Make a careful exploration of who you are
and the work you have been given,
and then sink yourself into that.
Don't be impressed with yourself.
Don't compare yourself with others.*

GALATIANS 6:4 MSG

It's easy to become impressed with your accomplishments. You work hard and take pride in your work. People say things like, "We know we can count on you." The more praise you receive, the better you like it. And if you do make a mistake, others are surprised because you're usually so conscientious. Sound familiar? If you're one of the favorites or long-timers at your work, it probably does. At times I've been appreciated, too, and I have to admit that it felt great.

That's why it's good for us to remember this verse. It's pretty clear, isn't it? Basically, we're supposed to understand what we're supposed to be doing and then do it. . .with humility. We shouldn't become too proud of ourselves or hold ourselves up as the standard. We just have to remember that the talents we have are God-given and if we want to see real greatness, we only have to look to Him.

–GM

POWER PRAYER
Lord, You are the one who deserves praise. Help me not to compare myself to others.

SISTER PERFECT

*For when I am weak,
then I am strong.*

2 CORINTHIANS 12:10 NLT

My wonderful sister, Martie, was born in July. Do any of you have older, perfect sisters? If so, you'll understand when I say this—I've always felt like I've lived in her shadow—especially when it comes to spiritual things. Martie has always had the gift of gab, and I don't mean just small talk or polite party banter. No, I mean this gal can preach!

So when I was asked to preach at a ladies' luncheon in New Mexico earlier this year, I immediately said, "Oh, you must want my sister, Martie." I couldn't imagine why they'd want me. I only speak about writing and industry stuff. I'd never been asked to preach. "No, we want you to come," the voice on the other end of the line said. Before I had time to think, I heard myself utter, "Sure, I'd be happy to do it."

At that point, I had to quit comparing myself to my sister and focus on God. I knew I couldn't preach in my own strength, but I also knew that He was made perfect in my weakness. So I was giving Him a perfect opportunity to shine. And He did, through me! Let God shine through you today, and stop comparing yourself to others—even your perfect older sisters.

–MMA

POWER PRAYER
Lord, shine through me today! Amen.

AN ORIGINAL

*That means we will not compare ourselves with each other
as if one of us were better and another worse.
We have far more interesting things to do with our lives.
Each of us is an original.*

GALATIANS 5:26 MSG

Face it; there are times in our careers when we're on top of
the world. We've got the Midas Touch and everything is
wonderful, but there are also times when we can't seem to
chew gum and walk in a straight line without help. We're at
the bottom of the food chain and it's a long way to the top.
Can anyone relate? I know I can.

Like I mentioned before, there have been times when
I felt appreciated and admired for my work, but then there
were times when I was barely hanging on. For some reason,
I just missed a series of things—due dates, lost information,
misplaced files, you name it and it had my name on it.

It's easy during those times to look around and feel like
the ugly duckling among beautiful swans, but don't give up.
God can use you and teach you how to do things better.
Like His Word says: You are an original.

–GM

POWER PRAYER

*Lord, help me to be the original that You want me to be. I ded-
icate my work to You and pray that I honor You with it.*

FACETS OF THE SISTERHOOD

Be good friends who love deeply;
practice playing second fiddle.

ROMANS 12:10 MSG

One afternoon as I watched Judge Judy—one of my guilty pleasures—I heard her instruct a young woman about the "Sisterhood." The woman had become involved with a married man. Then, following the end of the relationship, she had begun to harass the man's wife. In Judge Judy's typical style, she told this woman to grow up, move on, leave married men alone, and respect the Sisterhood. I cheered.

As women, we can be hardest on each other. Instead of building each other up, we often drag each other down. As sisters in the Body of Christ, we should support and respect each other's choices. Often I've heard women criticize each other because of their choices. Does she work outside or inside the home? To what kind of school does she send her children? What's her education? Is she committed to her career? On and on we go.

Each woman has to make choices according to God's direction in her life. As members of the Sisterhood, respect that God made each woman differently. By doing this, you'll help the Sisterhood and the Body of Christ thrive.

–GM

POWER PRAYER

Lord, thank You for directing me in my life. Help me to
appreciate the differences in other women so that I can
encourage and be a blessing to them.

BEAUTIFUL COATS

*For wherever there is jealousy and selfish ambition,
there you will find disorder and every kind of evil.*

JAMES 3:16 NLT

Remember the story of Joseph and his coat of many colors? Remember how his brothers sold him into slavery and then told their father that he had died? Usually, when we hear this story, we focus on Joseph and his trials. But I want to talk about Joseph's brothers today. Have you ever wondered how Joseph's brothers went from loving him to hating his guts in no time flat?

Jealousy. But do you know how that jealousy started? My guess is the brothers started comparing how their father treated them to how he treated Joseph. Suddenly, they looked around and noticed, "Hey, none of us has a colorful coat! What's up with that? How come Joe has one?" Eventually, their comparing and wondering led to a raging jealousy.

Are you in the comparison mode today? Is there a coworker who is wearing "the coat of many colors" around the office, and you're wishing you could sell her into slavery? Well, before you dwell in that land of comparison too long, ask God to remove the jealous feelings stored in your heart and replace them with His supernatural love. Stay wrapped in His love. You don't need that colorful coat!

–MMA

POWER PRAYER

*Lord, please take away any jealousy within me and replace it
with Your love. Amen.*

GETTING NOTICED

As it is, you boast and brag.
All such boasting is evil.

JAMES 4:16

We all know Brenda Brag-a-lot. She seizes every opportunity to share all about her successes. There's at least one "Brenda" in every company. She's easy to spot because she is always talking, and those surrounding her have expressions on their faces that say, "We really don't care. Why don't you take a personal day or something!"

In this dog-eat-dog world, many feel the need to brag on themselves. They believe the old adage, "If you don't look out for Number One, who will?" Well, God will! You don't have to toot your own horn to move up in your company. God will cause you to outshine others, and you won't even have to open your mouth.

The Bible says that God has crowned you with glory and honor and favor. He will give you favor with your bosses and your coworkers. He will cause your efforts and accomplishments to get noticed by "the powers that be." God will do that for you. All you have to do is ask, then thank Him for it every day! Don't become a Brenda Brag-a-lot. Let God do your bragging for you. He loves to dote on His children!

–MMA

POWER PRAYER

Thank You, Lord, for giving me favor with my bosses and coworkers. I praise You that my accomplishments will not go unnoticed. Amen.

SECRET SANTA'S EVIL TWIN

*We're not, understand, putting ourselves in a league
with those who boast that they're our superiors. . . .
But in all this comparing and grading
and competing, they quite miss the point.*

2 CORINTHIANS 10:12 MSG

At one time, I worked in an office where Secret Santa was a yearly event. Once a week from December 1–25, everyone exchanged gifts with someone whose name they had drawn. Unfortunately one year, Secret Santa's Evil Twin showed up. Instead of small, $5–$10 "I Appreciate You" gifts, the standard was $20–$40 "How Can I Fulfill Your Christmas Dreams" gifts. You do the math. My coworkers were spending $80–$160 over the month. For some, that might not seem like much, but for me, it was steep. I tried to give nice gifts, but my $5–$10 gifts just couldn't compare, and they soon became the department joke. Needless to say, I was mortified.

People will always compare what they have or do with others, and in the workplace, the comparisons just don't stop. Someone always wins and someone always loses. But with God, you're never a loser. To Him, your value isn't based on external things. So even if Secret Santa's Evil Twin comes to visit, you can have peace knowing that your value comes from God, not man.

–GM

POWER PRAYER
*Lord, thank You for reminding me that my value is in You.
Help keep me from falling prey to comparing myself to others'
standards.*

IT'S MY OFFICE
AND I'LL CRY IF I WANT TO

As far as the east is from the west,
so far has he removed our transgressions from us.

PSALM 103:12

When I get mad, I cry. Are you like that, too? It's just as well, really, because my tears keep me from saying too many things I'd later regret. Why? Because it's hard to talk when you're blubbering like an idiot.

However, I've been known to say a few ugly remarks between sobs. Sure, I was sorry later, but I couldn't retrieve my words. Have you ever been there? Have you ever wished you could hit the REWIND button and retract the words you just screamed at your boss? Oh, yeah. . .we've all been there.

Well, I've got good news. Even though you can't take back the words you yelled at your boss, you can apologize and pray for God's intervention on your behalf. And here's more good news. You *can* hit the REWIND button with God. Once you ask for forgiveness, God doesn't remember your harsh, sinful comments anymore. He totally erases them from His memory. The Word says He removes our transgressions "as far as the east is from the west," and that's a good little piece, as they say in Texas. So dry your eyes. God isn't mad at you.

–MMA

POWER PRAYER

Thank You, Lord, for loving me—no matter what. Help me
to walk in Your love. Amen.

OUCH!

He who ignores discipline comes to poverty and shame,
but whoever heeds correction is honored.

PROVERBS 13:18

Now we come to a subject that no one likes to talk about: correction. It's definitely up there with submission and gluttony in the "Christian Principles We'd Like to Ignore" category.

I know. I know. None of us likes to admit we're wrong. We like to believe that we're either right or at least that we've made the best decisions with the information we had available. Translated: It wasn't our fault. We all make mistakes or errors in judgment.

The great thing is that as Christians we aren't beyond hope. As my pastor loves to remind us, "Nothing is fatal or final in Jesus." So then why is it so hard for us to turn around and admit when we're wrong?

Is it pride? Maybe.

Conviction? Sometimes.

Whatever the reason, you have to remember to graciously accept correction—from God and leaders. Even when you may not totally agree, you need to respectfully accept their decisions. Not only can it make your work lives easier, but as scripture reminds you "whoever heeds correction is honored." Now, isn't that a good thing?

–GM

POWER PRAYER

Lord, help me to remain humble and respectfully accept
correction.

SMILE!

A cheerful heart is good medicine,
but a crushed spirit dries up the bones.

PROVERBS 17:22

For those wanting to change their image in the workplace, here's some simple advice: Smile. Though it sounds simple, just walk through your office and see how many people consistently look bored or irritated. Then consider which coworkers you would trust with a new assignment or turn to in a pinch—probably those with a good attitude.

I've known several workers who desperately wanted a promotion, but they went through their days looking like they hated their job and sucked a lemon to prove it. They never smiled, and if you impositioned them in the slightest way. . .well, just forget about it. You wondered if they were going to slash your tires in the parking lot. The sad thing was that most of them just didn't know how to express themselves in a positive way. If they had just smiled and taken a more positive approach to their jobs, they probably would have been trusted with much more.

The Word says "a cheerful heart is good medicine," happiness is a choice. So if you're looking for a way to improve your standing in your office and enjoy your life in general, take this one simple step: Smile!

–GM

POWER PRAYER

Lord, thank You for giving me my job and help me to have a
good attitude as I do it.

TERRITORIAL STANDOFFS

A gentle answer turns away wrath,
but a harsh word stirs up anger.

PROVERBS 15:1

Once as a new hire, I found myself facing off with a veteran worker. At the time, I couldn't figure out what I had done to offend her, but it was apparent that my very presence was an irritation. Of course, I now realize that many of her responsibilities were shifted over to me. Obviously, there was a lot more going on with her than what I knew.

When you become the object of someone's scorn for no apparent reason, it probably has nothing to do with you personally. You're simply the catalyst. Anger is a difficult emotion to navigate, whether in the workplace, home, or even the dry cleaner's. God's Word instructs us to have a kind word for those who are angry, which unfortunately is a constant state of being for some.

If you're confronted with an angry person, pray for wisdom for the situation. Make the decision not to match their actions. Instead, remain calm, kind, and objective. By doing this, you may not see an immediate change in their demeanor, but you'll be a witness—possibly the only witness—of kindness in their life.

–GM

POWER PRAYER

Dear Lord, thank You for helping me to be kind to others, even when they're angry. Help me to be a witness for You today.

BAD DAYS

But David encouraged himself in the LORD his God.

1 SAMUEL 30:6 KJV

I want you to stop and think about the very worst day you've ever spent on the job. Okay, do you have a visual? Did you just want to throw your hands into the air and quit on that day? Did you feel like God had forsaken you? Did you want to head for a tropical island and never return? I think we've all been there. Even David had some bad days "on the job."

He was doing exactly what God had told him to do, fighting battles for God. But when he and his men returned from war on this particular day, they found their city had been burned and all of their wives and children had been taken. You talk about a bad day on the job! To make matters worse, all of David's men turned on him and plotted together to stone him. Things looked pretty bleak, but David didn't crawl into a hole and curse God. Instead the Bible says that David encouraged himself in the Lord. And you know what? It wasn't long before that entire situation turned around in David's favor.

So no matter how bad it may get at work—follow David's example. Encourage yourself in the Lord, and watch your situation turn around!

–MMA

POWER PRAYER

Thank You, Lord, for Your never-ending faithfulness! Amen.

MESSING UP

Neither height nor depth,
nor anything else in all creation,
will be able to separate us from the love of God
that is in Christ Jesus our Lord.

ROMANS 8:39

"Have you been to see the boss man yet?" my friend and coworker asked.

"No, why?" I inquired.

"You had an error in your story. . . . It's causing quite a stir in the newsroom," she shared.

I thought I would be sick. I had written an entire story, quoting the wrong man. I had lost my credibility with the readers. I had lost my credibility with my boss and my coworkers. And I had totally humiliated myself. It was a very bad day. I felt I had let everyone down—everyone but God. Not once did I feel condemned when I brought the dilemma to Him. In fact, I felt nothing but love. You see, nothing can separate us from the love of God.

No matter how many times you mess up. No matter how many things you do wrong. No matter if your mistake is on the front page of the local newspaper—God still adores you. He's right there with you, ready to help you pick yourself up and start again. So if you've made a gigantic mistake and you need some unconditional love, run to God. He wants to love you today.

–MMA

POWER PRAYER
Thank You, Lord, for loving me—even when I make big mistakes. Amen.

THE LILY LIFE

*"Therefore I tell you, do not worry about your life,
what you will eat or drink;
or about your body, what you will wear."*

MATTHEW 6:25

Every once in a while I catch myself obsessing about something—a past conversation or a project's due date. When I catch myself beginning to worry, I try to stop and pray for God's help to let the worry go.

In this hustle-bustle world, it's important to remember that God is still in control. He's masterfully created the universe and our place in it. Nothing illustrates this better than Matthew 6. In this chapter, Jesus reminded the people that God created the lilies of the field. Nothing they do helps them to grow, and as beautiful as they are, God cares for us even more. He ended by saying, "Do not worry about tomorrow, for tomorrow will worry about itself" (Matthew 6:34).

If you find that you worry about things, consider this verse. Then when something disturbing arises, let God's Word comfort you. As His Word becomes more real to you, you'll rest knowing that you are more precious and cared for than the lilies of the field.

–GM

POWER PRAYER

*Lord, You are greater than anything else. I trust You with my
life and ask You to help me not worry about tomorrow or
anything in my life.*

MOUNT EVEREST

"I tell you the truth,
if you have faith and do not doubt. . .
you can say to this mountain,
'Go, throw yourself into the sea,'
and it will be done."

MATTHEW 21:21

I recently read a bumper sticker that said, "Focusing on our problems blinds us to our blessings." Okay, while I'm not one who likes bumper stickers very much, I love that one. It is so true, isn't it? If we look long enough at our problems, they seem to get bigger and bigger. What started as a molehill, suddenly looks like a big old mountain—a mountain that blinds you to all of the blessings in your life. Before you know it, you're facing the Mount Everest of problems!

Rather than dwelling on how big your problems are today, why not think about how big your God is? Why not count all of the blessings in your life?

If you have trouble meditating on God's goodness instead of on your problems, I have an assignment for you. Start keeping a little praise journal. Every day, find something to praise God for—the sunny day, your pay raise, your health, and so on. Thank Him for the little things, and pretty soon your big problems won't seem so big anymore.

–MMA

POWER PRAYER
Thank You, God, for all of the blessings You shower down on me every day. I love You. Amen.

WHAT-IFS

*"The LORD himself goes before you
and will be with you; he will never
leave you nor forsake you.
Do not be afraid; do not be discouraged."*

DEUTERONOMY 31:8

"Courage is not simply one of the virtues," C. S. Lewis said, "but the form of every virtue at the testing point."

In your work, there are moments when you need courage. Maybe you've been given a tough assignment, earned a much desired promotion, or had to give a presentation. Whatever it is, you're more than a little nervous.

Well, take a deep breath; you're not alone.

Everyone has faced situations that have left them unsure of whether they can accomplish what they've been asked to do. A thousand what-ifs may be racing through your mind: what if I stammer, what if I fail, what if they're sorry they hired me, what if, what if, what if?

If you're doing what God has called you to do and you're on the career path He's laid out for you, then you're going to be fine. It doesn't mean that everything will always be easy, but you can relax knowing that the Lord is with you.

–GM

POWER PRAYER

Dear Lord, thank You for going before me and being with me. Help me to have courage and to trust You to show me everything I need to do.

SOMETHING TO WORK WITH

*"How long will this wicked community grumble against me?
I have heard the complaints of these grumbling Israelites."*

NUMBERS 14:27

"Nobody knows the trouble I've seen. Nobody knows the sorrow. . . ." Have you been singing the blues lately? Have you been complaining about your job? Your coworkers? Your life? When you open your mouth, are you spewing words that sound like they could be the chorus for a bad country song? Well, I've got news for you—God is not moved by our sad songs or our complaints. No matter how bad your situation is at work, you need to praise God.

Have you ever heard the expression, "Complain and remain or praise and be raised"? It's really true. Complaining never changes anything for the better, but praising changes the condition of our hearts and the atmosphere of our workplace. Not to mention, God appreciates our praise.

You have to give God something to work with in order to change your situation. You tie God's hands with your negative words and sour attitude. C'mon, now. Take off those dark glasses. Put away that harmonica. Stop singing the blues. Give God praise, and give Him something to work with today!

–MMA

POWER PRAYER
Father, I praise You today for all that You've done in my life, and I praise You for all that You're going to do. I love You. Amen.

SHE MEANT WELL

*At that point Peter got up the nerve to ask, "Master, how
many times do I forgive a brother or sister
who hurts me? Seven?"
Jesus replied, "Seven! Hardly. Try seventy times seven."*

MATTHEW 18:21–22 MSG

I had been teaching my little heart out at a writers' conference, and I was really tired by day five. As you might imagine, there was little time to eat. So rather than dive into a
full-course meal, I opted for a Snickers and a Diet Coke. In
fact, I had that same meal a few times throughout the week.

As I headed up the dining hall steps, a woman approached me. She said, "I've been watching you all week.
You give so much to others." I smiled, feeling pretty good
about myself. She continued, "I've also been watching your
eating habits, and I'm worried for you." I thought that was a
bizarre statement, but I kept listening. "So" she said, "I have
something for you." I smiled, thinking another conferee had
a gift for me. Just then, she whipped out a diet plan and said
I should prayerfully consider it. Okay, I hadn't seen that one
coming.

I wanted to dump my Diet Coke on her head! Sometimes, it's really difficult to not become offended. Ask God
to help you. And have a Snickers on me!

–MMA

POWER PRAYER

Lord, help me not to become easily offended. I love You. Amen.

ON THE BRIGHTER SIDE

She is clothed with strength and dignity;
she can laugh at the days to come.

PROVERBS 31:25

For quite a while I worked with two women who had a gift for seeing the humor in almost any situation. Stacy had an outspoken wit. She said—in a very funny way—what everyone else thought. She had a gift for speaking the truth in a way that completely disarmed others. Amber was much more understated but equally funny. A true Southern belle to the core, she could see situations from a different perspective and find humor in them.

I'm thankful for both women.

When the time comes to either laugh or cry, wouldn't you much rather be laughing? I think we all would. When pressures start to mount, look for the person who sees the humor in the situation. That doesn't mean someone who can never be serious or wields sarcasm, but look for people who can joyfully rise above a situation. Those people are blessings, and you can learn a lot from them. The next time your work has you down, ask God to help you find the humor in it. You never know who He might send your way.

–GM

POWER PRAYER

Lord, thank You for helping me see the humor in things so that I can stay positive in my life and job.

DRAMA QUEEN

But when the Holy Spirit controls our lives,
he will produce this kind of fruit in us:
love, joy, peace, patience, kindness, goodness,
faithfulness, gentleness, and self-control.
Here there is no conflict with the law.

GALATIANS 5:22–23 NLT

I saw a T-shirt the other day that had "Drama Queen" printed on the front of it. I almost bought it because I've been known to be a drama queen from time to time. How about you? Do you have a little theater blood running through your veins, too?

Sure, we all go through our drama queen stages in life, but by the time we enter the workforce, we should have outgrown that phase. However, that's not always the case. Maybe you have a lingering drama queen inside of you, or perhaps you work with a drama queen? If so, you know that "drama queen syndrome" disrupts an office. In fact, it can destroy an otherwise smooth-running workplace. There's no place for drama in the office.

If you wear the drama queen crown from time to time, ask God to help you become more consistent in your Christian walk. Ask Him to help you grow in the fruit of the Spirit. The Bible says that God has crowned you with glory and honor. You don't need that drama queen crown anymore!

–MMA

POWER PRAYER
Lord, help me to grow in the fruit of the Spirit. Amen.

SINNER VS. SIN

*Jesus said, "Father, forgive them,
for they do not know what they are doing."*

LUKE 23:34

Have you ever heard someone say, "Hate the sin not the sinner?" Isn't that difficult? When people are cruel or unfair, it's hard to separate them from their actions. I've struggled with this at times. If I know that someone has been rude to me or a loved one, I have a hard time getting past it. Eventually, though, I feel convicted and have to take my emotions to God. I can't say that it's always a pleasant or easy thing, but I try to forgive and move past the hurt, realizing that even though what they did was wrong, I still need to forgive.

If you have a hard time forgiving others, can you imagine how Jesus must have felt? After being falsely accused and tortured, He still had the strength to say, "Father, forgive them, for they do not know what they are doing." He separated their sinful actions from their need for forgiveness.

As you face difficult people, remember Jesus' example. Try to separate the sin from the sinner and bless them. It may not be easy, but whether they know it or not, they need your forgiveness.

–GM

POWER PRAYER
Lord, please help me to distinguish between the sinner and the sin and give me strength to forgive those who offend me.

JOY ROBBERS

*"He will yet fill your mouth with laughter
and your lips with shouts of joy."*

JOB 8:21 NLT

Have you been robbed lately? No, I don't mean robbed of material things. I'm talking about something else—your joy. See, there are joy robbers in every company. They sneakily cozy up to you, only to steal all of your joy, leaving you drained and depressed. Some joy robbers skillfully put you down. Others give a negative report. Still others criticize you on a personal level. And they are trained to come at you when you least expect it.

When I sold my first devotional book, I shared my joyful news with a colleague who said, "You sold your manuscript to *that* company? I guess it's fine for you, but I wouldn't want my name on the cover of the poor quality books they produce. Of course, that's just me." Nice, huh? Yes, I had encountered a joy thief.

If you are dealing with joy thieves in your workplace, ask God to help you guard your joy level. You need joy, because the Bible tells us "the joy of the Lord is our strength." Dive into God's Word today and get a joy refill. It's even better than a power shake!

–MMA

POWER PRAYER

*Lord, help me to avoid the joy robbers in my life. Keep me
filled up with Your joy, Lord, that my strength might be
renewed. Amen.*

THE GOOD FIGHT

*Fight the good fight of the faith;
lay hold of the eternal life to which you were summoned
and [for which] you confessed the good confession
[of faith] before many witnesses.*

1 TIMOTHY 6:12 AMP

Need some good news? No matter what battle you are fighting right now, you're going to win. Do you know how I know that? Because it's a fixed fight. Psalm 34:19 says, "Many are the afflictions of the righteous: but the Lord delivereth him out of them all." All means all, right? So no matter what you're going through at home or at work, victory is on the horizon.

When your boss hollers at you in front of all of your coworkers, you can smile and say under your breath, "Hey, I already know I am going to come through this trial a winner, so I am going to rest in God's supernatural peace today." When the newspaper prints an article that says six hundred people will be laid off at your company over the next year, you don't have to worry. You can say, "I am not going to stress over this situation because the Word says that God will supply all my needs."

So go ahead, fight the good fight of faith, knowing all the while that, in the end, you win!

–MMA

POWER PRAYER
Lord, thank You for delivering me from all of my troubles. Amen.

CUTTING BACK

But people are declared righteous because of their faith,
not because of their work.

ROMANS 4:5 NLT

The company was cutting back, and the trickle effect had reached the lowest level: office supplies. Usually, something as simple as a thirty-five-cent ballpoint pen could be purchased with relative ease, but think again. My boss called me to her office. "We have to cut back," she said, "so here ya go." Out of her pencil drawer, she handed me a hodgepodge of capless old pens. I stood there a moment feeling confused and more than a little irritated. I wondered, *I'm not even worth a decent ballpoint pen?* I walked back to my office, sat down, and stared at the pens. *How had it come to this?* I thought, deciding to foot the bill for my own pen.

Now a pen may seem pretty petty, but in the workplace many things can make us feel unappreciated. Over the years, I've tried to remember that the inconsideration usually isn't personal. It's just part of the system.

If you feel unappreciated, try to remember that most of the time, it isn't personal. It's just the way things work sometimes. Then ask God to give you insight into management's decisions. Understanding what it's facing will help you have more compassion for the decisions.

–GM

POWER PRAYER

Lord, give me the insight and understanding to take
management's decisions in stride.

STOP THE RAIN

[Jesus said,] I have told you these things,
so that in Me you may have [perfect] peace and confidence.
In the world you have tribulation and trials
and distress and frustration;
but be of good cheer. . . . I have overcome the world.

JOHN 16:33 AMP

"Into each life a little rain must fall. . . ." Ever heard that expression? Yeah, well there have been days in my life when that "little rain" became a torrential downpour. I wondered if the flood would simply carry me away—never to be heard from again. Maybe you're there today. If you've had your share of rain lately, let me encourage you.

Though it's tempting, crying in your office won't change your negative circumstances. (Plus, your eyes will get all puffy, and that's bad, too.) Instead, I want you to meditate on this—you have Jesus living on the inside of you, and He has already overcome every kind of trouble there is. It doesn't matter if your husband just told you that he's found someone else. It doesn't matter if your boss just informed you that your position is being discontinued. It doesn't matter if your teenage child is away from God. I'm telling you, Jesus can handle every situation. Cast your cares on Him today. Tell Him all about the rain you've been experiencing, and then thank Him for victory in every area. Be of good cheer. . . . You are an overcomer!

–MMA

POWER PRAYER
Lord, thank You for my impending victories! Amen.

NOW'S A GREAT TIME
FOR A BREAKDOWN

*"You're going to wear yourself out—and the people, too.
This job is too heavy a burden
for you to handle all by yourself."*

EXODUS 18:18 NLT

There are times when, as women, our emotions get the best of us. We try to handle pressure in stride, but we just can't keep it inside any longer. Even if we're not overly emotional, we can't keep the tears down. All the stress and frustration come to the surface and we find ourselves crying in the bathroom stall or in our cars on the way home.

Believe it or not, letting the emotions out is generally healthier than trying to bury them. Now I'm not suggesting that you fly into hysteria or run over anyone in the parking lot, but having a good cry, hard workout, or even screaming into your pillow may be just what the doctor ordered. Once you're calm again, go to the Lord so He can comfort you. Then talk to an objective, Christian friend who can give you perspective and encouragement. Don't let the stress build into a physical or emotional ailment. God didn't make you out of stone. He created you with emotions, so instead of denying them, take them to Him and let Him help you deal with them.

–GM

POWER PRAYER
Lord, show me how to handle the stress in my life.

FORGET IT

Joseph named his firstborn Manasseh and said,
"It is because God has made me forget all my trouble
and all my father's household."

GENESIS 41:51

Remember the story of Joseph? His brothers resented him because he was his daddy's favorite, so they sold him into slavery. But Joseph had favor wherever he went and eventually became a ruler in Egypt. Still, he had to endure much in his lifetime. Not only did his brothers sell him into slavery, but also he spent time in prison for a crime he didn't commit.

When Joseph's wife gave birth to their firstborn son, Joseph named him "Manasseh," which means "made to forget." He did this as a sort of tribute to God because the Father had done so much for him, causing him to forget his past hurts and mistreatment.

Maybe you feel you should change your name to "Manasseh" today because of all the persecution you've endured at work and in your life. Let me encourage you—no matter how many hurts you have to forget, God will make them up to you. He hasn't forgotten you. Honor God with your decision to let the past be the past and press forward into your bright future. You have much to look forward to!

–MMA

POWER PRAYER
Lord, help me to leave behind my past hurts and move forward with You. Amen.

THE DARK PATH

Don't sin by letting anger gain control over you.
Think about it overnight and remain silent.

PSALM 4:4 NLT

Have you ever gotten angry at work? Sure you have. It's normal. Someone treats you badly or overturns one of your decisions and you want to take them to the woodshed. Or thoughts of walking out the front door flash across your mind. Boy, if you haven't been there, then you're more mature than I am.

Everyone has irritating days. It's how we deal with them that separates us from the world. As Christians, we should avoid the dark path—the one filled with revenge, hostility, or verbal assaults. Instead, we should find our peace in the Lord. We should take our anger to Him—first—before we say anything to others. Then we should take a deep breath and deal with the situation with grace. That's not to say we should always roll over and take abuse, but we should keep our emotions from ruling our actions and words.

If you're facing situations that leave you livid, take it to God. Let Him help you filter through your emotions so that you handle them in the most constructive way. That way, you'll continue to be an example for Him, even in your anger.

–GM

POWER PRAYER

Lord, I'm angry and I need Your help. Help me to handle my emotions in the best way.

WISH ME LUCK

*[Jesus said,] "This is My commandment:
that you love one another
[just] as I have loved you."*

JOHN 15:12 AMP

Do you know the song that goes, "What the world needs now, is love sweet love"? I've always loved that song. It's not only a great little melody but also packs a powerful message. You know, the world really does need love. But not the kind of love that the world can offer. That love is temporary and artificial. The world needs God's love—the everlasting, unconditional kind of love.

Just a guess, but I bet your workplace could use a healthy dose of love, too. No matter how ugly people are acting today, answer them with love. Yes, it's tough, but you can do it with the Lord's help. I speak from experience.

On my last day of work at a monthly magazine, one of my coworkers poked her head in my office and said, "Just wanted to wish you luck and say that I'll always remember you as the girl who *way* overdressed for work." Nice, eh? Nothing like getting the last word in. I so wanted to say, "Yeah, well I'll remember you as the coworker that no one liked." But the Lord wouldn't let me say it. See, God wants us to answer low blows by walking the high road of love. Take that walk today.

–MMA

POWER PRAYER
Lord, fill me up with more of Your love. Amen.

BE AN ANGEL

*And live a life of love, just as Christ loved us
and gave himself up for us
as a fragrant offering and sacrifice to God.*

EPHESIANS 5:2

I was so homesick. I wanted desperately to move back to Indiana, but I couldn't tell my husband that. After all, we had moved to Texas to accommodate my new job. I knew I was where God wanted me to be, but that didn't make me miss my family and friends in Indiana any less.

In the midst of this homesickness, I was also struggling to find my identity at this magazine. As a former award-winning newspaper writer, I walked onto the job with an attitude the size of Texas. It didn't take long to realize that my awards and experience didn't mean squat to the people at my new job. I was an emotional wreck.

I needed a touch from heaven, and that touch came through Ron and Edna. My managing editor, Ron, also a former newspaper reporter, understood my background and helped me transition into the magazine world. He and his wife, Edna, became family to me. God knew what I needed and He used this sweet couple to help me. They were like angels on earth to me. I'll never forget their kindness. Why don't you see if you can be an angel in a coworker's life today? Ask God to use you.

–MMA

POWER PRAYER

Lord, use me to touch someone's hurting heart today. Amen.

IT'S A DRILL!

Be prepared. . . . Take all the help you can get,
every weapon God has issued,
so that when it's all over but the shouting
you'll still be on your feet.

EPHESIANS 6:13 MSG

Don't you love fire drills at work? You're working peacefully in your office and all of a sudden a loud shrill pierces the air. Often workers roll their eyes at the thought of leaving their desks for a false alarm, but if the alarm was ever real, they'd be thankful that they knew exactly where to go. Though it seems frivolous, the preparation is good.

In our lives, it's good to be prepared, too. Instead of being afraid or overwhelmed when challenges arise, stay close to God. It doesn't mean that you'll always avoid difficult situations, but you will be able to handle the pressure when it comes. You won't be caught by surprise when the shrill of a problem comes up.

So if you want to be prepared for the fires of life, start preparing now by staying close to God through prayer, reading His Word, attending church, and socializing with other Christians. When you do, you'll be much more ready to take on tough situations.

–GM

POWER PRAYER

Lord, thank You for always helping me prepare for the problems that come up in life. Help me to stay close to You so they don't overwhelm me.

THE PLAGUE

Repent, then, and turn to God,
so that your sins may be wiped out,
that times of refreshing may come from the Lord.

ACTS 3:19

A few years ago, I made a huge mistake that involved an e-mail and my big electronic mouth. A close friend had confided that she was having trouble with a coworker. In a moment of unrestrained cattiness, I sent an e-mail telling my friend how I would respond to this woman's verbal assault. Here's the really horrible part: Because both women had the same last name, I ended up sending it to the other woman—not my friend. It was an ugly scene. My sin had found me out. Though I apologized, you can guess that my witness had been irretrievably lost.

All of us have experienced guilt over something we've done or said. Unfortunately, sometimes that guilt can plague us for years. Though we try to rectify the situation, the feeling can still remain. It's only through a heart-to-heart with Jesus that we can get rid of it.

If you're struggling with guilt over a past wrong, take it to Jesus, and if you need help, talk to a pastor or Christian counselor. Whatever method He uses, either instantaneous or through a counseling process, Jesus will help you settle the situation.

–GM

POWER PRAYER

Lord, please forgive me of my sins and help me get rid of any
guilt in my life.

GIVE ME A DOSE

"For the joy of the LORD is your strength."

NEHEMIAH 8:10

Have you ever met someone and thought, "I want the kind of joy he has?" You can tell that without a doubt the joy of the Lord is his strength. I have. I once had an associate pastor who had that kind of joy. He just radiated the love of God. Everyone—other ministers, the congregation, people on the street—noticed it and couldn't help being influenced by it. Then I discovered how amazing his joy really was. Not too many years earlier, he and his wife had lost their only child in an accident. For some, this devastating event could have turned them bitter and angry with God, but not him. He endured. In fact, he more than endured. He discovered a God-given strength.

If you need the joy of the Lord, begin to talk to God about it. Pray and consider what His joy is and how you can receive it. Ponder who God is and commit to serve Him at all costs. As His truth and character become more real, you won't be able to help getting a good dose of His joy. Then the joy of the Lord will be your strength, too.

–GM

POWER PRAYER

Lord, I need Your joy today. Show me how I can develop a joy that isn't affected by anything that comes my way.

THE POWER OF WORDS

*Those who love to talk will experience the consequences,
for the tongue can kill or nourish life.*

PROVERBS 18:21 NLT

As a former sportswriter for a daily newspaper in southern Indiana, I love sports—especially college basketball (Go Hoosiers!)—but I'm also quite partial to golf.

I recently saw a special on the Golf Channel about golf legend Gary Player. In this interview, Player said that from the time he took up golf at age 14, he would wake up, look himself in the mirror, and say, "I'm going to be the best golfer in the whole world." It's no wonder that in 1965 at age 29, he won golf's Grand Slam—the Masters, the U.S. Open, the British Open, and the PGA. At that time, he was the youngest competitor to ever reach that pinnacle. How did he do it? He saw himself as a winner and a champion long before his talents merited such talk. He understood the power of words, vision, and dreams.

Do you understand the power of words? Why not learn from Gary Player? Wake up each morning and look yourself in the mirror and say: "Everything I touch prospers and succeeds. I am well able to accomplish the task that God has put before me." Speak words of victory, and you'll experience victory in and out of the office!

–MMA

POWER PRAYER
Lord, help me to only speak words of victory. Amen.

WHAT LIGHT?

"Record the vision
And inscribe it on tablets,
That the one who reads it may run."

HABAKKUK 2:2 NASB

Have you ever felt so discouraged in your job that you just wanted to crawl under your desk, eat some chocolate, and cry? I think we've all been there. On those days, my mother would always say, "Into each life a little rain must fall," or "This, too, shall pass," or "There's a light at the end of the tunnel." All three statements are quite true, but when you're right smack-dab in the middle of a discouraging day, it's hard to see that promised light at the end of the long tunnel.

Well, I have some good news for you—Jesus is the Light! And He is there for you right now. No matter how desperate your situation at work may seem, the Lord can deliver you from it. No matter how hopeless you feel, Jesus can restore your hope and your vision today.

Grab some notebook paper and write your vision. Write the dreams that God has placed into your heart. Like the Word says, keep that vision before you. Stick it inside your planner or tuck it away in your desk drawer. Don't let discouragement rob you of your vision. Come out from under your desk and run with your vision today!

–MMA

POWER PRAYER

Thank You, Lord, for restoring my hope and vision today.
Amen.

EMOTIONAL ROLLER COASTER

*And the people, that is, the men of Israel,
encouraged themselves.*

JUDGES 20:22 NKJV

If you're having an emotional roller-coaster kind of day, you need to jump off that wild ride and take a few minutes to encourage yourself in the Lord. Have you ever done that before? If not, this is a good day to start.

Don't listen to the devil's lies today. When he whispers in your ear, "You're going to lose your job. You're not working to your potential. You're a big, fat failure," simply say: "I am a child of the Most High King! I am more than a conqueror! Everything I touch prospers and succeeds! No weapon formed against me is going to prosper!" It's important to take every thought captive, like the Word of God says. In order to counteract those negative thoughts that the devil drops into your mind, you actually need to speak the Word. Shout it out!

When you feel that emotional roller coaster starting to climb a hill, stop it in its tracks and say, "This is the day that the Lord has made, and I will rejoice and be glad in it!" It's amazing how speaking the Word can totally transform your mood and your day. Fight the devil with your mouth. Gain control of your emotions. And truly, have a good day!

–MMA

POWER PRAYER
Lord, help me to get off this emotional roller coaster. Amen.

SURVIVING TECHNOBABBLE

"When you pass through the waters, I will be with you;
and when you pass through the rivers,
they will not sweep over you. . . .
For I am the LORD, your God."

ISAIAH 43:2–3

A few times, I have found myself sitting across a conference table from a computer genius, listening to him discuss some information technology hang up. As he droned on, I sat there thinking: *Why can't I just push a button?* Of course, I never wanted to admit that I was lost, but seriously, does any nontechnical person really understand the information technology world with its symmetric multiprocessing configuration without a kernel recompilation? No!

Regardless of where it comes from, confusion is awful, and you know when you're in over your head. You need help. Mercifully, God hasn't left you sitting across the heavenly conference table listening to Him talk incomprehensibly about your seemingly unfixable situation. No, He's waiting to help you cut through the confusion with clarity. Through studying His Word and praying, you *can* find the answers to any situation. With His help, even the technobabble won't be quite so baffling.

–GM

POWER PRAYER

Lord, I need Your clarity in everything I do—every project on my desk and every person I come in contact with. I trust You for it.

SINGING THROUGH THE TROUBLE

About midnight Paul and Silas were
praying and singing hymns to God.

ACTS 16:25

When in a crisis, the last thing you want to hear is something along the lines of: "When God closes a door, He opens a window," right? I understand; however, in difficult situations, God does work in remarkable ways.

You've probably experienced difficult situations, and you know that even through them, God was faithful. Eventually, you learn to trust Him so that when the challenges come, you know He'll come through for you or at least you recognize that the persecution is small in comparison to His greatness.

That's why the story of Paul and Silas is so encouraging. Even though they had been thrown into prison, they still praised God. They recognized that their suffering was only temporary and that God was greater than anything they had to endure.

The next time you face a setback, don't let discouragement and fear overwhelm you. Trust God and follow Paul and Silas's lead, praying and singing praises to Him. As you do, He *will* show Himself faithful.

–GM

POWER PRAYER

Lord, I trust You. You know my circumstances better than I do.
I commit to praising You regardless of the outcome because I
know You will take care of me.

THERE AIN'T ENOUGH ROOM FOR THE TWO OF US

For God is not a God of disorder but of peace.

1 CORINTHIANS 14:33

Have you ever been in a situation where you felt so strongly that you were right, yet you were unable to voice your opinion because of your lack of authority? It's tough, isn't it? There have been times I have almost bitten clean through my tongue just to keep myself from speaking.

Difficult as it is, we have to honor those in authority over us. That doesn't mean we have to agree with our bosses all of the time, but we do have to show them respect. See, God is a God of order—not a God of confusion. To come against those in authority over us would never be God's way.

Need more convincing? Read Numbers 12. Miriam and Aaron didn't like it when Moses, their leader, married a Cushite woman, and they talked badly about him. Well, the Lord heard them, and the Word says, "The anger of the Lord burned against them." And there were some serious consequences.

So if you're feeling badly toward your boss, ask God to forgive you. And if you truly feel that the leaders in your company are going in the wrong direction, pray for God to change their hearts. But don't come against them. Bite your tongue, and walk in peace.

–MMA

POWER PRAYER
Lord, help me to honor those who are in authority over me. Amen.

SOLITAIRE

*Agree with each other, love each other,
be deep-spirited friends.*

PHILIPPIANS 2:2 MSG

You've probably heard of companies that have removed the game of solitaire from their computer systems because of too many employees' wasted time. If you're like me, the thought of people spending their workday playing solitaire sounds pretty ridiculous.

Unfortunately, many people play "solitaire" at work—and I'm not talking about a computer. They play solitaire by trying to accomplish everything themselves and avoiding working with groups. If they're put on a team, they feel like they're beating their heads against the wall because other workers just can't do the work as well as they could alone—or so they believe. Sound familiar? Effectively working in groups doesn't always come easy. It's a practiced art, but a group can accomplish more than a single person.

Just as you aren't meant to go it alone at work, you shouldn't try to go it alone in your spiritual life. God wants you to have relationships with other Christians. Together, you'll accomplish more for Him than you would alone. So the next time you cringe when joining a group, take time to appreciate all you can do together. As you work toward a common goal, you'll see the benefits in the outcome.

–GM

POWER PRAYER

*Lord, thank You for the coworkers You've place around me.
Help me to be a positive team player with them.*

WALK IN LOVE

Love is kind.

1 CORINTHIANS 13:4

"Happy birthday, Michelle!" shouted three of my closest co-workers. They had decorated my office and sprinkled it with fun-sized chocolate candy bars. They knew I'd need an extra lift. After all, it was my thirtieth birthday. I had been dreading it for weeks. Leaving behind my twenties was a tough one. I feared that crow's-feet were just around the corner. But my buddies were there to cheer me up—except for Claire.

As I headed downstairs for my morning Diet Coke, she stopped me in the hallway. "So how old are you today?"

"I'm thirty," I whispered.

"Really?" Claire said, raising her eyebrows. "I thought you were *way* older than that."

With that curt comment, she took her size-4 body down the hall, leaving me feeling deflated and miserable. She was great at spewing hurtful comments on a daily basis. Oh how I longed to say some zingers back at her. I had crafted them carefully in my mind, just waiting for the right time. But whenever that opportunity arose, the Lord wouldn't let me speak. I kept hearing that inner voice saying, "Walk in love."

Maybe there's a "Claire" in your office that you'd like to throttle. Well, don't. Instead, kill her with kindness. Walk in love. Yes, it's difficult, but you don't have to walk it alone. God will help you.

–MMA

POWER PRAYER
Father, help me walk in Your love. Amen.

ONE-UPMANSHIP

*For where you have envy and selfish ambition,
there you find disorder and every evil practice.*

JAMES 3:16

Ever worked with someone who always one-ups you? Uh-huh, you know the type. If you have an idea that will save the company hundreds of dollars, she comes up with a plan to save thousands. Irritating, isn't it?

Be honest. That old green-eyed monster occasionally rears its ugly head when she enters the room. Jealousy is a funny thing. It sort of sneaks up on you when you least expect it. Unfortunately, it brings a few of its friends like anger, frustration, and strife. Let's face it—that's no way to live.

Instead of focusing all of your energy on the "one-upper," turn your attention to God. Ask God to help you see her through *His* eyes. Ask Him to fill you up with so much love that there won't be any room for jealousy, anger, frustration, or strife.

Be happy when your coworker succeeds. Rejoice with her, because until you can celebrate her accomplishments, you'll never have any success of your own. Remember, God is no respecter of persons. What He has done for her, He will also do for you—if you'll keep your heart right.

–MMA

POWER PRAYER

*Father, please help me to get along with all of my coworkers.
Change my heart, Lord. I love You. Amen.*

POWERFUL WORDS

The tongue that brings healing is a tree of life,
but a deceitful tongue crushes the spirit.

PROVERBS 15:4

Have you ever considered how powerful your words are? I can remember things that people have said to me—both positive and negative—that still resonate in my mind. I've been called a creative problem solver, but then I've also been told that I'm a pushover. The good is nice to hear, but the bad is hard to swallow. I have to consciously remind myself not to see myself that way.

Why? Because words are powerful. They can build up or tear down; it's that simple. The amazing thing to realize is that our words can have a similar power over other people. What we say can build them up or tear them down, affecting how they view themselves.

As an ambassador of Christ, you're in a powerful position where it is necessary to build others up, being a positive influence in their lives instead of a destructive force. You have that power and responsibility. So today, as you work with coworkers, some of whom may grate on your nerves, determine to build them up. You never know, your kind words may be the only ones they hear.

–GM

POWER PRAYER

Lord, as an ambassador for You, help me to bring healing and encouragement to others today.

PICK YOUR BATTLES

A gentle answer turns away wrath,
but a harsh word stirs up anger.

PROVERBS 15:1

One of the greatest lessons I've learned in business is to pick my battles wisely. In stressful environments with intense people, I've seen some people roll with the punches and others explode over every little frustration, causing coworkers to hide under their desks or at least avoid working with them.

Though there are times when you have to go to battle to correct a wrong, there are other times when peacefully working out a solution with creativity is more effective. By being proactive instead of constantly looking for a fight, you'll instill trust and cooperation in your coworkers instead of fear and wrath.

Just imagine if every time you approached God, He beat you over the head with your failure. Wouldn't you finally stop approaching Him or live in fear of His reaction? Yes, He still corrects you and His Holy Spirit still convicts you for wrongdoing, but you can be peaceful knowing that He only wants what's best for you.

–GM

POWER PRAYER

Lord, thank You for my coworkers. I pray for Your blessings on
them and ask that You help me to work well with them.

THE BEST KIND OF THINKING

As charcoal to embers and as wood to fire,
so is a quarrelsome man for kindling strife.

PROVERBS 26:21

One of my managers, JoAnn, was a great team builder. She could rally a group of people to work harder and longer than ever. When challenges came her way, she wasn't always happy about it, but she always gave people the benefit of the doubt. Through experience, she'd learned that workers sometimes faced unusual challenges, and her example taught me a valuable lesson: Think the best of others.

Over the years, I've tried to keep this lesson at the forefront of my mind. Of course, there will be those few difficult, incompetent workers, but usually people want to be good at their jobs. So though you may have to deal with a few bad apples, wouldn't you rather err on the side of thinking the best of someone who didn't deserve it than the other way around?

God wants you to be a peacemaker wherever you go. He wants you to stand out as someone who avoids strife and builds others up. As you do, you'll continue to be a light that others will trust and follow.

–GM

POWER PRAYER

Lord, help me to see the best in others. Help me to be a peace-maker and build others up so that I can be a light for You in everything I do.

MR. GRUMPY

A cheerful look brings joy to the heart.

PROVERBS 15:30

He was always grumpy. He hated his marriage. He hated his job. He hated his life. And from what I could tell, he hated everyone in the office. Call me crazy, but it became my mission to get a grin out of this guy. However, he made it very difficult. He grouched and grumbled on a daily basis. Once, I offered to get Mr. Grumpy a soft drink since I was on my way back to the lunchroom, and he grumbled, "Are you trying to kill me? Do you know what's in that junk?"

This guy was a real piece of work. I never made much progress with this grumpy old guy, but I did manage to muster a smile or two over the years. When I moved to take another job, he even gave me a hug at my going-away luncheon! The entire office gasped, sure he was lunging toward me to swing at me, not hug me.

You know, there are grumpy people at every workplace— people who'd rather scowl than smile. But don't let their grumpiness steal your joy. Instead, share your joy with them! Go out of your way to be nice to them. Just think. . . you may be the only Christian in their lives.

–MMA

POWER PRAYER

Lord, fill me with Your joy that I might share it with others.
Amen.

BUILD A NEW CLIMATE

Be imitators of God. . .and live a life of love.

EPHESIANS 5:1–2

I was fresh out of college with a journalism degree and no place to use that degree. I had interviewed with a few area newspapers, but no one was hiring. So a local optometrist took mercy on me and hired me to do receptionist-type work. Eventually, he even taught me how to pretest patients on his expensive equipment. He showed me how to do a frame selection with patients. He helped with billing when I couldn't get the numbers to add up. He had great patience with me. In fact, he looked for ways to compliment me. (And the Lord knows there weren't many things he could choose from—I was clueless to this type of work!) I've never forgotten his kindness.

You know, we can take a lesson from Doc Poling. We should look for the best in our coworkers. We should find ways to encourage them. We should be patient when someone drops the ball. We should help one another and point out one another's strengths instead of magnifying each other's weaknesses.

When you sow good things into your coworkers, you'll reap a harvest of good things—kindness, mercy, grace, patience, and more. Look for ways to build up your coworkers today, and watch the climate of your office change.

–MMA

POWER PRAYER
Lord, help me to build others up, not tear them down. Amen.

INTUITION? MAYBE.
DISCERNMENT? OH YEAH!

The heart of the discerning acquires knowledge;
the ears of the wise seek it out.

PROVERBS 18:15

Have you ever had a feeling about taking a course of action but didn't really know why? You just sensed it. Some may consider this intuition, but for the Christian, it goes beyond intuition. We can have discernment. In our spirits, we can just know the right things to do or how to handle situations. And when it comes to working with people, you just can't beat discernment. It can help you accomplish your goals more quickly and effectively.

This verse says it all: "The heart of the discerning acquires knowledge; the ears of the wise seek it out." You can't get much clearer than that. As wise, working women, we should seek discernment. In fact, if we're smart, we won't be able to help turning to God to do our jobs better.

If you need to work effectively and efficiently with others, ask God for discernment. Listen when the Lord leads you to handle things a specific way. As you rely on His Spirit, you'll enjoy more success.

–GM

POWER PRAYER

Lord, thank You for giving me discernment. I want to see
things the way You see them.

9-11

Why, you do not even know what will happen tomorrow.
What is your life?
You are a mist that appears for a little while
and then vanishes.

JAMES 4:14

September 11, 2001, forever changed our world. Every year when this day rolls around, we are reminded of those who lost their lives at the hands of ruthless terrorists. Images of billowing smoke and an ash-filled sky are still vivid in our minds.

Following that devastating day, we put aside our differences and worked together to rebuild our country and mend the broken pieces—no hidden agendas, nothing expected in return. We found out that we truly needed each other. Barriers were broken. Walls came down. And we discovered that it would take a lot more than some evil terrorists to destroy the spirit of the United States. This is God's country—it always has been, and it always will be.

Today, as we reflect on that fateful day, I challenge you to take a few minutes to pray for those who lost loved ones on 9-11-2001. And I urge you to let your friends, family, and coworkers know how much you appreciate them. If we learned anything from 9-11, we learned that we're not promised tomorrow. Every day is a gift. What will you do with your gift today?

–MMA

POWER PRAYER
Thank You, Lord, for the freedoms we enjoy in this country.
Bless those who are hurting today. Amen.

WORKLOADS

Moses' father-in-law replied,
"What you are doing is not good.
You and these people who come to you
will only wear yourselves out.
The work is too heavy for you; you cannot handle it alone."

EXODUS 18:17–18

Have you ever heard the expression, "Two heads are better than one"? That's so true, or at least it can be. When you're assigned a project at work, don't be afraid to ask for your colleagues' input. Who knows? One of them may have the final puzzle piece you've been struggling to find.

Why do we have such a hard time asking for help? Do we fear that we'll have to share the credit with somebody else? Are we afraid that we'll be admitting we're not perfect if we reach out for help? Well, we do need help.

Even Moses needed help when his workload became overwhelming. He was sitting as judge over the Israelites, helping them settle disputes from morning until nightfall, and he was exhausted. His father-in-law suggested that he appoint some godly men to help him judge the simple cases and only leave the really difficult ones to Moses. The plan was a "God idea," and it worked beautifully. See, teamwork is of God. He never told us to "go it alone." So ask for help today.

–MMA

POWER PRAYER
Lord, I give my fears to You. Help me to be able to reach out
for help. Amen.

DON'T GO IT ALONE

As iron sharpens iron,
so one man sharpens another.

PROVERBS 27:17

It's interesting to notice how many people try to do everything themselves. They want to believe that they don't need anyone else, but actually, others help strengthen them. Maybe they can earn success on their own, but they'll work harder for it and won't have others to celebrate with them once they achieve it. Just ask those who have spent all their time grasping for success without taking time out to invest in others. Most would trade some of the success for real friendship and love.

God never meant for any of us to travel through life alone, not personally or professionally. He has given you family members, mentors, and Christian brothers and sisters to make the journey easier, more successful, and more fulfilling. Even Jesus had friends and companions in His ministry, and after He died, they continued the work that He had begun. So as you work, take time to invest in the people around you. Though it may seem like a sacrificial effort at first, in the end, you will reap the reward of it.

–GM

POWER PRAYER

Lord, help me to remember to take time to invest in others.
Show me those with whom I could develop a true friendship.

GETTING THE WORK DONE

*From him the whole body,
joined and held together by every supporting ligament,
grows and builds itself up in love,
as each part does its work.*

EPHESIANS 4:16

Everyone has a job to do. And without everyone working together, things wouldn't run smoothly or, possibly, at all. Imagine a grocery store. What would happen if those who ordered the food didn't do their jobs? How about the cashiers and stockers? Each person plays a role in getting the work done.

It's the same way in the Body of Christ. Everyone has a job. If you're called to teach others, you've got one job. If you're called to help administrate, you work behind the scenes, but your role is still important. If you're called to prayer, your work may be done completely in secret, but that doesn't make it any less important.

We're all part of the team of the Body of Christ. And your role is just as important as anyone else's. As long as you are doing what God has shown you to do, then you are successful. Take your job—your work and your ministry— seriously. In both, you're part of getting the work done.

–GM

POWER PRAYER

Lord, thank You for calling me to be part of the Body of Christ. Help me to accomplish all that You need me to do.

KEEPING THE PEACE

Love one another deeply, from the heart.

1 PETER 1:22

September is the month that my wonderful husband, Jeff, was born. Jeff was my high school sweetheart, so we have practically grown up together. However, during that first year of marriage, we found out that we didn't know each other nearly as well as we thought we did. I couldn't believe how moody he was, and he had no idea that I was so high maintenance. (Okay, he had some idea. . . .) We had to learn the true meaning of the word "compromise," or we never would have made it through those first twelve months. Now, thirteen years later, we're still compromising and finding that middle ground in order to keep peace in the home.

You know what? It works the same way in the office. No, you're not married to your coworkers, but you are with them at least eight hours a day. Spending that much time together is an absolute breeding ground for strife. You're going to disagree with your coworkers—it's a fact of life. But how you handle those disagreements "separates the men from the boys," to borrow a cliché. Choose your battles wisely. Be willing to compromise. And look for that middle ground in every situation. If you will, God will take you to a higher ground!

–MMA

POWER PRAYER

Lord, help me to promote peace in every situation at work. Amen.

THE DEVIL'S ADVOCATE

*Let there be real harmony
so there won't be divisions in the church.
I plead with you to be of one mind,
united in thought and purpose.*

1 CORINTHIANS 1:10 NLT

There's always one in a crowd, one person who takes it upon himself to play devil's advocate because no one else knows how things should be done, right? I worked with one of these for quite a while. Jerry was detailed, talented, intelligent, passionate about his work, and completely irritating. Nothing anyone else ever did was good enough. If he could point out problems, he would. Our team would be running in one direction, and Jerry would be standing back shaking his head, because to him, we were so clueless. As talented as he was, his constant criticism stifled his influence in the group.

If you're working on a team, support that team. No, the group isn't going to get it right every time, but you'll be able to make a bigger impact with constructive teamwork rather than destructive criticism. Working with other people can be a challenge, but if we recognize that we don't always have all the answers, we'll be more apt to recognize that others' input and talents are just as valuable.

–GM

POWER PRAYER

*Lord, teach me to work in harmony with others so that we can
be united in thought and purpose.*

FOR THE TEAM

Just as our bodies have many parts
and each part has a special function,
so it is with Christ's body.
We are all parts of his one body,
and each of us has different work to do.

ROMANS 12:4–5 NLT

Not long ago, I was watching the National Cheerleading Association finals on television, and I was amazed at the skill level of these athletes. I was also so sad for this one squad who dropped a very important stunt. It collapsed somewhere in the middle, and down came the formation, totally throwing off the entire routine. Needless to say, that squad didn't win.

You know, we can learn from cheerleaders when it comes to our workplaces. First off, they're cheery and they're leaders—both good qualities for the office. We can also take a lesson in teamwork from these fine athletes. See, if we get out of sync with one of our coworkers due to a disagreement or a lack of understanding, it throws off the entire office. Or if someone is relying on you, and you're off doing your own thing, the whole "formation" is going to fall. So get in sync! Be a team player. If you learn to do those things, you and your coworkers will really have something to cheer about!

–MMA

POWER PRAYER
Father, help me to support my coworkers as we work together
to accomplish great things. Amen.

PART OF THE WHOLE

We are all one body,
we have the same Spirit,
and we have all been called to the same glorious future.

EPHESIANS 4:4 NLT

Recently, a pastor said, "Relational joining is necessary in order to enjoy the fullness of what God has to offer." By relational joining, he meant that God doesn't want us to focus solely on ourselves and our individual salvation. Instead, God wants us to be a part of a whole. As someone who is leery of joining groups, this was a good message for me.

At times, I haven't always felt "in sync" with other women in the church because of my career. I've attended women's retreats only to be so exhausted from my workweek that I just wanted to sleep—a big no-no at women's retreats. Or I've attended church classes and found little to talk about with the other women. Eventually, though, I found other working, Christian women who shared my interests. Their friendships have proven to be some of the closest of my life.

Don't give up on finding other Christian women with whom to connect. Even if it seems like a hopeless task, make the effort. As you connect with other women in the Body of Christ, you will enhance your faith.

–GM

POWER PRAYER
Lord, help me to find close Christian friends with whom I
can share my walk and grow.

HUMILITY FIRST

"Whoever wants to be first among you must be your slave."

MATTHEW 20:27 MSG

Do you have a "me" problem? Do you think of yourself before everyone else in your office? Do you always have an agenda? If you do, you're right in line with the world's way of thinking. The world says, "If you don't look out for number one, nobody else will." But the Word says, "Whoever wants to be first among you must be your slave." Those two statements are in direct contradiction, aren't they?

Well, let me give you some additional reasons to go the Word way. Proverbs 16:18 says, "First pride, then the crash—the bigger the ego, the harder the fall" (MSG). The Word also says a lot about humility. It says that God gives grace to the lowly and that He promises to save the humble. Sounds like God looks out for those who aren't so concerned with looking out for themselves, doesn't it?

See, you don't have to look out for numero uno because the Creator of the Universe is looking out for you. Stop the "Me, Me, Me" mentality and begin focusing your attention on God. You don't have to do a single thing except trust in the Lord. He is your protector and defender.

–MMA

POWER PRAYER

Father, help me to get my eyes off of myself and back onto You. Amen.

CHEERLEADER

I long to see you so that I may impart to you
some spiritual gift to make you strong—
that is, that you and I may be mutually encouraged
by each other's faith.

ROMANS 1:11–12

Everyone needs a cheerleader, a friend who believes in them when everything seems to be falling apart. Thankfully, I have one of those friends, and I hope you do, too. When either of us is hit by career disappointments, harsh coworkers, or family trauma—sometimes all at once—we meet for lunch, which must include a *huge* smothered-in-chocolate dessert, and remind each other that God loves us and has called us for this time. It's the best kind of therapy.

If you need a cheer from a special friend but don't have one nearby, let these scriptures encourage you. They're the words that your heavenly Father has said about you: He loves you (John 15:9), and nothing you have ever done or ever will do will separate you from His love (Romans 8:38). God knows everything about you and considers you valuable and precious (Luke 12:7). You are chosen by Him to be used for His glory (Ephesians 1:11). Every step you take is ordered by Him and He delights in you (Psalm 37:23). Ponder these verses today, because they are part of God's personal cheer to you.

–GM

POWER PRAYER
Lord, thank You for Your love, acceptance, and direction in
my life.

DIVA ON THE LOOSE

"Do to others as you would have them do to you."

LUKE 6:31

Compromise—easier said than done, eh? But in order to have a happy and productive company, you have to find that middle ground. As a writer, I am constantly battling with the "art guys." They *always* need more white space, meaning I *always* have to cut my articles in half. And those of you who are creative types will understand my frustration with this routine. I mean, I feel like I've given birth to each word of those articles. I hate to see any of it cut, especially for the sake of "more white space." I just don't get it. But guess what? I don't have to get it. In fact, it's not my job to get it. It's my job to compromise and not be the diva with an attitude, demanding my way in every situation.

Be honest. . . . Are you the office diva? Are people calling you Whitney and Madonna behind your back? If so, it's time for a change. Ask God to help you become more agreeable in the office. Look for ways to find that middle ground. Choose your battles wisely, and do unto others as you'd have them do unto you. Your boss will be pleased, and so will God.

–MMA

POWER PRAYER

Lord, help me to treat others as I'd like to be treated. Amen.

BIG TASKS

LORD, you establish peace for us;
all that we have accomplished you have done for us.

ISAIAH 26:12

Have you ever had to do something but knew you needed help? The task took determination and hard work, but it was bigger than one person.

In the Old Testament, three men were given a task like this. After years of captivity in Babylon, God wanted Israel to return to Jerusalem. Since the city had been destroyed, the process took almost 100 years. First, Zerubbabel returned to Jerusalem with over 42,000 people. Then, 79 years later, Ezra returned with 1,754 men. Finally, 13 years after Ezra, Nehemiah returned as governor to rebuild the city.

Imagine a task like this, the rebuilding of God's holy city. It may sound daunting, but so is growing a company, managing a group that doesn't peacefully coexist, or even raising children alone. Whatever the task, remember that if God has called you to do it, then it is doable. But don't assume that just because it's part of your calling you can't have help. Even for Jerusalem's rebuilding, Zerubbabel, Ezra, and Nehemiah had help. As they set out to accomplish their tasks, they had many workers with them. Just like them, with God's guidance and the help of the people around you, you can accomplish your task, too.

–GM

POWER PRAYER

Lord, accomplish through me and those around me all that You want to do.

THE LEAST IS THE GREATEST

An argument started among the disciples
as to which of them would be the greatest.
Jesus, knowing their thoughts,
took a little child and had him stand beside him.
Then he said to them, "Whoever welcomes
this little child in my name welcomes me;
and whoever welcomes me welcomes the one who sent me.
For he who is least among you all—he is the greatest."

LUKE 9:46–48

If you're struggling to get along with a coworker today, don't feel bad. Even the disciples—the chosen twelve—had trouble. Obviously, from this passage in Luke, we see that they had a little jealousy going on in the ranks. They were jockeying for position. They wanted to know who would be the greatest among them. Notice how Jesus answered them. He said, "Whoever is the least among you, he is the greatest."

It's not hard to see that Jesus frowns on competitive jealousy. He wouldn't tolerate it back then, and He still won't. Why? Because He knows it will eventually destroy us. The Word says, "For where envy and self-seeking exist, confusion and every evil thing are there" (James 3:16 NKJV).

If you're striving to outshine someone else in your company or if you're in constant strife with another colleague over "who's the greatest," end it today. Love your neighbor as yourself and let Jesus promote you.

–MMA

POWER PRAYER
Lord, keep my heart right where my coworkers are concerned.
Amen.

YOUR HELPER

*I know that through your prayers
and the help given by the Spirit of Jesus Christ,
what has happened to me will turn out for my deliverance.*

PHILIPPIANS 1:19

Do you ever wonder how people manage their lives without Jesus? I do. The thought of making daily decisions without His guidance is pretty scary.

There was a time in my life when I tried doing everything myself. I made my own decisions and lived by my own rules. And it was short-lived. I remember praying, "Lord, I can't do it alone. I'm Yours." I'll never forget the peace, joy, and love that filled my heart at that moment. Within weeks, the things in my life that were displeasing to Him were gone—and not by my own hand. He orchestrated all of it.

If you're struggling to do everything and make every decision by yourself, let it go. Jesus is the best coach, friend, big brother, and teammate that you'll ever have. He will never leave you and He'll continually be interceding to the Father on your behalf. Go ahead and turn your entire life—every career decision and relationship—over to Him. It'll be *by far* the best decision you'll ever make.

–GM

POWER PRAYER

Lord, I surrender everything in my life to You. Direct and use me however You choose.

Isn't It Obvious?

Serve only the LORD your God and fear him alone.
Obey his commands, listen to his voice, and cling to him.

DEUTERONOMY 13:4 NLT

There is a funny dynamic that happens in some meetings when everyone states the obvious. Maybe you've noticed it in some of your meetings, too. Deciding on how to handle a new project or evaluating how effective something is, the meeting opens with everyone looking perplexed. Then the observations begin. Someone says something that any sixth-grader could come up with, and everyone nods with deep contemplation. "Oh yes, that's true," they affirm. Then someone else says something equally insightful and again everyone nods in agreement. At the end of the hour-long meeting, little has been determined, or the most obvious plan of action was taken. The attendees aren't wrong or dense; they just don't know what to do.

That's why it's nice to know that God always has a plan for our lives. In the great meetings of our life, He's right there in the midst of us, giving us truly insightful and creative ideas of what we can do and where we can go. He's our own personal leader who is ready and willing to lead us, if we're just ready to follow Him.

–GM

POWER PRAYER

Lord, I serve, honor, and cling to You. I will follow Your voice wherever You lead.

FEELING THE LOVE

Love is patient, love is kind.

1 CORINTHIANS 13:4

Pfsst. Ahh. . .the wonderful sound of a Diet Coke opening first thing in the morning. I've never been much of a coffee drinker. My drink of choice? I love to mix Diet Coke and Classic Coke for a winning combination of caffeine and fizz.

When I worked full time for a local magazine, the first thing on my morning agenda at work was to run downstairs and fill my Indiana Hoosiers mug with ice so that I could "mix" my drink. One morning on my way downstairs, my supervisor stopped me and said, "You'll need to take care of getting ice before the workday begins. New rule." Now I was a salaried employee—not a time clock puncher, and I almost always worked more hours a week than I was required to work, so I didn't see the problem. Besides, she ran to the coffeepot that was stationed in our work area at least four times a day. I wanted to dump my cup of ice on her head, to be honest. But that still, small voice whispered, "Love is patient. Love is kind."

Let me share, I wasn't feeling the love that day, but love is a choice. If you're struggling with a difficult boss or coworker today, choose to walk in love.

–MMA

POWER PRAYER

Lord, help me to walk in love even when I don't feel like it.
Amen.

GENERALISTS VS. SPECIALISTS

All these gifts have a common origin,
but are handed out one by one by the one Spirit of God.
He decides who gets what, and when.

1 CORINTHIANS 12:11 MSG

As you know, in business there are generalists and specialists. The generalists are those who know a little about a lot. Specialists, on the other hand, are just what they sound like. They specialize in one area, like a computer programmer who knows the ins and outs of one language. Both of these are necessary for a company to run smoothly. We need the generalists to see the big picture and the specialists to make sure every minuscule base is covered. Without the generalists, the specialists may not know how to fit all the parts together, and without the specialists, something small, yet important, would be overlooked.

Even in church, God has given people these kinds of gifts. Many times, pastors are the generalists. They set the vision, and they surround themselves with great helpers, specialists, who make sure every detail is covered. Why is this important? Because we all need to work together to do what God has called us to do. God brings people into our lives, and whether they're specialists or generalists, their roles are important. Together, we can succeed.

–GM

POWER PRAYER
Lord, help me to serve You in the best possible way and to appreciate the gifts You've given to others.

KEEP PRAYING

"But I say to you, love your enemies,
bless those who curse you, do good to those who hate you,
and pray for those who spitefully use you and persecute you."

MATTHEW 5:44 NKJV

Okay, so you've tried to find that middle ground, but your coworker continues to be impossible. There are some people who are just flat out difficult. (You're getting a mental picture of that person right now, aren't you?) No matter what you try, that person won't cooperate. If you say "black," she says "white." If you say "up," she says "down." I know you'd like to punch her, but what you must do is pray for her.

Matthew 5:44 says just that—pray for those who spitefully use you and persecute you. So that's what you have to do—no matter how you feel about that person. Feeling has nothing to do with it. Ask God to change her heart. Confess favor with her, standing on Psalm 5:12. Be diligent. Even if you don't see an immediate change in her, keep praying.

God will either move her out or move you up. He will give her a chance to change, but if she won't, God won't allow His will for your life to be hindered by a difficult coworker. Keep praying and go to work each day with great expectancy. It will get better.

–MMA

POWER PRAYER

Lord, I pray for my difficult coworker. Show me favor with
her. Amen.

IT'S A JUDGMENT CALL
"Do not judge, or you too will be judged."

MATTHEW 7:1

Don't you hate being around judgmental people? I know I do. Unfortunately, I've caught myself being that judgmental person. I assumed that I knew the best way something should be done or thought that someone should've handled or said something differently. I've asked the Lord to help me with this because I know it's a bad habit.

Though there's nothing wrong with being a black-and-white type of person, it's dangerous for us to set ourselves up as the standard for others. It divides people, breaking down trust, so that none of us wants to be vulnerable. And the scripture is pretty clear that to judge is a sure way to be judged.

If you're like me and you struggle with being too judgmental, ask God to help you become more mindful of what you think and say. Start sifting those thoughts and words through this scripture. When you catch yourself thinking or saying something judgmental, correct yourself. In time, you'll break yourself of that destructive habit and enjoy closer, more trusting relationships with those around you.

–GM

POWER PRAYER
Lord, help me to not be judgmental toward others so that I can build trusting relationships with them.

PRAYER PARTNER

"Again, I tell you that if two of you on earth
agree about anything you ask for,
it will be done for you by my Father in heaven."

MATTHEW 18:19

I looked up at the poster above the conference table. It read: "T-E-A-M: TOGETHER, EVERYONE ACHIEVES MORE." Maybe you've seen a similar sign in your workplace. It's a catchy little saying that speaks great truth. It reminds me of Matthew 18:19, which says if we agree together in prayer, it will be done by our heavenly Father. That's like the ultimate in teamwork, isn't it?

If your "team" at work has trouble working together to accomplish a common goal, you may need to find another Christian team member and begin praying for your overall team. Two prayer warriors in a company can totally transform the atmosphere of your office.

When I worked for a daily newspaper, I had a prayer partner named Glendora. I always teased her, "Glendora, when I need prayer, I come to you. I think you have a direct line with the Father." She'd always get tickled when I'd say that, but truly, Glendora knew how to touch heaven. If there's no "Glendora" in your company, why not fill that void? Start praying diligently for your coworkers, your bosses, and those you serve. And while you're at it, pray for God to send you a prayer partner.

–MMA

POWER PRAYER
Lord, please send me a prayer partner. Amen.

IF YOU NEED ME, I'LL BE UNDER MY DESK WITH BONBONS

*"Don't be afraid," the prophet answered.
"Those who are with us are more than
those who are with them."*

2 KINGS 6:16

Ever felt like you were all alone in your company? Ever felt so outnumbered by your adversaries that you wanted to crawl under your desk and hide? We've all been there, and it's not an easy place to be.

But isn't it comforting to know that we don't have to go it alone? God says He will never leave us or forsake us.

Need some more convincing? Read about Elisha in 2 Kings 6. The king of Aram was angry with Elisha and came after him. When Elisha and his servant awoke the next morning, the servant saw the enemy's army with horses and chariots surrounding the city. The servant was scared and asked, "What shall we do?" Elisha assured him, "Those who are with us are more than those who are with them." Then Elisha prayed for the servant's eyes to be opened so he could see the real situation—the hills full of horses and chariots of fire all around them. God had the situation under control.

Even though you may feel alone today, just know that God has an army working for you. Ask God to help you see your situation through His eyes. And rejoice in your impending victory.

–MMA

POWER PRAYER
Thank You, Lord, for protecting me from my enemies. Amen.

NOBODY LIKES ME

*You made him a little lower than the heavenly beings
and crowned him with glory and honor.*

PSALM 8:5

Whenever I used to have a feel-sorry-for-myself day, my mother would sing this silly little song: "Nobody likes me. Everybody hates me. Guess I'll go eat worms."

How about you? Have you felt like eating a big, fat juicy worm lately? Are you feeling sorry for yourself? Do you feel as though you'll never be able to succeed in your job? If you answered "yes" to any of those questions, you need to give your insecurities to God and ask Him to replace them with confidence and supernatural favor.

Here's what the Bible says about you in Deuteronomy 28:13: "The LORD will make you the head, not the tail." I like being the head, how about you? And John 12:26 says, "My Father will honor the one who serves me." Did you get that? God will honor you! So stop feeling badly about yourself.

Start thinking, feeling, believing, and saying what God says about you, and pretty soon, others will think highly of you, too. It works! But you have to walk in it every day. C'mon, now. Put down that big, juicy worm and start walking in God's divine favor. It's the only way to walk!

–MMA

POWER PRAYER

*Lord, replace my insecurities with Your kind of confidence.
Amen.*

JUST SAY "NO"

*Pride goes before destruction,
a haughty spirit before a fall.*

PROVERBS 16:18

Do you have trouble saying "no" to your superiors? I have a classic case of "Sure, I can do that," even though I know I'm saying "yes" when I should be saying "no." For instance, last summer I signed two book contracts with a deadline of September 1. When both publishers asked if I needed more time, I proudly said, "No, I can totally meet that deadline." I didn't want to admit that I needed more time. I was afraid they might see it as a sign of weakness and lose confidence in me.

So I practically killed myself to meet those deadlines. I even ended up having to ask for an extension on one of the deadlines! Ugh. I learned that one the hard way.

Looking back, it was fear and pride that kept me from being honest with myself and my bosses. I was afraid of disappointing anyone, and I was too proud to admit that I couldn't do what they were asking me to do.

Maybe you're on that same merry-go-round today. If so, jump off! Ask God to help you say "no" when "no" is the needed answer. And ask Him to help you swallow your pride and admit when you need help. There's no shame in being human.

–MMA

POWER PRAYER

Lord, help me to walk free from fear and pride. Amen.

THE GREAT UNKNOWN

Fearless now, I trust in God;
what can mere mortals do to me?

PSALM 56:11 MSG

As much as the fear of failure can hinder us, the fear of success can hold us back, too. This is a difficult fear to overcome because the end results are unknown. You know what's expected in your current position and the thought of leaving it makes you scared and nervous.

The only way to rid yourself of any fear is with the Word of God. By studying the Word of God and discovering what God says about you, your faith in Him will increase. You'll begin to view the obstacles in your career as small in comparison to Him.

So if you're struggling with the fear of success, take time to read and meditate on God's Word. Find the scriptures with which you can relate, copy them down, and put them in a place where you can see them every day—your Bible, your desk drawer, your purse. Don't just read them like you're reading your grocery list, read them as though they are personal words from your heavenly Father. Continue to pray and surround yourself with positive Christian friends who will encourage you. With all this, you're sure to succeed.

–GM

POWER PRAYER

Lord, as I meditate on Your Word, I trust You to fulfill Your
plan in my life and to help me follow that plan without fear.

WILL THIS STORM EVER END?

*But God remembered Noah and all the wild animals
and the livestock that were with him in the ark,
and he sent a wind over the earth,
and the waters receded.*

GENESIS 8:1

Can you imagine being on a boat with a bunch of smelly animals for 150 days? (Remind you of your workplace?) Well. . .Noah and his family did just that. Some people think they only had to survive on that boat for 40 days and 40 nights, but the Bible says it *rained* for 40 days and 40 nights, but it took 150 days for the water to go down enough for Noah and the gang to exit the boat.

I'm sure there were days when Noah and his family wished they hadn't been chosen for the ark assignment. But Noah knew God, and he believed that God would deliver them—no matter how many days he looked outside and saw nothing but water. For almost seven months, the Lord caused the wind to blow and push back the floodwaters. God was working behind the scenes the whole time.

Maybe you feel like you're on a big boat, floating on a sea of insecurities right now. You may not be able to see a change today, but just trust in Him. God hasn't forgotten you. In fact, your miracle may blow in on the very next breeze.

–MMA

POWER PRAYER
Lord, help me to trust You more. Amen.

DRIVEN TO SUCCEED

Don't panic. I'm with you.
There's no need to fear for I'm your God.
I'll give you strength. I'll help you.
I'll hold you steady, keep a firm grip on you.

ISAIAH 41:10 MSG

I once sat in a seminar where a successful female executive admitted that the catalyst that drove her to succeed was a fear of failure. She owned several businesses, including a consulting firm and two employment agencies. Personally, she had faced a divorce, remarriage, stepparenting, and a substance abuse problem. While I admired her success, it saddened me that she'd faced it alone.

As a Christian, you have such an advantage in Jesus. You are never alone. I know that when fear has gripped me, I haven't had my eyes focused on Jesus. Instead, I've tried to do everything in my own strength. As women, we often fall into doing things in our own strength. We try to accomplish so much—personally and professionally—that it's easy to forget that we don't have to carry everything ourselves. Jesus is there to help carry our burdens and overcome our fears. Trust Jesus to help you increase your faith and destroy your fear through His Word.

–GM

POWER PRAYER

Lord, I am struggling with a fear that's making it difficult for me to make the decisions I need to make. I trust that through Your Word my faith and peace will increase.

SPEAK UP

For God has not given us a spirit of fear and timidity,
but of power, love, and self-discipline.

2 TIMOTHY 1:7 NLT

Have you ever been afraid to voice your opinion? It seems
that everyone else in the company has no problem saying exactly what is on her mind, but you can't even manage to utter
one syllable? While I am usually capable of saying exactly
what I think (sometimes too easily, I might add), I remember
a time when I couldn't move my mouth either.

I was in a brainstorming meeting with my peers, de-
bating whether we should run a very controversial comic
strip in our ultra conservative newspaper. Politically correct
comments rolled off of everyone's tongues. My peers
seemed to be in favor of running the comic. When it came
around to me, my heart beat fast and hard. I wanted to say
something insightful and uplifting. I wanted to change the
atmosphere of the conference room. Instead, I said nothing.
I've relived that moment many times, wishing I wouldn't
have been so afraid to say what I thought.

If you've ever stifled your comments for fear of upsetting
someone or saying the wrong thing, you know how icky you
feel afterwards. But don't live in regret. And don't let fear stop
you from speaking your mind or, better yet, His mind.

–MMA

POWER PRAYER
Lord, help me to always speak Your mind. Amen.

NO LIMITS

The Spirit itself beareth witness with our spirit,
that we are the children of God:
And if children, then heirs;
heirs of God, and joint-heirs with Christ.

ROMANS 8:16–17 KJV

When you look in the mirror, what do you see? Do you see a woman who is smart and talented, or do you see a woman who never quite measures up? Often the limitations that we place on ourselves have nothing to do with who we really are or the strengths God has given us. They're more about how we see ourselves. Even if the rest of the world sees us as confident, smart women, we can limit ourselves by our own view.

If you're limiting your success and peace of mind because of how you see yourself, begin to immerse yourself in God's Word. If necessary, talk to a pastor or counselor. God doesn't want you to live with the heaviness of never thinking you're good enough. If you are a child of God, then you are more than good enough. You are His heir and a joint-heir with Jesus. Through the sacrifice of Jesus Christ, you are good enough—regardless of what others say or have said, regardless of what you've ever done. If you don't believe me, just ask your heavenly Father.

–GM

POWER PRAYER

Jesus, thank You for Your sacrifice. Help me to see myself as
God's heir and a joint-heir with You.

ADMIT IT

*You can't whitewash your sins and get by with it;
you find mercy by admitting and leaving them.*

PROVERBS 28:13 MSG

Okay, so you missed it. You dropped the ball. You made a big, whopping mistake. It happens. We're only human, and we're going to miss it once in a while, but how you handle your mistake is key. Your first instinct might be to hide under your desk or figure out a masterful way to defend yourself. Neither is the best course of action.

Proverbs 28:13 tells us that we shouldn't whitewash our sins and try to get by with it. In other words, take responsibility for your mistakes. Go to your boss and say, "Hey, I messed up. My intentions were good, but I missed it. I am sorry." That's much better than covering up your misdoings and blaming somebody else farther down the food chain.

See, if we are quick to admit our mistakes and ask for forgiveness, we open up the door for a second chance. God is a God of mercy. He wants to see you prosper and succeed in your endeavors, but you must be honest and sincere with Him and others. Freely admit when you are wrong, and watch Him reward your honesty.

–MMA

POWER PRAYER

Lord, help me to be quick to admit my shortcomings and just as quick to receive Your mercy. I love You. Amen.

PUTTING OUT FLAMES

"When you walk through the fire, you will not be burned;
the flames will not set you ablaze."

ISAIAH 43:2

Firemen aren't the only ones who put out fires. At times, I've felt like I was one crisis away from donning the red hat and fireproof jacket. Okay, so maybe part of me just wanted to climb the nearest ladder to get away from the flames.

No matter what position you hold, there are days when you feel that you've accomplished nothing more than standing in your office holding an imaginary hose to put out the projects that inexplicably combust. When those days come, don't let feelings of failure, anger, or panic get the best of you. Remember, God will give you the wisdom you need to prioritize your work, handle the crisis, and get the job done. Step back and take a breath. Collect your thoughts. Don't just react, but pray and ask God for wisdom. Then, when the day is over, thank Him for giving you inspiration and keeping you calm. More than anyone else, He's with you, not as a silent partner, but as the One who is helping you work things out and be a success.

–GM

POWER PRAYER

Lord, thank You for Your wisdom and Your peace, regardless of
what comes across my desk. I give You all the thanks for it.

GOING PUBLIC

"He who speaks on his own does so to gain honor for himself,
but he who works for the honor of the one who sent him
is a man of truth;
there is nothing false about him."

JOHN 7:18

One of the greatest fears among adults is public speaking.[2]
Some say it is even more prominent than the fear of death.
As someone who dislikes public speaking, I understand how
overwhelming it can be. Through practice, the fear lessens.
While I still don't enjoy it, I can do it. When facing my fear
of public speaking, I realized something that helped me, and
maybe it'll help you, too. I realized that if I have an idea or
comment to share, the goal isn't to elevate myself, but rather
to get the job done in the best possible way.

If you're terrified of public speaking, begin looking for
ways—at church, work, or other organizations—to overcome
your fear. Know that when you hold back from speaking up
in a meeting or at work, you're withholding the talents that
God has given you because what you have to share is just as
worthwhile as that of your coworkers. Ask God to show
you how to gain confidence. Through practice and prayer,
you'll succeed in ridding yourself of that fear.

–GM

POWER PRAYER

Father, I pray that You'll teach me to speak Your words in
every situation.

THE WISDOM OF SOLOMON

So God replied, ". . .I will give you what you asked for!
I will give you a wise and understanding mind such as
no one else has ever had or ever will have!"

1 KINGS 3:11–12 NLT

Have you ever felt like you were wearing a big "C" for "Clueless" in the middle of your forehead? When I worked for a monthly magazine, every time I had a computer glitch, I dreaded the phone call to "Tech Support." After I had tried everything I knew to fix my computer (which was basically shutting it down and rebooting), I'd resort to calling the company's computer gurus. Inevitably, the guy on the other end of the line would talk techno gibberish to me, and I would have to wave my "Clueless Flag" high in the air and surrender.

Let's face it, we are going to feel clueless once in a while. We can't possibly know everything there is to know about our jobs. But that's okay because we have a secret weapon—a wisdom weapon. Pray this with me: "Lord, I know You are no respecter of persons, so I am asking that You give me wisdom just like You gave it to Solomon, and I thank You for it. Amen."

That's it. Now thank Him for your newfound wisdom every day and put that Clueless Flag away. You don't need it anymore.

–MMA

POWER PRAYER
Thank You, Lord, for Your wisdom. Amen.

HE WANTS TO DO WHAT?

By [the help of] God I will praise His word;
on God I lean, rely, and confidently put my trust;
I will not fear. What can man, who is flesh, do to me?

PSALM 56:4 AMP

There is nothing quite as unnerving as a new boss who wants to make radical changes. When you've been doing things one way for a long time, mixing things up can cause widespread panic.

I've experienced this a few times. New bosses. New procedures. New insecurities. People either didn't know what to do or were so protective over their areas that the office was one scuffle away from selling ringside seats. Some of the changes I handled with ease; others left me nervously watching my back.

If you're facing new procedures or a new boss, try to keep a cool head, avoid becoming one of the malcontents (because there will *always* be malcontents), and take plenty of deep breaths. Continue to praise God and rely on Him. As you continue to honor the people in authority over you and trust God with your fears and insecurities, you won't get sucked into the boxing ring. You'll be able to do your job with confidence, knowing that you don't need to fear what any man can do.

–GM

POWER PRAYER
Lord, I rely on You and praise Your Word. I will not fear,
regardless of the situation.

ON CALL

Is any one of you in trouble? He should pray.

JAMES 5:13

If you're feeling insecure about yourself and unsure of your abilities today, I have good news for you. You don't have to know all the answers. You just have to know the One who does know all the answers. If you're lacking wisdom; if you're overwhelmed with responsibilities; if you're having trouble at work—go to God.

James 5:13 tells us to do just that—"Is any one of you in trouble? He should pray." Prayer changes things. Have you been hitting your knees on a regular basis? If not, you're missing out. God has all of the answers. He knows the exact information you need for your meeting tomorrow. He knows the way to win over your difficult client. He knows it all! And what's more, He is willing to share it all with you.

Prayer is your connection to the Creator of the entire Universe. And we have access to Him twenty-four hours a day, every day of the year. You just can't beat a deal like that! So why not put in some "on your knees time" today? After praising Him for all of your blessings and putting in all of your requests, make sure you take time to listen. God may want to impart some wisdom to you this very day.

–MMA

POWER PRAYER

Thank You, Lord, for being on call 24–7. Amen.

HIJACKED

May the God of peace. . .
equip you with everything good for doing his will,
and may he work in us what is pleasing to him,
through Jesus Christ.

HEBREWS 13:20–21

Have you ever handled an assignment differently from the norm? It may have been a better way but, unfortunately, this can sometimes incur a boss's wrath. We can be left feeling lost, a bit like we've been hijacked. We were flying along doing our work when suddenly out of nowhere our bosses jump our cases about doing things differently. It's confusing and can leave us frustrated and insecure.

In those times, trust God to be your God of peace. Though your boss may not be right in her assumption that there's only one way to accomplish a task, submit to her authority. Try to please her, but don't let her correction make you insecure about your work. You can do your job and if, after trying to please her, you feel that you need to work for someone else, trust God to direct your steps. You are valuable and your talents will be put to good use.

–GM

POWER PRAYER
Lord, thank You for being my God of peace and for equipping me to do Your will in my job.

THE INTIMIDATOR

Conduct yourselves in a manner worthy of
the gospel of Christ. Then. . .
I will know that you stand firm in one spirit. . .
without being frightened in any way
by those who oppose you.

PHILIPPIANS 1:27–28

I once worked closely with a coworker who, though talented, was a very angry woman. After several near misses, my boss and I agreed that I should limit my contact with her. In response, the woman accused me of being jealous of her. Her accusation took me back. *Was I jealous of her?* I wondered. I didn't think so, but I couldn't decide what about her affected me so much. After some soul-searching, it hit me—she intimidated the daylights out of me. It wasn't her talent; it was her anger and her ability to look like a victim in any situation. Basically, she scared me.

Intimidation is an ugly fear, because in essence you fight a battle within yourself. For me, I had to gain confidence in myself and my abilities. If you're struggling with an intimidator, ask God to help you build your confidence. Don't worry about the person or dwell on the fear. Instead, keep doing what you know to do. God *will* give you the strength to win your intimidation battle.

–GM

POWER PRAYER

Lord, help me to conduct myself in a manner worthy of You
and not to be frightened by those who oppose me.

DID I SAY THAT?

Friends, don't get me wrong:
By no means do I count myself an expert in all of this,
but I've got my eye on the goal,
where God is beckoning us onward—to Jesus.

PHILIPPIANS 3:13 MSG

Have you ever said something really stupid in an important meeting? Or maybe you've made a huge mistake that qualifies you for "incompetent employee of the month." I've so been there.

Early in my career as a newspaper reporter, I was asked to cover the filming of *Blue Chips*, a movie about basketball that was being partially shot in Indiana. I was quite excited the day I saw Rick Pitino, the then coach of the University of Kentucky, arrive on the set. I desperately wanted an interview, so I walked right up to him and asked for a few comments. He was so gorgeous, standing there in his Armani suit. He said, "Sure." And before I could stop myself, I said, "Wow, you smell really nice." It was one of those comments you mean to think, yet somehow it rolls off your tongue. He smiled, while I tried to regain my composure. It was a stupid comment. Thankfully, I wasn't escorted off the set.

No matter how badly you mess up, God can fix it. He is the God of our good and bad days. Leave your mistakes behind, and move forward with Him today.

–MMA

POWER PRAYER
Lord, help me to let go of my mistakes and move on. Amen.

INTIMIDATED

I can do everything through him who gives me strength.

PHILIPPIANS 4:13

Do you get intimidated easily? I do. I sort of "fell into" a speaking ministry, and now I teach at women's conferences and writers' conferences across the United States. I never dreamed I'd be speaking in front of hundreds of people, but God knew. I guess that's why He had me minor in speech in college. I thought I was minoring in speech because it was easier than minoring in earth science.

Even today, I still feel queasy each time I stand up to speak. Last fall, I was asked to teach a Continuing Education course for a national pharmaceutical group. My audience? A bunch of brilliant pharmacists. As I glanced over the roster of speakers, I realized I was the only one without a "Dr." before my name or a whole lot of initials after my name. I was a tad bit intimidated.

So I prayed, "Lord, Your Word says I have the mind of Christ, so I am calling upon that wisdom right now. Help me to speak with excellence." And guess what? He did help me. I actually sounded much smarter than I am. God always comes through. So don't be intimidated in your job. Even if you can't do it, God can do it through you.

–MMA

POWER PRAYER

Thank You, Lord, for giving me courage to be excellent. Amen.

SPIRITUAL GUMBO

Praise be to the God and Father of our Lord Jesus Christ,
who has blessed us in the heavenly realms
with every spiritual blessing in Christ.

EPHESIANS 1:3

Have you ever spent time around someone who considered themselves "spiritual"? I'm not talking about the Christian who isn't living right or *SNL*'s version of "The Church Lady." I'm talking about the newfangled spirituality that believes that nothing is wrong and we all need to just be "open" to whatever spiritual force comes our way. It's the religious version of gumbo. There's a little Christianity mixed with a dash of Eastern mysticism and a helping of humanism.

From spending time around people who believe this way, I've sensed that they're on a quest. For some, they may be seeking inner peace. For others, it may be power, a way for them to not feel so helpless.

Wasn't it nice to know that once you found Jesus, your search was over? Through Him, you experienced real peace and true power. Your fears or past mistakes didn't control you any longer. Thank Jesus for the freedom you've found in Him. Thank Him for saving you, setting you free, and walking with you every day.

–GM

POWER PRAYER

Jesus, thank You for saving me and setting me free. Thank You for fulfilling my need for peace and power and walking with me every day.

PLEASE TELL ME THIS ISN'T IT

*I cry out to God Most High, to God,
who fulfills his purpose for me.*

PSALM 57:2

Have you ever thought to yourself, *Dear Lord, please tell me
this isn't all there is?* You've been doing your job long enough
that you start to feel that the walls are closing in upon you.
You want to do something—anything—else, but just can't
figure out what it is. Well, rest assured, you aren't alone.

At times, I've become very restless in my work. Even
when I loved a job at first, after doing it for *y–e–a–r–s*, it lost
its appeal. I wanted to do more but couldn't figure out what.
It was during those times that I turned to God, and I hope
you'll do the same. I felt led to really think about what I
wanted and loved. It took time, but eventually I got the insight and courage to step out. And what God did for me,
He'll do for you.

If you're nervous that you're never going to do any
more than you're doing right now, start talking to God
about it. Prayerfully consider what you want to be doing
and what it would take to make your dreams a reality. God
will use you, so don't give up hope.

–GM

POWER PRAYER

*Lord, You know my dreams and talents. Please fulfill Your
purpose in my life.*

SWEET DREAMS

Yes, you will lie down and your sleep will be sweet.

PROVERBS 3:24 NKJV

Okay, I admit it. By nature, I am a worrier. I don't intentionally worry. In fact, my worrying usually starts as wondering, which leads to reasoning, which leads to worrying, which almost always leads to sleepless nights. Ever been there?

You're lying in bed. The lights are off. Everyone else, including the dog, is asleep, but you can't turn off your mind. Your brain continues to crank, trying to figure out how to solve some crisis at work. Slowly, the tension headache begins, creeping up your neck and spreading over your entire head. That's it. Now you're wide awake and in pain. So you watch *Mr. Ed* reruns on TV as the clock ticks into the wee hours of the night.

I have spent more nights living out that scenario than I'd like to admit. But you know what? Worrying about the problems at work never changed a single one of them. Now if I happen to have a restless night, I spend it in prayer. I thank God for watching over me. I thank Him for wisdom. I thank Him for favor with my boss. And I fall asleep in peace—no headaches, no worries. God promises us sweet slumber in Proverbs, so hold Him to it. Sweet dreams, sister!

–MMA

POWER PRAYER

Thank You, Lord, for giving me peaceful, restful nights. Amen.

WORKPLACE BULLY

*He will defend the afflicted among the people
and save the children of the needy.*

PSALM 72:4

Do you have a scary boss? One of those Attila the Hun types? People are afraid to tell him anything because he'll either yell, degrade, or retaliate? Or maybe he just seems to have it in for you. Just entering his office makes you nervous. These people can make life at work difficult. Even if they treat everyone that way, it still doesn't make it easier.

If you've got one of these leaders in your life, know that God will help you work to the best of your ability. Often in the psalms there is the promise that "He will defend the afflicted," and if you're working under an unfair tyrant, you may well find yourself afflicted. Pray for God's wisdom. Pray for the person. Then trust God to help you overcome the situation successfully. You don't have to be afraid of a workplace bully. Instead, focus on what God has given you to do and trust Him to defend you.

–GM

POWER PRAYER

Heavenly Father, You know the conditions under which I work, so I trust You to help me through it. Please give me wisdom, bless those who try to frighten me, and defend me from their attacks.

THE LONE RANGER

*"In the last times there will be scoffers
who will follow their own ungodly desires."
These are the men who divide you,
who follow mere natural instincts
and do not have the Spirit.*

JUDE 18–19

Working in a worldly workplace, you may feel like the Lone Ranger, standing alone for godly principles. While your coworkers party on the weekends or tell tasteless jokes, it can be tough to know that you'll never fit in.

For some, this knowledge doesn't matter. You're there to do a job, and you don't mind going against the grain. But others may find it difficult. You may not be a part of the in crowd. You may be considered a prude because you won't join in their "fun." Or others may distrust you because you don't have their same standards. It can be disheartening—even though you know standing for Jesus is the right thing to do.

If you feel like you're on the outside looking in at work, find a group of other Christian professionals outside of work to help you deal with the isolation. If your church doesn't have a working women's group, maybe you can start one. As you build friendships with other Christian women, you'll be stronger to stand against the ungodly influences.

–GM

POWER PRAYER
Lord, I feel very alone at work. There are so many ungodly influences. Please help me to stand strong.

THE NICHE

For we are God's masterpiece.
He has created us anew in Christ Jesus,
so that we can do the good things he planned for us long ago.

EPHESIANS 2:10 NLT

Okay, I have to fess up—I am hooked on the Fox reality show *American Idol*. I absolutely love it! I have watched it ever since its debut. During the 2003–2004 season, a contestant named John won the hearts of many. Only sixteen years old, this redheaded crooner took America by surprise. You see, he sang Tony Bennett and Frank Sinatra songs instead of pop and rock. So when he was forced to sing Latin music one night of the competition, he fell flat—literally. Simon Cowell, the mean-spirited judge, said, "John, you and Latin music go together like chocolate ice cream and an onion." Well, John was voted off after that performance, which proves one thing—you can't be the best at everything. While he can belt out Big Band tunes with the best, he can't sing a Latin lyric to save his life.

And that's okay. We can't be awesome at everything, so stop beating yourself up. Ask God to help you find your niche. He has a destiny for you, and like John, it may not include singing Latin music. Whatever God has for you will be great, and you'll be great at it!

–MMA

POWER PRAYER

Thank You, Lord, for helping me to succeed in my calling.
Amen.

OUT OF MY LEAGUE

*If you are willing and obedient,
you will eat the best from the land.*

ISAIAH 1:19

Over the years, I've met many women who felt out of their league in business. Sometimes they recently returned to the workplace after years of staying at home to raise their children, or they felt intimidated because of new responsibilities. All of these women were more talented than they gave themselves credit for. They just allowed their insecurities to convince them they were not good enough for the positions they had. The fact is, most of them could run laps around many of their veteran workplace sisters.

If you feel insecure because of your job or responsibilities, know that God uses those who are willing. He will equip you to accomplish what needs to be done. Don't let fearful and doubtful thoughts plague you or hold you back from giving your all. Step back and think objectively about the talents you need and the ones you have. You may just discover that God has prepared you more than you ever realized.

–GM

POWER PRAYER

*Lord, I am willing to do whatever You want me to do.
Please help me to be strong and confident of the talents
You've given me.*

SOMETHING BETTER

*And we know that in all things
God works for the good of those who love him,
who have been called according to his purpose.*

ROMANS 8:28

As Christians, we don't have to fear failure. Isn't that great? I once heard a great story about a businessman who was let go from his job of many years. But this businessman didn't let that setback destroy him. Instead, he put on his entrepreneurial hat and began working on a "God idea." That germ of an idea eventually blossomed into today's mega-earning Home Depot stores. Men across America thank God for this man every night. (My husband spends so much time in Home Depot, that if he wore an orange shirt, he'd be up for employee of the month.)

See, if we keep our hearts right—free from anger and bitterness and fear—God can use setbacks to thrust us forward. If you've recently lost your job, don't worry. God has a better position waiting for you. If you were passed over for a promotion at your company, don't be sad. He has something much better for you. God knows exactly what we need. His Word even says so in Matthew 6:32. So don't let disappointments depress you. Rather, see them as opportunities for God to bless your socks right off your feet!

–MMA

POWER PRAYER

*Thank You, Lord, for using even my failures as a means of
promotion. I love You. Amen.*

THE ULTIMATE TUMS

*For you did not receive a spirit that makes you
a slave again to fear.*

ROMANS 8:15

Lots of businesspeople live on a constant diet of Tums. They live in fear of not measuring up or getting all their work finished. They worry about impending downsizing or providing for their families. Fear comes in all shapes and sizes. It slips into one's life with little doubts and then grows, sending roots that penetrate every area, but it doesn't have to be that way.

Some Christians think of God as a last resort, turning to him only when all else fails. Others view Him as a Band-Aid that covers a gaping wound. He doesn't really help; He's more of a feel-good patch. But Jesus is so much more than that.

As a Christian, you don't have to live with fear. Jesus didn't just come to be your last resort or your feel-good image. He is your deliverer, and as much as He delivers you from hell, He delivers you from fear. He's the ultimate Tums. He won't just cover the problem; He eliminates it. If you're struggling with fear, turn to Jesus. He'll be the best medicine you'll ever take.

–GM

POWER PRAYER

Lord, I love You and realize that You are a real and personal God. Instead of just helping me deal with my fears, I pray that You'll eliminate them from my life.

INSECURITIES

"So don't be afraid;
you are more valuable to him
than a whole flock of sparrows."

MATTHEW 10:31 NLT

Okay, I love the Game Show Network (GSN). Does that make me a mega-nerd, or what? You can learn so many interesting tidbits from watching shows such as *Jeopardy* and *Hollywood Squares*. Recently, I learned that a person isn't born with shyness. It's a learned trait. Well, if that's true, we aren't born with insecurities, either. Those, too, must be learned as we develop into the adults we are today.

If you grew up in a household where you were constantly put down and criticized, you probably struggle with much insecurity. Maybe you weren't "the favorite child." Or maybe a cruel kid once called you fat and stupid, and that same old recording has been playing in your head ever since. Whatever the case, if you struggle with fear and insecurities, God can break those chains off of you.

As Christians, we don't have to stand for that bondage. When Jesus died on the cross for our sins, He also bore our sickness, disease, insecurities, and fear. He took care of it all that day at Calvary, so walk in the freedom that already belongs to you today. Hold your head up high as you go into work today. You are valuable!

–MMA

POWER PRAYER

Lord, I give You all of my insecurities. Thank You for loving
me exactly the way I am. Amen.

SIX-MONTH TRIAL PERIOD

*So we say with confidence,
"The Lord is my helper; I will not be afraid.
What can man do to me?"*

HEBREWS 13:6

I once worked for a boss who was intelligent, resourceful and. . .difficult. The first six months that anyone worked for her were a challenge. During that time, new employees doubted that she even liked them. In meetings, she spoke to everyone but the new person, and she avoided their company in social situations. Just when the person was certain that she disliked him, the six-month period ended and she embraced the new worker.

New workers—both men and women—would comment on her behavior. Veterans tried to encourage them. "Just hang in there," they said. "She's just getting used to you." Eventually, they discovered that was true.

Fearing what others think of you can be paralyzing. It can inhibit you or cause you to desperately try to win their approval. But as the writer of Hebrews said, "The Lord is my helper. . . . What can man do to me?" As you develop your relationship with Jesus, your confidence will grow. You'll have peace knowing that your security rests with Him.

–GM

POWER PRAYER

Lord, I trust You, love You, and serve You. As I pursue a deeper relationship with You, I pray that You'll give me the confidence to face anyone and anything that comes my way.

ROUND THE MOUNTAIN, AGAIN

*He went on a little farther
and fell face down on the ground, praying,
"My Father! If it is possible,
let this cup of suffering be taken away from me.
Yet I want your will, not mine."*

MATTHEW 26:39 NLT

Think of the biggest problem you have at work—a difficult boss, a coworker who is driving you crazy, a client who won't pay his bill, or whatever. Now think back; have you dealt with this exact same dilemma before? It might be that God is trying to teach you something through this adversity in your life. My mom calls it "going around the mountain again" whenever you have to go through a problem again because you apparently didn't learn what you needed to on the "first lap around."

There are some areas in my life where I've practically worn out my track shoes going around that mountain, but eventually I get it. I finally see what God was trying to show me through the negative situation, and I get to move on!

If you're going around the same aggravating mountain today, seek God's wisdom on the matter. Pray, "Lord, what are You trying to show me through this? Help me not to miss it, Lord." Then, praise Him, and trade in your track shoes for a classic pair of pumps!

–MMA

POWER PRAYER
Lord, help me to learn through every adversity I must face. I trust You. Amen.

QUIET WITNESS

*"Stand up for me against world opinion
and I'll stand up for you before my Father in heaven."*

MATTHEW 10:32 MSG

When I used to work for the daily newspaper in Indiana, every year about this time, several kindergarten classes would "trick or treat" through our building, showing off their cutest-ever costumes. Some wore scary masks. Some wore costumes their "Martha Stewart mothers" had made. Others wore face paint. But all of them were disguised and animated as they paraded through the office.

Later in the year, we hosted those same kindergarten students for a morning field trip, showing them how the newspaper was printed. Without their masks and clever costumes, they weren't nearly as confident. Some even hid behind the teachers!

Maybe you're the same way. You feel pretty confident when you're wearing your "Christy Christian" costume at church, but when you go to work without it, you're scared to live out your life of faith—especially if no one else at your workplace is a Christian. But hey, you don't have to be afraid. You don't have to be fake and say, "Praise God!" every other breath to be a Christian at work. You don't even need that "Christy Christian" costume that comes with a nifty Bible bag. You can simply give a quiet witness and let the Lord's light shine through you as you go about living your Christian life.

–MMA

POWER PRAYER

Lord, help me to be a good witness at work. Amen.

DOES THIS CUBICLE
COME IN A BIGGER SIZE?

*I am not saying this because I am in need,
for I have learned to be content whatever the circumstances.*

PHILIPPIANS 4:11

Recently, I heard a preacher say you should enjoy the journey on the way to where you're going. I wish I'd known that truth when I first started my career as a reporter for a daily newspaper. My first writing gig? I was hired as a police beat reporter. I had to work long weekday hours and most Friday nights. I desperately wanted to work in a different area of the newspaper—anything but the police beat. I spent so much time dreaming about a new assignment that I didn't enjoy the one I had. I took for granted that I was able to hang out with the cool sports guys on Friday nights. I took for granted that working on Friday nights allowed me to work side by side with the managing editor. I took many things for granted.

Looking back, those days were critical to my development as a writer. God had placed me in that job for a season. It wasn't my "dream job," but before the dream job could manifest, I had to learn some stuff. Maybe you're in that "learning stuff" place today—on the way to your dream job. If so, hang in there. Be content where you are. Enjoy the journey.

–MMA

POWER PRAYER
Lord, help me to enjoy the journey. Amen.

PASSED OVER

The LORD is a refuge for the oppressed,
a stronghold in times of trouble.
Those who know your name will trust in you,
for you, LORD, have never forsaken those who seek you.

PSALM 9:9–10

When I graduated college, I interviewed for five different positions in one company, and yet I kept losing the positions to other people, some of whom were much less qualified. During that three-month period, I worked in a temporary position, just waiting for something—anything—to open. Then, right before my temporary commitment was over, a vacancy came open in a great area. I went from feeling like a wallflower to feeling very blessed. Looking back, I saw how faithful God was—He made sure I got the best possible job.

If you've been passed over for a job, don't get discouraged or doubt your worth. You are valuable and God is still working on your behalf. He hasn't forgotten you and though you may not be able to see it now, He has your best interest at heart. So don't give up on Him—because He certainly hasn't given up on you.

–GM

POWER PRAYER
Lord, Your Word says that You will never forsake those who seek You, and that's just what I'm doing. You are my refuge during this difficult time and I trust You.

DREAMS CAN BE REAL, CAN'T THEY?

*"If you believe,
you will receive whatever you ask for in prayer."*

MATTHEW 21:22

I have a friend whose actual job is to go into people's homes and organize them from top to bottom. I can't even imagine doing that. I mean, I have so many "junk drawers" in my house, it takes me thirty minutes to locate the scissors each time I need them. Can I have an amen? Obviously, organization is not one of my gifts.

I have another friend who teaches twenty-five kindergarteners for a living. Yes, she is a wonderful teacher. While I adore children, I knew I wasn't called to be a teacher after substitute teaching for a brief stint. Who knew 8 a.m. to 3 p.m. could last so long?

But you know what is so cool? Both of my friends absolutely love what they do, and they are awesome at their individual callings. They are truly walking in their professional dreams.

That's what I love about our heavenly Father. He gives each of us unique dreams; then He equips us to accomplish those dreams if we'll only believe. It gives Him great joy to see us pursuing the ambitions He has placed within us. So hang in there! God can't wait to see you walking in your dream.

–MMA

POWER PRAYER

Lord, thank You for placing unique dreams in my heart. Amen.

THE CHOICE

*I have learned the secret of being content
in any and every situation,
whether well fed or hungry,
whether living in plenty or in want.
I can do everything through him who gives me strength.*

PHILIPPIANS 4:12–13

Paul is a great example of someone who chose to be content. Though he was imprisoned for preaching the gospel and his surroundings were filthy, he continued to teach other Christians through his letters. In fact, while he was in prison, he wrote: "I have learned the secret of being content in any and every situation." He knew that his personal comfort wasn't as important as his eternal calling. What a challenge for everyone!

Regardless of what position you have now or in the future, you are first called to be a child of God and a light to the world. Though it isn't wrong to pursue promotions, you need to realize that true happiness and contentment doesn't come because of outward circumstances. It's a choice—one you make every day.

As you work at your job—one you may love or hate—choose to be a light for Jesus. Through your attitude and work ethic, you could be more of an example and blessing to one of your coworkers than you could ever know.

–GM

POWER PRAYER
Lord, I choose to be content today. I know that, more than anything else, I'm called to be a light for You.

TENDING THE SHEEP

From that day on the Spirit of the LORD
came upon David in power. . . .
But David went back and forth from Saul
to tend his father's sheep at Bethlehem.

1 SAMUEL 16:13, 17:15

Everyone knows that David was a great leader, but at the beginning of his life, when he was out tending sheep, he didn't
really look like one. He was the youngest of seven brothers,
probably picked on by the older ones and given the chores
that no one else wanted to do. That's when God chose him
to be king. God saw David's potential even though David
didn't ascend to the throne until much later. From the time
that Samuel anointed him until he became king, he worked
as a professional musician, then as a military warrior. And
even then, he still tended sheep. He wasn't exactly on the fast
track.

You may find that even though God calls you to do
something, it'll take patience and perseverance for it to
happen. You may know that you're going to have your own
company or a higher position, but, until then, allow God to
equip you for that position, so you are prepared for it.
Through patience and perseverance, you can see your plans
fulfilled.

–GM

POWER PRAYER

Lord, thank You for preparing me for Your plans. I submit to
You in all I do.

BIG PICTURE

Where there is no vision, the people perish.

PROVERBS 29:18 KJV

I've learned from some wonderful bosses how important it is to continually keep the vision of a project in front of a team. In fact, the most successful projects that I've ever been a part of have been when everyone knew the goal and her place in bringing it to pass.

Even in our lives, having a vision is vital. I've met many women who struggle with knowing the vision God has for their lives. They jokingly say they want to know what they're going to be when they grow up—regardless of their age.

Though it may sound simple to do, discovering your life's goal can be challenging. Sometimes it takes time for the pieces to come together, but don't get discouraged. Be faithful to what He's put in front of you right now. Continue to pray, read His Word, and talk to your pastor or mentor. As you do, you'll eventually see the pieces come together. You'll understand that God was preparing you, even when you felt like you were just spinning your wheels. Never doubt that He has a vision for you!

–GM

POWER PRAYER

Lord, thank You for directing me in every area of my life. I ask that You give me a clear vision of what I should do now and in the future.

ON YOUR WAY
TO THE CORNER OFFICE

*A heart at peace gives life to the body,
but envy rots the bones.*

PROVERBS 14:30

Staring at the inside of my green cubicle, I wondered if God even knew that I existed. It seemed everyone around me was moving up in the company, but not me. No matter how hard I worked, no one seemed to notice or care. Ever been there?

It's an unpleasant place to be. That "What about me?" mentality eventually leads to jealousy, envy, bitterness, and hopelessness. So if you're dwelling in that "What about me?" land, head for the border!

If you can't be happy for your coworker when she finally gets promoted, God will never be able to bless you with your dream job. If you can't celebrate with your boss when he is awarded a Caribbean cruise for a job well done, God will never be able to bless you with company perks.

In the midst of everybody else's dreams coming true, we have to keep our hearts right. If we don't, we'll never get to walk in ours. Keep your eyes on God, and He will make your dreams come true, too. Don't worry when you see others getting blessed. He has more than enough blessings to go around.

—MMA

POWER PRAYER

Lord, help me to be happy when my coworkers realize their dreams because I know my dreams will also come true. Amen.

STRAIGHT FROM THE TOP

*Your word is a lamp to my feet
and a light for my path.*

PSALM 119:105

"If you want to know God's will, you've got to study His Word," a minister said. He also said that if anyone wants to know someone—really *know* him—they've got to spend time listening to him, because you can't separate someone's character from his words. The two go hand in hand.

As simple as his message was, it resonated with me. Instead of discovering God's will through His Word, we sometimes haphazardly throw up a prayer, attaching an "if it's Your will" to it. We treat God like an absent parent we barely know. Of course, God sees the big picture in our lives and His ways are not always our ways (Isaiah 55:8), but that doesn't mean we can't more clearly grasp His character through His Word.

If you're struggling with a dilemma—a job change, an illness, an ethical question, or whatever—turn to God's Word to better understand His will in the situation. Don't treat Him like an absent parent. Get to know Him as your Father who loves you and cares about the things that concern you.

–GM

POWER PRAYER

Lord, I trust You and pray that through Your Word, I'll discover Your will.

WAIT

Since before time began no one has ever imagined,
No ear heard, no eye seen,
a God like you who works for those who wait for him.

ISAIAH 64:4 MSG

Do you remember the story of Sarai, Abram, Hagar, and Ishmael? God told Abram that He would give him a son and that his offspring would outnumber the stars in the sky.

No doubt he shared the news with his wife, Sarai, who desperately desired to give Abram an heir. But she was getting too old to bear children, and she grew tired of waiting. So she convinced Abram to sleep with her maid, Hagar. Hagar became pregnant and eventually gave birth to a son— Ishmael. But Ishmael wasn't the promised heir. If Sarai had waited on God, she would've discovered that God already had a good plan—a plan for Sarai to become pregnant and give birth to Isaac—the promised heir. I'm sure every time Sarai looked at Ishmael, she was reminded of her mistake. Sure, God still gave her Isaac, but only in *His* time.

Have you birthed any "Ishmaels" lately? Have you been so impatient, waiting on God's perfect plan for your life, that you've jumped ahead and worked out a plan of your own? If so, go back to God. Wait on His plan. It's a really good one!

–MMA

POWER PRAYER

Lord, help me to wait patiently on Your plan for my life.
Amen.

FACETS

*And let the loveliness of our Lord, our God,
rest on us, confirming the work that we do.*

PSALM 90:17 MSG

Women know that life is a balancing act. Many work to keep their professional life intact while doing what they need to do in their personal life. But what about fun? Often, women think that they don't have time for fun, but actually, without a little fun, they lose the thrill of doing their jobs. No one is meant to work all the time.

Consider a diamond. A diamond shines the best when it has as many facets as possible. That is the only way for light to shine through it so that it can glimmer brightly. Similarly, you have to have facets in your life. You have to have different aspects—work, church, family, friends, fun—that make your life shine.

On the road to success, make time for fun in your schedule, even if you have to pencil it into your calendar. This isn't a frivolous treat; this is necessary for you to succeed and be content in that success. Yes, life is a balancing act, but don't just limit it to the must-dos on your to-do list. Make time for fun so that you can shine brightly for Jesus.

–GM

POWER PRAYER

Lord, let Your loveliness rest on me. Let me balance my life and work so that it's pleasing to You.

SMALL BEGINNINGS

*"Do not despise these small beginnings,
for the LORD rejoices to see the work begin."*

ZECHARIAH 4:10 NLT

My sister and her husband can totally relate to this verse. When God told them to start a church in their hometown in Indiana, they were excited. He had been a pastor years before, but he'd been building houses and just "preaching here and there" for some time. My sister, an interior designer, worked for him in his homebuilding business, but she believed what God had said. They thought it would happen overnight, but no doors opened. So they simply put that vision on the shelf and took another opportunity—working for a worldwide ministry.

My sister was hired as a communications coordinator, which sounded impressive; however, it was actually a glorified gofer position. It was a difficult, not-very-glamorous job, but she worked at it faithfully. Eventually, she was promoted to an important position. Her husband remodeled houses and did other odd jobs. Then, seven years later, the doors began opening for their own church.

When my sister was making copies for others, she did it with a joyful heart. When Jan was remodeling homes, he simply waited on God with anticipation. They didn't despise their small beginnings, and now they are walking in their dream. Maybe you're in "the waiting process." If so, rejoice! God hasn't forgotten your dream, either.

–MMA

POWER PRAYER

Lord, help me to rejoice in small beginnings. Amen.

MY VERY OWN CUBE

Always giving thanks to God the Father for everything. . .

EPHESIANS 5:20

Do you know what I find interesting? They tell you to "think outside the box," and then they put you in a boxlike cubicle for eight hours a day. Silly, isn't it?

When I worked for a monthly magazine, we had green "cubes." They were small, and they weren't very attractive. But you could always tell the positive folks in the group, because they had decorated their little cubes with great pride. One woman had pearls hanging down over the corners, with lace doilies and satin ribbons everywhere. She was obviously going for that Victorian cubicle look. Another woman had chosen a Disney theme, with Poohs, Piglets, and Eeyores all over her "Hundred-Acre Cubicle." Very cute!

Instead of whining about not having an actual office, my coworkers made the very best of the situation. They may not have loved working in a cube all day, but you never heard them complaining about it. They were determined to enjoy every day on the job.

Maybe you're in a "cubicle" kind of situation today, feeling unimportant and depressed. Don't give in to grumbling and complaining. Instead, start thanking God that you have a job that comes with your very own cubicle. Make the very best of your journey—even the cubicle rest stops.

–MMA

POWER PRAYER

Lord, help me to make the best of every situation. Amen.

WHAT? FORGIVE?

Bear with each other and forgive whatever grievances
you may have against one another.
Forgive as the Lord forgave you.

COLOSSIANS 3:13

Is there someone in your office who has offended you, and
you just can't seem to let it go? You see that person and your
stomach immediately ties into a knot or your heart races.
The feelings of hurt and anger continue to hang on.

Though you may have been wronged, you'll never find
true contentment and peace until you've forgiven her. You
may think, "Yes, but you don't know what she did!" True, I
don't know, but God does. And He doesn't tell us to forgive
some of the time. He just tells us to forgive.

You may have to forgive her several times before it becomes real. You'll decide to forgive her and the next time
you see her, the anger and hurt rise back up. So you have to
forgive her again. Not only is it important for your spiritual
health, but it's important for your emotional health, too.
Until you forgive and let go of the pain and anger, you'll
never have the peace that God wants you to have. So determine to forgive that person, not just for her, but also for you.

–GM

POWER PRAYER

Lord, I choose to forgive this person just as Your Word instructs
me to do. Please heal me from the feelings of hurt and anger.

I THOUGHT I HAD IT TOUGH

*It is strength that endures the unendurable
and spills over into joy,*
*thanking the Father who makes us strong enough to take part
in everything bright and beautiful that he has for us.*

COLOSSIANS 1:11–12 MSG

Less than 50 percent of Americans are satisfied with their jobs.[3] They're frustrated and some feel trapped. They long to do something else—pursue a dream, find an occupation they love, get additional education, anything to make going to work worthwhile. Though these are fine pursuits, desires that God may have given to us, part of finding contentment is realizing that we're part of a greater work.

When we read about the apostle Paul, we realize just how good we have it. He was a faithful minister who eventually died for his work, and many of his letters—Philemon, Ephesians, Philippians, Colossians—were written from prison. He was in dire circumstances, yet he persevered. The conditions weren't great and he probably wished he were somewhere else—doing something else—but he fulfilled his mission.

Today, thank God for the provision that He's made for you. Realize that through your work, He has provided for you and your family and probably helped others. Though you may eventually find another job, be thankful for the one He's given you right now.

–GM

POWER PRAYER
Lord, thank You for Your provision. I will persevere in what You've called me to do.

JOY SUPPLY

"Do not grieve, for the joy of the LORD is your strength."

NEHEMIAH 8:10

As a child, did you ever sing the song, "I've got the joy, joy, joy, joy, down in my heart. . .Down in my heart to stay?" That little song packs a powerful message.

If you've got joy down in your heart, you can accomplish anything, go through any circumstance, and do it all with a smile. The Word tells us that the joy of the Lord is our strength. The devil knows that, so he is going to try to zap your joy every chance he gets. If he can steal your joy, he can steal your strength. If he can steal your strength, he can infuse you with some hopelessness and depression. By the time he is done, you'll be so far down in a hole you won't even be able to see out. So don't go there. Keep your joy supply full!

Listen to praise music on the drive to work. Take a few minutes at lunch and read Psalms and Proverbs. Make sure you're getting enough sleep; take time to exercise; and take your vitamins (I sound like your mother, don't I?) so that you don't give the devil any entrance. Say: "I've got the joy of the Lord down in my heart," and then act like it today!

–MMA

POWER PRAYER

Thank You, Lord, for Your eternal joy supply. Amen.

RAIN

"Anyone who listens to my teaching and obeys me is wise,
like a person who builds a house on solid rock.
Though the rain comes in torrents. . .
and the winds beat against that house,
it won't collapse, because it is built on rock."

MATTHEW 7:24–25 NLT

Recently, I heard someone bring out a point in this parable that I hadn't before heard. In the lesson, both men built homes—one on solid rock, the other on sand. The example teaches us to build our lives on Jesus, our solid rock, so that we can live with certainty. Yet regardless of how you build your house, scripture says the rains *will* come.

Often, we want to find the equation to a content, happy life that is free from any problems. But in reality, building our lives on Jesus only means that we have the tools to withstand the storms when they come, not that we'll never face them.

If you're looking for the key to living an easy life, you probably won't find it. But if you're looking for a way to rise above challenges, Jesus will be there to help. Instead of praying for the trouble-free path, trust Jesus to show you how to live. It may not be the simplest way, but it will be the best.

–GM

POWER PRAYER
Lord, thank You for building my life on You so that I can
withstand the rains when they come.

WILDFLOWERS IN BLOOM

*Think about all he endured when
sinful people did such terrible things to him,
so that you don't become weary and give up.*

HEBREWS 12:3 NLT

Springtime in Texas is really beautiful. In fact, people come from all over the world just to view our gorgeous array of wildflowers—especially our Texas bluebonnets. It's breathtaking. But you know what I find fascinating? Every spring, the Indian paintbrush and the Texas bluebonnets pop up in the most unusual places. You'll even find them in the median of the highway, poking their yellow and blue heads up among the weeds and tall grass. It's as if they're saying, "Hey, we're blooming here despite the fact that no one waters us or pulls the weeds that surround us."

I want to encourage you today—become like a Texas wildflower. Bloom wherever you are planted—in spite of the weeds surrounding you. Maybe you're not working in a very nice environment right now, but you can still make the best of it. Do your best work, and keep your eyes on God. He will water you. He won't let the weeds choke the life out of you. Just keep trusting Him, and pretty soon you'll be blooming in a much better environment. God has a way of transplanting us at just the perfect time. Until then, keep growing!

–MMA

POWER PRAYER

*Father, help me to bloom where I am planted. I love You.
Amen.*

WORK PERKS

*You should praise the LORD for his love
and for the wonderful things he does for all of us.*

PSALM 107:21 CEV

I once heard actress Reese Witherspoon share that she gets
to keep all of the cute shoes that her character Elle Woods
wears in the *Legally Blonde* movies. Talk about a work perk!
(I especially love the ones she slips on in the beginning of
the first *Legally Blonde* movie.)

I'm sure if you think hard enough, you can think of a
few work perks that you have. Okay, so maybe your job
doesn't have a "cutest-shoes-ever" allowance, but surely you
have some perks. Maybe you have flextime. Maybe you
have four-day work weeks. Or maybe you have casual Friday every day! Whatever the perks, be grateful!

The next time your annual review rolls around and
you're asked for feedback, take a minute to thank your company for the office perks. Better yet, why not write a note
to the head of your company, thanking him for the perks
that you enjoy? Bosses like to be bragged on once in a
while. Company presidents like to feel appreciated by their
employees. And God likes it when we honor those that He
put in authority over us. So why not perk up someone's day
and thank your boss for the work perks!

–MMA

POWER PRAYER
Father, help me to always have a grateful heart. Amen.

THANKSGIVING

Let the peace of Christ rule in your hearts,
since as members of one body you were called to peace.
And be thankful.

COLOSSIANS 3:15

There really is nothing that helps put life back into perspective like a tragedy or loved one's illness. A few days ago, I received news that an acquaintance's young husband had died suddenly from a heart attack. Then, out of the blue, my own husband asked if I'd make a doctor's appointment for him because he'd been experiencing some potentially dangerous symptoms. Thankfully, his checkup was clear except for some unusually aggressive allergy attacks.

Until this week, I'd focused on some frustrating personal business and disappointing career news. Things that I thought would work out easily have been tough. But all of that has been put into perspective, and I'm reminded once again of God's blessings.

All of us have something for which to be thankful. It may be our job or our health or our family or our friendships or, above all, our salvation. If we think about it—and some may need to think hard—God has blessed our lives. During this season, be content and peaceful knowing that your heavenly Father has blessed your life and called you to be a member of His family.

–GM

POWER PRAYER

Lord, thank You for calling me to be a member of Your family
and for blessing my life with so many good things.

BEACON OF JOY

*"You are the light of the world.
A city on a hill cannot be hidden."*

MATTHEW 5:14

When my father suffered four strokes over a two-year period of time, we spent many hours in and out of various
hospitals and rehabilitation units. After a while, you start to
notice things. For instance, I learned quite a bit of medical
terminology. I also learned something else—a good nurse
makes for a pleasant stay, while a bad nurse makes every
second seem like an eternity.

My father had one nurse named "Joy" who was appro-
priately named, because she was a light in our time of dark
ness. She just bubbled with the love of Jesus, and she was
such an encouragement to my father. You could tell that she
truly enjoyed her work. She didn't have to announce to the
world that she was Christian. Her life told the story. She was
kind and helpful to everyone.

I don't know about you, but I want to be more like Joy.
I want to be a beacon in my workplace. I desire to walk the
walk, not just talk the talk. Just as I observed Joy, people are
observing us every day. Let's give them something worth
watching. Let's shine with the love of Jesus as we go about
our workday.

–MMA

POWER PRAYER

*Lord, I want Your light to shine through me as I go about my
work. Amen.*

ON THE WAY

*Humble yourselves therefore under
the mighty hand of God,
that he may exalt you in due time:
Casting all your care upon him;
for he careth for you.*

1 PETER 5:6–7 KJV

Have you ever wondered who actually works in those really cool jobs? For instance, who gets to be the taste tester for new Bubble Yum flavors? Or who gets to name all the latest OPI nail colors? Or who gets to test ride wild roller coasters? Or who gets to go to the finest spas in the world and write those reviews? Those are pretty awesome jobs.

Okay, so you may not have the most glamorous job. Maybe you don't have the most enjoyable job. Maybe you're not yet working in your dream job, but the key word in this sentence is "yet." If you'll keep your heart right in your current work situation, God will promote you.

So what if you're the custodian? God can make it happen—in spite of your current work situation. Trust in God's Word. It says He has a good plan for you (Jeremiah 29:11), so you can hold on to that promise. Keep believing for your dream job, but all the while, do your very best in your current position. Pretty soon, you'll be walking in your dream!

–MMA

POWER PRAYER

*Lord, help me to be content with where I am on the way to
where You are taking me. Amen.*

HAPPY THOUGHTS

*Finally, brothers, whatever is true, whatever is noble,
whatever is right, whatever is pure, whatever is lovely,
whatever is admirable—if anything is excellent
or praiseworthy—think about such things.*

PHILIPPIANS 4:8

Martha Washington said, "The greater part of our happiness or misery depends on our dispositions, and not our circumstances." In essence, our thoughts determine our contentment. If we ponder doom and gloom, then we will only see doom and gloom; but if we think about God's goodness and blessings, we will see His goodness and blessings.

Today's verse is especially powerful when you consider that the apostle Paul wrote this when he was in prison. During his life—over the course of thirty years—he had been beaten, mobbed, and stoned. Yet, still he focused on joy. He didn't let the harshness of his life overwhelm his attitude. He was still thankful for his salvation and focused on God's blessings.

As you search for joy and contentment in your life and work, focus on those things that are noble, right, pure, lovely, and admirable. There will always be things that don't quite measure up, but by focusing on the good, you'll find more contentment and joy than ever before.

–GM

POWER PRAYER

Lord, today I commit to think on things that are noble, right, pure, lovely, and admirable and trust You to take care of everything else.

MY EVERYTHING

As the deer pants for streams of water, so I long for you, O God.

PSALM 42:1 NLT

There's a beautiful song by the group Avalon that goes: "You're everything to me. You're more than a story. More than words on a page of history. You're the air that I breathe. The water I thirst for. And the ground beneath my feet. You're everything to me."

If we truly feel that way about our Lord, we can be content no matter if we're the CEO or a letter-opener-in-training. Contentment—true contentment—comes only from the Lord. Sure, we can get "temporary career contentment fixes," but that lasting peace and sense of fulfillment comes only from heaven.

No promotion. No pay increase. No corner office. Nothing can fill the hole in our hearts that yearns for Jesus. Only He can fill that void. Only He can cause contentment to be a way of life. That's why Paul and Silas could sing praises to God while locked up in a stinky prison. They were content—even joyful—in their circumstances. Why? Because Jesus was everything to them—period. Is Jesus everything to you today? If you've lost that passion you once had for Christ, spend some time with Him today. If He is your everything, you'll be content in everything.

–MMA

POWER PRAYER

Lord, You truly are everything to me. Help me never to lose sight of that. Amen.

Enjoying Your Workspace
on the Way to the Corner Office

NOVEMBER

24

CHAPTERS

"For I know the plans I have for you," declares the LORD,
"plans to prosper you and not to harm you,
plans to give you hope and a future."

JEREMIAH 29:11

I look at my life like chapters in a book. Looking back, I can see God's hand direct me from one phase to another. In fact, even when I couldn't see how a job or experience applied to the big picture, I eventually discovered that it did. Nothing was a waste of time. God used each and every experience to mold me so that He could use me today.

And what He's done for me, He'll surely do for you.

If you are at a place where you're wondering whether what you're doing really matters, take heart; God is using and preparing you for the next chapter. Just as He said in His Word, "I know the plans I have for you," He's preparing your way. If you work retail, He may be molding your interpersonal skills. If you're in finance, He may be teaching you about financial trends. If you're in education, He may be equipping you to be a better teacher. Whatever your job, God will use your talents to glorify Him.

–GM

POWER PRAYER
Lord, I know that You have exciting plans for me, and I trust You to fulfill them in my life.

DETAILS, DETAILS

But the Lord said to her,
"My dear Martha, you are so upset over all these details!
There is really only one thing worth being concerned about.
Mary has discovered it—
and I won't take it away from her."

LUKE 10:41–42 NLT

In the midst of never-ending paperwork, office politics, possible layoffs, and office strife, it's hard to be content in your current job, isn't it? I remember days when I would drive into the parking lot of my workplace and wish I could be anywhere else at that moment. But guess what? I survived that time in my life, and I even ended up liking my position.

No, my job didn't change, but my attitude did. Instead of dreading work on my drive to the office, I began praising God that I had a job. Instead of looking at the mounds of paperwork on my desk and resenting every piece, I thanked God that my boss had such confidence in me to give me so much work. I started seeing my situation through new eyes—through God's eyes. And I stopped getting so weighed down by all the "stuff." I chose to do what Mary did, and that was simply rest in Jesus. If you're weary today, rest in Him. And start looking at your job through His eyes. The view is a lot better!

–MMA

POWER PRAYER
Lord, help me to see my job through Your eyes. Amen.

DO YOU LOVE WHAT YOU DO?

The LORD will fulfill his purpose for me.

PSALM 138:8

A friend recently asked my husband, "Do you love what you do for a living?" My husband thought about it and responded, "I love the life I have because of what I do." Later, he explained that though he may not enjoy every part of his job, he loves his work environment, schedule, and the time he is able to spend with his family. Though it may sound simple, he's realized something about finding contentment in his work: Workplace contentment isn't based solely on the work. It's also based on the rewards you have because of it, rewards that may have nothing to do with money or things.

If you're in a job that, though somewhat fulfilling, leaves you wondering if there's anything more, try to focus on what you have because of it. Do you make a difference to people? Do you make a good salary? Do you use your God-given skills? Is there room for advancement? Sure, you're going to have jobs that are less than stellar, but they may be in preparation for something better down the road. Focus on what you gain from your job and you'll find more contentment than you expected to find.

–GM

POWER PRAYER

Lord, help me to remember all the good things that I have because of my job.

COMMITTED CONTENTMENT
Therefore, since we have been justified through faith,
we have peace with God through our Lord Jesus Christ.

ROMANS 5:1

A lot of people try to fill the voids in their lives with temporary things—money, fame, power, relationships, and more. They assume that if they just attain one more thing or one more promotion, finally, they'll achieve happiness and contentment. Unfortunately, that doesn't happen.

Every person is created with a spirit, and until that spirit comes alive through Jesus Christ, peace will be an illusion. And it doesn't work just to believe in Jesus or just to attend church. True peace and contentment only come through a committed relationship with Jesus. For some, the thought of serving Jesus wholeheartedly is scary. They worry that they'll have to live by a lot of rules or they'll be deprived of fun and relationships. But becoming solidly committed to Jesus brings so much more peace and contentment than they ever thought possible.

If you're considering becoming 100 percent committed to Jesus and committed to living your life for Him, don't wait. It's the most rewarding decision you'll ever make.

–GM

POWER PRAYER
Lord, I am ready to live completely committed to You. I trust
You to make my life whatever You want it to be.

PUMP IT UP

Through Him, therefore,
let us constantly and at all times offer up to God
a sacrifice of praise,
which is the fruit of lips that thankfully acknowledge
and confess and glorify His name.

HEBREWS 13:15 AMP

Be honest. . .you were feeling pretty content in your job and
your overall life until you ran into her. She drove up in her new
Cadillac Escalade, pulled in next to you, and shared how she'd
just been hired to a new position that pays three times what
you currently make. And to top it off, she just lost fourteen
pounds on the South Beach Diet. Suddenly, all of your con
tentment vanished. Instead, that contentment was replaced
with resentment, jealousy, and a little bit of anger.

If you've ever experienced a situation similar to this one,
you know how miserable it can make you. It can totally rob
your joy. There's only one way to fight off the resentment and
jealousy that follow an encounter like the one described
above. You have to pump up the praise. That's right—praise
the Lord like you've never praised before. Don't dwell on
what you don't have. Meditate on what you do have. Praise
God for the good things in your life. And praise Him for the
blessings in your friend's life, too. Praise will bring peace and
contentment to your heart, and it's a lot more fun than the
South Beach Diet.

–MMA

POWER PRAYER
I praise You, Lord, for the blessings in my life. Amen.

LEAVING EGYPT

"I am the LORD your God,
who brought you out of Egypt,
out of the land of slavery."

EXODUS 20:2

"Sometimes it's easier for people to stay in tough circumstances because it's familiar. They're content because at least they know what to expect," a friend recently said. As she spoke, I remembered times when things had been difficult at work. I had tried to love my job. I had prioritized and delegated—all of the things that are supposed to make things work. Eventually, I realized that I was unhappy, yet scared to make a change. I was content in my discontentment, just like the Israelites after they were freed from Egypt. They considered returning to slavery just because it was familiar.

For me, I had to gain the courage to make a change, and if you're in the same place, I challenge you to do it, too. God will always be there to catch you if you fall, and more likely than not, He's just waiting for you to be willing to take a chance on Him. Don't be content with discontentment. Make a decision to trust God and follow Him out of Egypt.

–GM

POWER PRAYER

Lord, I trust You to take me out of the Egypt in my life. Don't
let me be content in my discontentment, but help me to have
the courage and faith to follow You.

WHERE AM I GOING?

Where there is no vision, the people perish.

PROVERBS 29:18 KJV

Do you know any people who took early retirement and totally lost their drive for life? I've seen it happen. They lose their vision. They lose their reason for getting up in the morning. But you don't have to be of retirement age to lose your vision. I've seen women of all ages lose their hope and drive. In fact, I've been there myself. How about you? There have been times in my career when I felt as though I was drifting on a sea of pointlessness.

No matter where you are in life—right out of college working your first job or approaching retirement—you need to have a goal, a dream, a vision. If you don't, you'll wind up drifting on that same sea of pointlessness or possibly heading down the river of "I hate my job."

So do you know God's plan for your life? If not, ask God to show you His vision. Seek His plan, and once you discover it, write it down, and keep it before you. Thank Him for that vision every day. Keep the vision close to your heart. Remind yourself of God's plan every time you're asked to do menial tasks at work. Remember, you're on your way to something greater.

–MMA

POWER PRAYER

Lord, help me to never lose the vision that You've given me.
Amen.

IF I'M THE EMPLOYEE OF THE MONTH, EVERYONE ELSE MUST BE ON VACATION

*He said, "If I have found favor in your eyes,
my lord, do not pass your servant by."*

GENESIS 18:3

"Michelle Adams to the Marketing Conference Room, please."

As I heard the page over the company PA system, I wondered, *What have I done?*

I took one deep breath and entered the conference room, where a dozen of my coworkers, my boss, and my director all stood.

Suddenly, they started applauding.

"Michelle, I just wanted to congratulate you on a job well done in front of your peers," my director said. "That is the best annual report I've ever read."

It was official—I was the Golden Child of the moment.

That feeling of elation lasted about two days. Then, for reasons unknown to me, I couldn't even write my name with any accuracy in my supervisor's eyes. What had changed? I was the same writer who had written "the best annual report ever" just days before!

You see, you can easily fall out of favor with man, but you can't fall out of favor with God. So even if you're not the Golden Child at your company, you're a Golden Child with your heavenly Father, and that's more than enough.

–MMA

POWER PRAYER
Thank You, Lord, for loving me unconditionally. Amen.

THE POWER OF POSITIVE SPEAKING

Death and life are in the power of the tongue:
and they that love it shall eat the fruit thereof.

PROVERBS 18:21 KJV

Have you ever used the expression, "Well, I just tell it like it is," in order to justify your negative commentaries? I know I have. If you've spent your whole life "telling it like it is," stop! We shouldn't use our mouths to comment on the negative state of our workplaces or our difficult bosses. The Word says to "calleth those things which be not as though they were" (Romans 4:17). So instead of using your mouth to report the sorry state of things, use it to speak faith over your situation.

What exactly does that mean? It means to say things that agree with the Word of God—not your negative circumstances. No matter how ugly your boss treated you yesterday, confess that you have favor in her eyes today. No matter how many people have been laid off in your division, confess that your job is secure. No matter how many of your ideas have been shot down in the past, confess that your ideas rise to the top. Use your mouth to speak good things, and watch your world change around you. Stop telling it like it is, and start telling it like it's going to be!

–MMA

POWER PRAYER

Lord, help me only to speak words that line up with Your
Word. Amen.

PUTTING THE
GOLDEN RULE TO WORK

*"So in everything,
do to others what you would have them do to you."*

MATTHEW 7:12

Honestly, bosses have a tough time of it. Yes, there are those who only pay lip service to serious issues or get a thrill out of flexing their authoritative muscles, but most bosses try to do a good job. They walk a fine line between being too lenient and too harsh. They need to get a job done while preventing their natives from becoming too restless, and they're held accountable for the work of every person under them.

At one time or another, I think everyone has been critical of their boss. As unfair as it may be, employees can demand perfection from their boss while expecting mercy with regards to their own work. A double standard to be sure.

Scripture says to "do to others what you would have them do to you." Remember this in regards to your boss as you go through your week. If you don't want your boss to expect perfection from you every day, then you can't expect perfection from him, either. He's in a tough place, and in addition to your good work, he needs your support and understanding.

–GM

POWER PRAYER

*Lord, I want to be a support to my boss this week and show
favor toward him. Show me how to do that.*

IN HIS SHADOW

*He who dwells in the shelter of the Most High
will rest in the shadow of the Almighty.
I will say of the LORD,
"He is my refuge and my fortress,
my God, in whom I trust."*

PSALM 91:1–2

I love the Ninety-first Psalm. At times in my life when
things looked uncertain, the Ninety-first Psalm has been a
comfort. Just look at the first verse, "He who dwells in the
shelter of the Most High will rest in the shadow of the
Almighty." Isn't that a beautiful picture? As a child of God,
you dwell in God's shelter, and because you do, you can rest
in His shadow.

So when things look bleak or upsetting, you aren't forgotten. Often people envision God either as a taskmaster
who's ready to wallop them when they step out of line or as
a distant, disinterested figure. But both of these views are
incorrect. Psalm 91 is a great reminder of the protection
that He offers to His children.

I challenge you to read Psalm 91 and consider it in
light of your situation. As you do, you'll begin to see that
God is very interested in your life and He's available to help
you through difficult situations.

–GM

POWER PRAYER
*Lord, thank You for allowing me to rest in Your shadow and
protecting me. I trust You as my refuge and fortress.*

IT GOES A LONG WAY

So then, just as you received Christ Jesus as Lord,
continue to live in him,
rooted and built up in him,
strengthened in the faith as you were taught,
and overflowing with thankfulness.

COLOSSIANS 2:6–7

Have you worked around people who complained constantly? They didn't like the boss's decisions or the company's policies or the receptionist's attitude. Everything was a problem; nothing was easy. Their complaints were like nails on a chalkboard. All they had to do was start talking and everyone around them cringed. Needless to say, they didn't win any Miss Congeniality awards.

Every office has challenges, but having someone constantly point them out is draining. You'd rather be around positive people who are thankful for their jobs and peers.

Thankfulness goes a long way toward developing a positive attitude. It shows that you acknowledge that God is in control and works through, or sometimes in spite of, the people around you. So develop an attitude of thankfulness, realizing that it'll help you become a favorite among your peers and strengthen your relationship with the Lord.

–GM

POWER PRAYER

Lord, I thank You for Your provision. I thank You for the job
You've given me and the people You've placed around me. I
trust You in all I do.

AN OPEN LINE

Then Jesus told his disciples a parable to show them that
they should always pray and not give up.

LUKE 18:1

Recently I attended a meeting with a woman who, in the midst of our meeting, received a phone call. Then a few minutes later, while she was still on the phone, she received another call on her cell phone. Over the next five minutes, I watched as she juggled both calls at once—one phone on each ear—never breaking her stride.

As Christians, we need to have two receivers open, too—one to those around us and the other to God. In Luke 18, Jesus told the disciples to "always pray." As eager as you may be to get that helpful phone call at work with just the right information, as a child of God, you should be just as eager to get direction and information from God. Some people assume that if you're not in a certain place or praying in a certain way, it doesn't count. But actually, God never hangs up the spiritual phone; He's always on the line, hoping that you'll have your receiver pressed against your ear.

As you go through your day, keep your prayer line open, becoming even more in tune with Him.

–GM

POWER PRAYER
Lord, I love You and trust You today and I make a commitment to keep the communication between us open.

FAVOR FOR A LIFETIME

For surely, O LORD, you bless the righteous;
you surround them with your favor as with a shield.

PSALM 5:12

Finding favor with your coworkers and your superiors is a good thing. It certainly makes your work environment a lot more pleasant, right? But if you have to achieve that favor through natural means, you'll have to keep that place of favor the same way.

In other words, if you are your director's favorite employee because you baby-sit for her children every Friday night, you better get ready to do some more baby-sitting. See, after a while, Friday nights won't be enough. You'll be asked to watch her children on Saturday nights, too. Eventually, you'll be picking up her dry cleaning and washing her toilets. That's the funny thing about gaining favor through your own means—you always have to "work it" to stay in that favorable place.

That's not the kind of favor the Bible speaks of. Psalm 30:5 says the Lord's favor lasts a lifetime. Isn't that good to know? We can't fall out of favor with God for not doing enough good deeds in a week. He is a God of mercy. He loves us. You don't have to earn His favor. You can just simply enjoy it.

–MMA

POWER PRAYER

Thank You, Lord, for crowning my head with Your favor.
Help me to walk in Your supernatural favor with my cowork-
ers and superiors. Amen.

START GLOWING!

*When Aaron and all the Israelites saw Moses,
his face was radiant.*

EXODUS 34:30

Have you ever been around someone who actually glows? You can't really explain it, but that coworker simply beams. He or she outshines everyone else in the office. Yeah, we all know someone who walks in absolute favor. Usually, those folks are the ones who rise to the top with great ease. You know why? They are filled with God's presence! They glow with the glory of the Lord. That's why they outshine everyone else. That's why they are so attractive to others. That's why everyone is open to their ideas. That's why they are promoted when others are being let go.

Did you know after Moses had spent time with God, he would have to wear a veil over his face because he glowed too brightly for the Israelites to behold him? See, if you spend time with God—reading your Bible and talking to Him and praising Him—you will begin to glow, too! You'll start changing from the inside out. It'll be just like that *Extreme Makeover* show on TV, but you'll be extremely made over on the inside, which will overflow to your outside.

Why not spend some time with God today and begin your Master Makeover. You glow, girl!

–MMA

POWER PRAYER

*Lord, fill me with more of You that I might radiate Your love.
Amen.*

BLESSING

"The LORD bless you and keep you;
the LORD make his face shine upon you and be gracious to you;
the LORD turn his face toward you and give you peace."

NUMBERS 6:24–26

The Lord gave the above blessing to Moses. He instructed Moses that this was how Aaron and his sons should bless the Israelites. I particularly love this blessing because my pastor has used it for years at the end of his sermons. Each week, these words are like a warm blanket that he wraps around his congregation to remind them of the Lord's love and favor.

As you go through your day, remember this blessing. Recite it to yourself or write it down where you'll be able to see it. Remember that these words weren't man's creation, but God's. This is His blessing to His people. It is for you and me and every other believer. If there are people in your office who don't know the Lord, pray that they'll come to know Him so that this blessing can become theirs and "the Lord will make His face shine upon" them, too.

–GM

POWER PRAYER

Lord, thank You for Your favor and blessing. Thank You for blessing and keeping me, for making Your face to shine upon me and being gracious to me, and for turning Your face toward me and giving me peace. I love You.

SUPERNATURAL FAVOR

*The LORD had made the Egyptians
favorably disposed toward the people,
and they gave them what they asked for;
so they plundered the Egyptians.*

EXODUS 12:36

Do you know that God can cause people who don't particularly like you to do nice things on your behalf? It's true. When the Israelites left Egypt headed for the Promised Land, they left in a hurry as Moses had instructed. But on their way out of town, they asked the Egyptians for articles of gold and silver and for clothing. Now the Israelites and the Egyptians weren't exactly bosom buddies, yet the Israelites were given all they asked for and more!

I can just imagine the Egyptians loading up sacks of silver and gold to give to the Israelites and saying, "I don't know why I am giving these precious items to you, but enjoy them. Have a good trip!"

See, God can cause even your enemies to treat you favorably. He can cause that supervisor who despises you to recommend you for a raise. He can prompt your grouchy boss to grant you those vacation days you put in a request for many months ago. Just honor God. Obey His voice, and thank Him for His supernatural favor that is causing your enemies to bless you. It works!

–MMA

POWER PRAYER

*Lord, I thank You that even my enemies desire to bless me
because of Your supernatural favor. Amen*

TIDAL WAVES

*For surely, O LORD, you bless the righteous;
you surround them with your favor as with a shield.*

PSALM 5:12

Have you ever noticed that when you're good at your job, you tend to get more responsibility? It isn't necessarily bad, but it can lead to overload. As new projects come up, your boss—who is constantly impressed by your efficiency and good attitude—gives it to you without considering the five hundred other assignments on your desk. You're flattered, but it's kind of hard when you're barely treading water with the tidal waves slamming against your desk.

Ah, the price of good work ethics! As women, we're notorious for believing that if we just reorganize or reprioritize, we can handle immense loads, but in all honesty, we need to be realistic and honest—with ourselves and our bosses. When your work responsibility becomes overwhelming, pray for direction and, if the Lord leads you to, speak to your boss.

When sticky situations arise that need to be addressed, prepare with prayer. Then remember that just like this verse says, God will "bless the righteous" and "surround [you] with favor as with a shield."

–GM

POWER PRAYER

*Lord, thank You for Your favor. Please direct me in how to
handle the load.*

DISTINGUISHED FAVOR

May the favor of the Lord our God rest upon us;
establish the work of our hands for us—
yes, establish the work of our hands.

PSALM 90:17

Deborah was a woman who enjoyed favor with God and man. She was a prophetess, judge, and military leader for Israel. Judges 4:5 says that "people came to her for judgment." Obviously, they trusted her. Though Deborah was married and possibly a mother, she still worked for the good of her people. She was vital in freeing her people from the tyranny of Jabin, king of Canaan. When the fight for freedom came, she went with the army and counseled Israel's commander.

Did she accomplish these feats on her own? No, she was a godly woman who sought God's will and did what He told her to do.

We can learn from Deborah. She was strong, smart, courageous, and deeply devoted to following God's laws. She didn't allow difficult situations to keep her from serving Him. She didn't spend her days complaining because her people were oppressed. Instead, she rose above the circumstances, followed God, and helped her people.

As you go about your work, remember Deborah's example. Work hard. Help people and love God. As you determine to follow God's wisdom, you'll find His favor waiting for you.

–GM

POWER PRAYER

Heavenly Father, I love You and serve You today. Thank You for Your favor and honor.

F.O.G.

For the LORD God is a sun and shield;
the LORD bestows favor and honor;
no good thing does he withhold from those whose
walk is blameless.

PSALM 84:11

Have you ever heard the expression, "Walking in the F.O.G."? It stands for, "Walking in the Favor of God." I use this expression a lot, like when I pull into work and there's a parking spot right up front. I immediately thank the Lord for saving that parking place just for me, and I'll say to whomever is with me, "Yep, I'm just walking in the F.O.G." It's become sort of a fun activity. My friends and family and I look for opportunities to thank God for His favor.

Have you ever intentionally looked for God's goodness and favor in your life? If not, why not start today? It's fun, and you know what? Once you start praising God for His favor that is operating in your life, you'll start walking in much more favor. God appreciates that you notice all of the nice things He does for you each day.

So when your boss says, "Why don't you take the rest of the day off today—you've been working so hard," take a moment and thank God for His favor. Start walking in the F.O.G. today!

–MMA

POWER PRAYER
Thank You, heavenly Father, for the F.O.G. I praise You for all
that You do for me. You're awesome! Amen.

THE UNPLEASEABLE

I know that you are pleased with me,
for my enemy does not triumph over me.

PSALM 41:11

There are times when no matter what we do, we'll never please someone. Some people won't return our friendship. Some bosses won't look on us kindly. Some people will never believe that we measure up. That's why our confidence needs to be based on what God says about us. For everyone else, we can only do what God's Word instructs us to do.

My friend Rachel once called me in tears. After a long, sisterlike friendship with Christine, Rachel had finally realized that their friendship was over. For several months, she had tried to *save* the friendship through encouragement, gifts, and just "being there." Unfortunately, Christine wouldn't accept it. After the falling out, Rachel realized that she'd placed Christine's opinion of her above God's. It had become a twisted relationship that thankfully ended with Rachel rediscovering the importance of pleasing God instead of man.

If someone—a boss, friend, husband, or boyfriend—has you questioning your value, turn to God. If necessary, talk to an objective third party who is a Christian. Remember that you belong to God's family and your value depends on Him. For everyone else, you can only do what God calls you to do.

–GM

POWER PRAYER
Father, thank You for Your love. Help me to seek Your favor above anyone else's.

REJOICE

*"May the LORD show you his favor
and give you his peace."*

NUMBERS 6:26 NLT

I had worked a ten-hour day, and I still had another story to write before morning. I was tired. I was discouraged. I was frustrated. And for a brief moment, I wondered if I'd even chosen the right profession. Ever felt that way? How about when you have worked like a dog all month, and when it comes time to pay the bills, you're still short? It's enough to make you want to give up, isn't it? I know. I've been there.

But I have good news for you. One moment of God's favor is worth a lifetime of labor. In other words, God can turn things around for you in an instant! He can cause that screenplay you've been trying to get published to fall into the hands of a famous director. He can orchestrate a divine meeting between you and the president of your company. He can cause a large bill that's been hanging over your head to be canceled.

So don't be discouraged. Don't complain when you have to work late. Don't whine when you have to pay bills. Rejoice! Praise God that He is granting you favor with those who can help you. Just think, your moment of God's favor may happen today.

–MMA

POWER PRAYER

*Thank You, Father, for causing me to have favor with the
right people. Amen.*

SHOWING FAVOR

Then the King will say,
"I'm telling the solemn truth:
Whenever you did one of these things to someone
overlooked or ignored, that was me—you did it to me."

MATTHEW 25:40 MSG

This is the time of year when I love to find the perfect gift for the special people in my life. I enjoy watching their eyes sparkle when they open it, whether it's an electronic thing-amajig for my husband or yummy-scented lotion for my mother. It's a small way that I can share how much they mean to me and show them favor.

I'm sure that you have loved ones you want to bless with the perfect gift this holiday season, too. And yet, don't only reserve this for loved ones. Look for ways to bless others, too—the receptionist at work who always gives you a smile, the person who delivers your mail, your boss, or the janitor. As much as you enjoy giving special treatment to loved ones, you may also come to love showing kindness to the others around you. Remember that as you show kindness and favor to them, you also show it to Jesus.

–GM

POWER PRAYER
Lord, help me to show favor and kindness to the overlooked and ignored people around me.

THE KING'S OWN

*"For every animal of the forest is mine,
and the cattle on a thousand hills."*

PSALM 50:10

What if your father owned the company where you work? If he did, you'd probably have some fabulous fringe benefits, wouldn't you? Yes, that would be nice. But even if your father doesn't own the place where you work, you can expect great favor. Why? Because you are a child of the King of kings. The Bible says that God owns all of the cattle on a thousand hills. Now I live in Texas, and I can tell you—that's a lot of cows!

We serve a very wealthy God, and He loves to shower blessings down on His children. If you are born again, then you qualify! And if you aren't saved, we can take care of that right now. Simply pray, "Lord, I repent of my sins. Thank You, Jesus, for dying on the cross so that I might live. I make You the Lord and Savior of my life. Amen." That's it. You're in the "favor club."

As a child of the Most High God, you can expect favor and blessings. Become favor minded. Expect good things to come your way, because He has good things in store for you.

–MMA

POWER PRAYER

*Thank You, Father, for salvation, favor, blessings, and so much
more. I love You. Amen.*

THE GIFT

"Today in the town of David a Savior has been born to you;
he is Christ the Lord. This will be a sign to you:
You will find a baby wrapped in cloths
and lying in a manger." . . .
So they hurried off and found Mary and Joseph,
and the baby.

LUKE 2:11–12, 16

During this Christmas season, it's easy to get caught up in the commercialism, isn't it? I am guilty. I love the twinkle lights on all the houses. I love the holiday home shows. I love the traditional Christmas movies like *White Christmas* and *It's a Wonderful Life*. And I absolutely love to shop. I already have all of my gifts purchased and wrapped neatly under the tree. (Okay, I do have a few stocking stuffers left to purchase, but I'm pretty much done!)

Speaking of gifts. . .I wanted to take this opportunity to talk about the greatest Gift in the history of the world. Talk about favor! God so highly favored mankind that He sent His only Son to earth to save us.

So take time to celebrate Jesus this season. Don't get so caught up in the commercialism of it all. Instead, praise God for His favor and for sending Jesus to earth as a baby more than two thousand years ago. Keep your eyes on Him and have the happiest holiday season ever!

–MMA

POWER PRAYER
Thank You, Father, for the gift of Jesus. Amen.

IT'S FREE!

*[Jesus said,] Freely (without pay) you have received,
freely (without charge) give.*

MATTHEW 10:8 AMP

"I can never outgive God," a friend once told me. The working mother of five, she and her husband weren't wealthy, but she freely gave to anyone who needed it—money, clothes, time, or service. Whatever she had, she gave. I once even witnessed her giving a beautiful, leather jacket—something she adored—to someone because she believed that she should. Why? Because she understood an important truth: Everything she had came from God, and if she felt the Holy Spirit telling her to do it, she should be ready to give it away without reservation.

James 1:17 (NIV) says, "Every good and perfect gift is from above." It's a good reminder that our possessions don't belong to us, but rather to God. He's the one who gave them to us, and He's the one who can direct us to pass them to others.

During this season, prayerfully consider giving to others. Don't just think about the people to whom it is easy to give—children, family, and friends—but consider those who are not so easy—the homeless, widows, single parents, and orphans you don't know. Remember that just as you have freely received, you should freely give.

–GM

POWER PRAYER
*Lord, I realize that all I have is from You, so please show me
how, when, and where to continue giving to others.*

THANKS FOR THE FAVOR

Let the favor of the Lord our God be upon us.

PSALM 90:17 NASB

Okay, so you desire the favor of God in your life, but you're just not sure how to get it, right? Favor comes through prayer, faith in His Word, and obeying His leading. Bottom line—favor comes when you spend time in God's presence.

When I was looking for a publisher for *Living the Love Chapter*, I had submitted it to many places and received loads of rejection letters. But after I understood this favor principle, I began praying favor over my book proposal, and I thanked God that I had favor with whatever editor opened my e-mail. Guess what? I sold that book! Later, when I met with the publisher to sign the contract, he said, "You know, it's a miracle I even received your book proposal. You sent your e-mail to an account I never check anymore. But for some reason, I knew I was supposed to check that account the very day your message came through. Funny, huh?"

I smiled and said, "That's my God! He does favors for me all the time." And you know what? He will do favors for you, too. He loves doing nice things for His children. So go on. Spend some time with Him today, and thank Him for His favor.

–MMA

POWER PRAYER
Thank You, Lord, for Your favor. I love You. Amen.

A CHANGE OF HEART

*The king's heart is like channels of water
in the hand of the LORD;
He turns it wherever He wishes.*

PROVERBS 21:1 NASB

Do you work for someone who obviously dislikes you? It's difficult, isn't it? But don't worry. God can change your supervisor's heart.

I once interviewed a man named Pete who had lived a life of crime and ended up in prison. He had been serving his debt to society for armed robbery and had excellent behavior in prison. The guards all liked him. His fellow prisoners liked him. He was a light in a dark place because while he was in prison, he had become a Christian. He was a perfect candidate for early release, but every time his parole hearing came around, the chairperson of the parole board denied Pete's request without ever letting him speak. Pete was praying about his situation, and the Lord took him to Proverbs 21:1. Immediately, Pete started praying that God would change the chairperson's heart. When that next parole hearing rolled around, Pete was allowed to speak for the first time. Amazingly, the chairperson was kind to him. Shortly after, Pete walked out of prison a free man.

If your boss dislikes you, pray Proverbs 21:1 every day, and like Pete, you'll find favor, too!

–MMA

POWER PRAYER

Thank You, Lord, for changing the hearts of those who dislike me. Thank You for Your supernatural favor. I love You. Amen.

RENEWAL

Great is his faithfulness;
his mercies begin afresh each day.
I say to myself, "The LORD is my inheritance;
therefore, I will hope in him!"

LAMENTATIONS 3:23–24 NLT

What a beautiful reminder of the Lord's character! This verse shows us once again that God is merciful and faithful to His people, and our hope is in Him. It's interesting that this passage was written after a very dark time in Israel's history. The city of Jerusalem was in ruins, yet the prophet Jeremiah, who lamented the loss, still acknowledged God's kindness.

Aren't you glad that the Lord's mercies are new every day for you, too? I know I am. It's comforting to know that in our darkest days, when we miss it—totally and completely miss it—God is faithful. He is ready to give us a fresh start, never abandoning or leaving us to get ourselves out of the messes we create. Instead, His mercies are new every day, and we can put our hope in Him.

If you are struggling to accept God's forgiveness because you feel that you are too far gone, meditate on this scripture. Allow it to become real to you so you know that He is faithful. His mercies are new every day, and you can hope in Him.

–GM

POWER PRAYER

Lord, thank You for Your faithfulness and Your renewed
mercies. I love You!

DO WHAT?

God blesses those people who want to obey him.

MATTHEW 5:6 CEV

Have you ever received an assignment that left you wanting to roll your eyes? Or what about the *brilliant* idea that someone has for handling a project in a way that you know won't work? Face it; when you already have a hundred projects and only eight hours in each day, you can only do so much.

When it comes to doing what we're told to do at work, sometimes we just have to grin and bear it. There really is no other way. When it comes to our spiritual work, it's the same. God loves obedience. Of course, if we read this verse closely, we realize it isn't just obedience that God desires. We should *want* to obey Him, meaning we need to have a good attitude. In fact, this verse says that He blesses us when we do.

If you are eager to have God's favor and blessings in your life, commit to living a life of eager and joyful obedience. Guard against rolling your spiritual eyes at God. As you do, you'll receive His blessings and enjoy His favor.

–GM

POWER PRAYER

Lord, I am committed to following Your Word and doing Your will. As I do, I appreciate Your blessings.

I THINK I CAN

*I can do everything through him
who gives me strength.*

PHILIPPIANS 4:13

Remember the Little Golden Book about the little engine that could? You know the story. He tries really hard—against many odds—chugging along and puffing "I think I can, I think I can" until he proves everyone wrong and reaches his goal. I've always loved that little book. You know why? Because it's packed with powerful teaching. If we can keep a can-do attitude, we can achieve many things.

My eleven-year-old daughter, Abby, is a great gymnast. In fact, she is a member of a competitive gymnastics team. When Abby is preparing for her tumbling pass, I can always tell if she's going to do well just by the look on her face. If she approaches the mat with a can-do facial expression, I know she's going to nail it. But if she shows fear on her face, I know she's not going to give her best performance. It's all in the attitude.

Maybe you have a goal that seems impossible to reach—sort of like that little engine that could. Maybe your boss has put you in charge of something that seems impossible. Well, God says that you can do all things through Him, so go for it! Keep a can-do attitude and watch your dreams become a reality!

–MMA

POWER PRAYER

Lord, help me to have a can-do attitude. Amen.

KEEP REACHING

*You save the humble
but bring low those whose eyes are haughty.*

PSALM 18:27

I love to watch biographies about famous folks on TV, don't you? I once watched a program about an actress whose mother is also a famous actress. When asked what piece of motherly advice had most helped her in her film career, she said, "My mom told me not to believe anything that is written or said about myself—good or bad—or it would destroy me." The interviewer said, "Well, I can understand not believing the negative press, but what about the good press and favorable reviews?" She answered, "They are just as bad because if you start believing you're all those wonderful things people say you are, you'll stop growing and believe you've already arrived."

While most of us are probably not in the Hollywood scene, this is still good advice. If you receive a good review at work, rejoice but don't stop reaching. If your boss compliments you, be thankful but don't be satisfied with status quo. Keep reaching. Keep growing. Don't become haughty. If we remain humble, we remain teachable. As they say in Texas, "Don't get too big for your britches." Favor is a good thing. Just don't let it go to your head. Instead, be thankful in your heart.

–MMA

POWER PRAYER

*Thank You, Lord, for the favor I'm being shown at work. Help
me to remain humble. Amen.*

BONUSES

*And my God will meet all your needs
according to his glorious riches in Christ Jesus.*

PHILIPPIANS 4:19

The office memo read: "Due to a financially challenging year, we will not be able to give Christmas bonuses this year. . . ."

There was outrage within the office. Many of my co-workers had really been counting on that Christmas bonus to pay for their Christmas shopping sprees. In fact, several had already spent the bonus (charging on their credit cards) because they knew they'd be receiving a Christmas bonus. (Okay, yes, I fell into that last group.) After all, the company *always* gave Christmas bonuses—but not this year. Fear swept through the office like a swift, cold breeze. I heard "What are we going to do?" asked many times throughout the day. Others grumbled about the company's overspending on other things throughout the year.

But you know what? I didn't join in the Grinchfest. I rarely get it right, but the Holy Spirit really talked to me that day. I knew in my heart that God would supply for Christmas (and He did), and I also knew that if my company's leaders could've given bonuses, they would've. If you're in a similar situation this year, don't grumble—praise God for His provision. He is your source, and He gives supernatural bonuses!

–MMA

POWER PRAYER
Thank You, Lord, for supplying all of my needs. Amen.

GOOD THINGS

For the LORD God is a sun and shield;
the LORD bestows favor and honor;
no good thing does he withhold from those
whose walk is blameless.

PSALM 84:11

Have you seen the movie *Shadowlands*? If not, I highly recommend it. Just make sure you have a box of tissues next to
you when you do. It's the love story of C. S. Lewis and his
wife. At the beginning, Lewis is shown preaching hellfire
and brimstone. Very hard. By the end, Lewis, who has lost
his wife to cancer, has greatly changed. He's shown ex-
plaining the gentle vastness of God's love to his stepson. It's
very moving.

God loves His children; we know that. But that love is
more than just a lofty thought. It's real. This verse says, "no
good thing does He withhold from those whose walk is
blameless." That's a powerful statement of God's love and
favor. He's not a hard God, but He does want us to obey
Him. Of course, when we do, He gives us His best.

So don't wait. Commit to walking obediently before
Him. Then observe the good things He brings into your life.

–GM

POWER PRAYER

Lord, I commit to worship You blamelessly and obediently,
and I thank You in advance for the good things You bring
into my life.

EVEN IN THE TOUGH TIMES

*But while Joseph was there in the prison,
the LORD was with him;
he showed him kindness and granted him favor
in the eyes of the prison warden. . . .
The LORD was with Joseph
and gave him success in whatever he did.*

GENESIS 39:20–21, 23

God's favor can follow you wherever you go, even when things are tough. The story of Joseph is proof of that. First, Joseph was sold into slavery by his brothers, yet the Lord blessed him. Then he rose in favor to become the head of his master's household. When his master's wife falsely accused him of coming on to her, he was thrown in prison. And yet again, God's favor followed him, and he was eventually released and even promoted. On and on, obstacles came, yet God continued to show him favor.

Even when things get tough, God will still bless you. When someone accuses you, He can defend you. If you lose your job, He can care for you. You just have to look for it. When things are tough, God hasn't disappeared. If you'll willingly and obediently follow Him and look to Him for answers, He will come through for you every time.

–GM

POWER PRAYER
Lord, I want to obediently and willingly follow You, regardless of what's going on in my life. As I do, I know that You'll take care of me.

THE HIGHLY FAVORED

For the LORD God is a sun and shield;
the LORD bestows favor and honor;
no good thing does he withhold from those
whose walk is blameless.

PSALM 84:11

Growing up, I didn't understand God's favor. I thought I had
to earn it. I thought that maybe if I were good enough,
maybe He would toss me a bone once in a while. Is your
thinking as warped as mine used to be? Just in case—let me
shed some light on this favor matter for you. According to
Psalm 84:11, God does not withhold any good thing from
us. He takes great pleasure in sending down His blessings
to us. He adores us. The Word says we are the apple of His
eye. And because He is God, you can be His favorite child,
and so can I!

The Word also says, "For thou, LORD, wilt bless the
righteous; with favour wilt thou compass him as with a
shield" (Psalm 5:12 KJV). In other words, we are wrapped in
God's favor. It's all over us. But if you don't know it, you
can't walk in it. So now that you've been enlightened, walk
in His supernatural favor. Expect good things to come your
way at work today. Expect promotions. Expect pay raises.
Expect extra vacation days. You are highly favored!

–MMA

POWER PRAYER

Thank You, Lord, for Your favor. You are so good to me. Amen.

ALL HIS FAVORITES
"God does not show favoritism."

ACTS 10:34

Throughout this year, I've said that what God has done for me or others, He'll do for you. This lack of favoritism is a part of His character. God isn't up in heaven throwing dice to determine to whom He shows His favor. Once we accept Jesus as our Lord and Savior, we are made joint-heirs with Jesus and heirs of God (Romans 8:17). Just as God accepts anyone who calls on the name of Jesus, He accepts us. And as we've already studied, in Psalm 84:11, He doesn't withhold any good thing from those whose walk is blameless. As we do our part, He does His.

If you have a hard time believing that God will give you His peace (Psalm 85:8), show you His mercy (Isaiah 55:7), bless you with wisdom, knowledge, and happiness (Ecclesiastes 2:26), order your steps (Psalm 37:23), and empower you with the Holy Spirit (John 14:26), begin studying the scriptures in this sentence. They are His promises to you. So as you get ready to begin a new year, know that the favor of God follows you wherever you go, and it isn't just for everyone else; it's for you, too, His precious child.

–GM

POWER PRAYER
Lord, thank You for loving me as much as everyone else. Thank You that Your promises are real and that as I obediently serve You, I'll enjoy all of them.

WALKING IN GOD'S FAVOR

"Thou shalt arise, and have mercy upon Zion:
for the time to favour her, yea, the set time, is come."

PSALM 102:13 KJV

As this year ends and a new year begins, it's a perfect time to purposely walk in the favor of God. Start each day declaring God's favor over your life. Say, "This is the day that the Lord has made, and I will rejoice and be glad in it. The favor of God goes before me and surrounds me today!" Make it a habit of confessing God's favor in your life, and you'll be amazed at the doors that open before you and the way people receive you. You'll simply be amazed.

When I first started confessing God's favor on a daily basis, I just couldn't get over the change in my life. It's as if I opened a free gift from God that I didn't even know existed. Maybe you're the same way. Maybe you don't think you deserve God's favor or His best for your life. Maybe you think favor is only for super-Christians like Billy Graham. But guess what? It's for you, too! Now that you know about this great gift from God, you can walk in His favor every single day. So go ahead—get excited. This will be your best year yet!

–MMA

POWER PRAYER

Thank You, Lord, for the favor I walk in today and every day.
Amen.

NOTES

1. "Gender Differences in Communication,
      http://pages.towson.edu/itrow/wmcomm.htm.
2. Eggleston, Stephen, "Fear of Public Speaking,"
      http://www.the-eggman.com/writings/fearspk1.html.
3. www.workfamily.com/ConferenceBd.htm, "Job Satis-
      faction Hits Record Low," 9/18/03.

Scripture Index

ABOUT THE AUTHORS

Fellow Texans Michelle Medlock Adams and Gena Maselli are both full-time writers. Michelle, a former award-winning newspaper journalist, now writes magazine articles, women's devotionals, and children's picture books. Gena, who spent ten years developing materials for worldwide Christian ministries, now writes devotionals, nonfiction, and magazine and Internet articles.

For more information or to contact the authors, please visit:

www.michellemedlockadams.com
or
www.genamaselli.com

If you enjoyed

Daily Wisdom
for Working Women

be sure to check out Michelle Medlock Adams's

DAILY WISDOM FOR
MOTHERS

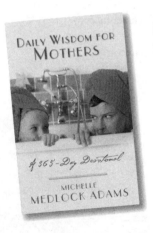

Especially for women with children at home, this book offers a year's worth of brief, relevant, biblical reflections with monthly themes such as worry, unconditional love, discipline, and praying.

ISBN 1-59130-175-9
$5.97, 384 pages

Also from Barbour Publishing or available wherever books are sold.